The EU and Conflict Resolution

This book analyzes the impact and effectiveness of EU foreign policy in promoting peace in five conflicts in the European southern and eastern neighbourhoods.

Conflict resolution features strongly as an objective of the European Union's foreign policy. In promoting this aim, the EU's geographical focus has rested primarily on its beleaguered backyard to the south and to the east. The EU's foreign policy instruments are well placed to promote peace in the neighbourhood. In particular, EU contractual relations, ranging from the accession process to looser forms of association, can play a constructive role in conflict resolution.

Through the study of five ethno-political conflicts lying on or just beyond Europe's borders, this book analyzes the impact and effectiveness of EU contractual relations on conflict resolution.

Taking a strong comparative approach, Nathalie Tocci explores the principal determinants of conflict dynamics in Cyprus, Turkey, Serbia–Montenegro, Israel–Palestine and Georgia in order to assess the impact of EU contractual ties on them. The volume includes topical analysis based on first-hand experience, in-depth interviews with all the relevant actors and photography in ongoing conflict areas in the Middle East, the eastern Mediterranean, the Balkans and the Caucasus. This revealing study shows that the gap between EU potential and effectiveness often rests in the specific manner in which the EU collectively chooses to conduct its contractual relations.

The EU and Conflict Resolution will be of interest to all readers who wish to acquire an excellent understanding of the EU's impact on conflict contexts and will appeal to scholars of European politics, security studies and conflict resolution.

Nathalie Tocci is a Senior Fellow at the Istituto Affari Internazionali, Rome, Italy.

The EU and Conflict Resolution

Promoting peace in the backyard

Nathalie Tocci

LONDON AND NEW YORK

First published 2007
by Routledge
2 Park Square, Milton Park, Abingdon, Oxon OX14 4RN

Simultaneously published in the USA and Canada
by Routledge
270 Madison Avenue, New York, NY 10016

Routledge is an imprint of the Taylor & Francis Group, an informa business

© 2007 Nathalie Tocci

Typeset in Times New Roman by Keyword Group Ltd.
Printed and bound in Great Britain by MPG Books Ltd, Bodmin

British Library Cataloguing in Publication Data
A catalogue record for this book is available from the British Library

Library of Congress Cataloging in Publication Data
Tocci, Nathalie.
 The EU and conflict resolution: promoting peace in the
 backyard/Nathalie Tocci.
  p.cm.
 Includes bibliographical references and index.
 ISBN 978-0-415-41394-7 (hardback:alk. paper) 1. European Union
 Countries–Foreign relations. 2. Conflict management–Case studies.
 3. Ethnic relations–Case studies. 4. International relations. I. Title.
 JZ1570.A5T63 2007
 327.1'72094–dc22
 2006037800

ISBN10: 0-415-41394-X (hbk)
ISBN10: 0-203-96092-0 (ebk)

ISBN13: 978-0-415-41394-7 (hbk)
ISBN13: 978-0-203-96092-9 (ebk)

To Kike

Tu me dis qu'ils te détestent? Mais qu'est-ce que cela veut dire, 'ils'? Chacun te déteste d'une façon différente et sois sûr qu'il y en a parmi eux qui t'aiment. Par sa prestidigitation, la grammaire sait transformer une multitude d'individus en une seule entité, un seul sujet, un seul 'subjectum' qui s'appelle 'nous' ou 'ils' mais qui, en tant que réalité concrète, n'existe pas.

Milan Kundera, *Le Rideau*.

Contents

Photographs

Maps

Tables

Preface

The European Union's *raison d'être* as a peace project ending centuries of war-fare in Europe has fundamentally shaped its external mission. In its treaties and declarations, the EU has in fact recurrently flagged conflict resolution as a primary objective in its fledging foreign policy. EU speech acts have also highlighted the importance of complementary foreign policy objectives, such as the promotion of democracy, human rights, the rule of law and regional cooperation. Hence, beyond conflict management and settlement, EU foreign policy theoretically aspires to conflict prevention, resolution and transformation, through the eradication of the root causes of conflict. In promoting these aims, the EU's geographical focus has rested primarily in its beleaguered backyard to the south and to the east.

The Union's foreign policy instruments are well placed to promote structural peace in the neighbourhood. In particular, EU contractual relations – ranging from the accession process to looser forms of association – can play a constructive role in conflict resolution. Through the study of five ethno-political conflicts lying on, or just beyond, Europe's borders, this book analyzes the impact and effectiveness of EU contractual relations on conflict resolution. Impact and effectiveness in Cyprus, Turkey, Serbia–Montenegro, Israel–Palestine and Georgia are assessed by contrasting the EU's declared aims in these conflicts with the conflicts' evolution on the ground.

The conclusions are sobering. Despite its potential to contribute significantly – and sometimes decisively – to conflict resolution, the EU has in practice punched well below its weight. On some occasions, it has contributed positively to conflict resolution, although underperforming in respect of its potential; on other occasions, it has unwittingly fuelled stalemate or retrenchment into conflict. The reasons underlying this underperformance need not be sought either in the objective limits of the EU's foreign policy instruments, or in the Union's much-quoted internal divisions. The gap between EU potential and effectiveness in practice often rests in the specific manner in which its contractual relations are conducted. At times, this has damaged the credibility of the EU, its norms and its obligations. At other times, contractual relations have been pursued with other EU interests and objectives in mind, which have thwarted peacemaking efforts in the neighbourhood.

This book was written as part of a research project financed by the European Commission's Marie Curie Fellowship Scheme and carried out at the Robert Schuman Centre for Advanced Studies of the European University Institute. Unlike most studies on EU foreign policy, the focal point of my research has been on the recipient regions themselves, rather than on the EU. By understanding the domestic, regional and international factors underpinning neighbourhood conflicts, I have sought to analyze how and why the EU has influenced peacemaking the way it did. In particular, through in-depth interviews with official and non-official sources within conflict situations, I have tried to understand the domestic perceptions of the EU and of its policies, and their ensuing impact on conflict resolution efforts.

As such, I am heavily indebted to all my friends, colleagues and interviewees in the Balkans, the Caucasus, the eastern Mediterranean and the Middle East. Without them, this research would not have been possible. Most importantly, without an appreciation of the views they represent, articulate and pursue, a thorough understanding of these conflicts and of the EU's influence on them would be eluded. With it, so would the aspiration to enhance the EU's role in conflict resolution in these regions. If this book succeeds in making a contribution – however modest – to this understanding, its cardinal objective will be fully met.

Rome, July 2006

Acknowledgements

The research for this book has been generously funded by the European Commission's Marie Curie Intra-European Fellowship Programme, which I have carried out at the Robert Schuman Centre of the European University Institute. I would like to thank all my friends and colleagues at the EUI, as well as at the Istituto Affari Internazionali in Rome, who have advised and supported me over the last two years. My special thanks goes to Charles Shamas, who has provided an important inspiration for this book. Many thanks also to Benoit Challand, Jonathan Cohen, Bruno Coppieters, Michael Emerson, Tamara Kovziridze, Liana Kvhvarchelia, Daniela Pioppi and Nicholas Whyte for their valuable comments on the draft chapters of this book. I would also like to thank Luigi Amici for his help and advice on the photographic material. Finally, I would like to thank my mother, my father and my partner Enrique for their constant love, patience and support during these years.

Abbreviations

AKEL	Anorthotikon Komma Ergazomenou Laou
AKP	Adalet ve Kalkınma Partisi
ANAP	Anavatan Partisi
CARDS	Community Assistance for Reconstruction, Development and Stabilization
CEECs	Central and Eastern European Countries
CFSP	Common Foreign and Security Policy
CIS	Commonwealth of Independent States
CTP	Cumhuriyetci Türk Partisi
DEHAP	Democratik Halk Partisi
DEP	Demokrasi Emek Partisi
DG	Directorate General of the European Commission
DIKO	Democratico Komma
DISY	Democraticos Synagermos
DOS	Demokratska Opozicija Srbije
DPS	Demoktatska Partija Socialista Crna Gore
DSS	Demoktatska Stranka Srbije
DTH	Demokratik Toplum HarekeTi
EC	European Community
ECHR	European Convention on Human Rights
ECJ	European Court of Justice
ECtHR	European Court of Human Rights
EDEK	Enie Democratiki Enosis Kyprou
EEA	European Economic Area
EMP	Euro-Mediterranean Partnership
ENP	European Neighbourhood Policy
ENPI	European Neighbourhood and Partnership Instrument
EOKA	Ethniki Organosis Kyprion Agoniston
EP	European Parliament
EPC	European Political Cooperation
ESDP	European Security and Defence Policy
EU	European Union

EU-COPPS	EU Coordinating Office for Palestinian Policing Support
EUSR	EU Special Representative
FRY	Former Republic of Yugoslavia
GAP	Güneydoğu Anadolu Projesi
HADEP	Halkın Demokrasi Partisi
HEP	Halkın Emek Partisi
ICJ	International Court of Justice
ICTY	International Criminal Tribunal for Yugoslavia
IDPs	Internally displaced persons
IFIs	International Financial Institutions
IGC	Intergovernmental Conference
IHL	International humanitarian law
IMF	International Monetary Fund
Inogate	Oil and Gas Transport to Europe
JCC	Joint Control Commission
MEP	Member of the European Parliament
NATO	North Atlantic Treaty Organization
ND	Nea Demokratia
NGO	Nongovernmental organization
OHAL	Olağanüstü Hal
OSCE	Organization for Security and Cooperation in Europe
OTs	Occupied territories
PA	Palestinian Authority
PASOK	Pannelion Socialistikon Kinima
PCA	Partnership and Cooperation Agreement
PKF	Peacekeeping force
PKK	Partiya Karkeran Kurdistan
PLC	Palestinian Legislative Council
PLO	Palestinian Liberation Organization
RoC	Republic of Cyprus
SAA	Stabilization and Association Agreement
SAP	Stabilization and Association Process
SEECP	South East European Cooperation Process
SHP	Sosysaldemokrat Halkçi Parti
SNP	Socijalisticka Narodna Partija
SSR	Socialist Soviet Republic
TACIS	Technical Assistance for the Commonwealth of Independent States
TIM	Temporary International Mechanism
Traceca	Transport Corridor Europe–Caucasus–Asia
TRNC	Turkish Republic of Northern Cyprus
UK	United Kingdom
UN	United Nations
UNFICYP	UN Peacekeeping force in Cyprus

UNOMIG	UN Observer Mission in Georgia
UNRWA	UN Relief Works Agency
UNSC	UN Security Council
UNSG	UN Secretary General
UNSR	UN Special Representative
US	United States

1 Introduction

The European Union, collectively, identifies peacemaking as a key priority in its neighbourhood, presenting it as an 'essential aspect of the EU's external action' (Commission 2004a: 3). It also views the promotion of human rights, democracy, the rule of law and regional cooperation as complementary and indeed necessary means to achieve peace in and beyond its borders (Commission 2003c; European Council 2003b). As stated in the draft EU Constitutional Treaty, these aims are considered as values underpinning the European project itself, as well as guiding principles of the Union's actions abroad (Article III-193(1), Article I-2 and I-3). The underlying assumption is that by pursuing these normative 'milieu goals', the EU helps shape the external environment in a manner conducive to its strategic 'possession' goals (Wolfers 1962: 73–6).

The preferred means to promote these objectives is through what EU institutions commonly refer to as 'constructive engagement' (Commission 2001b: 8–9, 2003c: 11). Constructive engagement is the use of a wide range of diplomatic, economic, social, cultural and military instruments, normally deployed through contractual arrangements with third countries. The concept behind this mode of foreign policy-making is that of achieving varying degrees of economic, social and legal integration into the EU through bilateral agreements. Other than degrees of integration per se, contractual ties are intended to foster in the long run structural change both within and between third countries, which in turn promotes conflict prevention and resolution (Commission 2001a: 4). Hence, the Union, which is based on a system of laws and rules, aims to promote its values abroad by embedding these rules within legal arrangements with third states, thus creating a complex web of contractual relations with its neighbours. The respect of the laws and rules that underpin EU contracts is essential to the pursuit of the EU's milieu and possession goals.

Based on these premises, this book assesses the EU's impact on, and effectiveness in, promoting conflict resolution in its backyard, through the use of contractual relations with conflict parties. Effectiveness is measured against the EU's declared objectives in the conflicts under scrutiny. More precisely, this study seeks to understand the effect of EU contractual relations on the incentive structure underpinning ethno-political conflicts, and thus on the prospect for their resolution along the lines advocated by the EU. It also aims to tease out the determinants of EU effectiveness in deploying its contractual relations at the service of conflict resolution.

Ethno-political conflicts in the EU neighbourhood

An assessment of external impact requires an in-depth understanding of the internal dynamics within ethno-political conflicts. Through the selection of five case studies – in Cyprus, Turkey, Serbia and Montenegro, Israel–Palestine and Georgia, this book explores the principal determinants of conflict dynamics. These dynamics are mapped against the EU's declared objectives in these conflict areas. On this basis, this study analyzes the impact and effectiveness of EU contractual relations. All of the selected conflicts either straddle or lie just beyond the EU's borders.

These conflicts share few similarities and many differences. In all five cases, the eruption of conflict is linked to a real and/or perceived violation of individual and/or collective rights, whose occurrence has been either justified by and/or has fuelled ethno-nationalism and exclusivist identity-politics. The Greek Cypriot struggle for self-determination triggered the violation of Turkish Cypriot rights and ignited reactive ethno-nationalisms, as did the Georgian, Turkish, Israeli and Serbian nation-state-building projects vis-à-vis the Abkhaz and Ossetians, the Kurds, the Palestinians and the Montenegrins respectively.

Yet historical specificities render the root causes of the five conflicts hardly comparable. In Cyprus, the nature of the Greek Cypriot struggle and of the Turkish Cypriot reaction was shaped by the respective nature of Greek and Turkish nationalisms, the historical animosities between the two kin-countries, the role of colonial power Britain and the wider international context in the emerging Cold War configuration. In Turkey, the dispute between the Turkish state and Kurdish nationalists emerged from the Ottoman legacy and great power politics in the early twentieth century, the ensuing contradictions of the Turkish republican project and the wider inter-state politics in the region. In Serbia and Montenegro, the dispute was triggered by Serbian nationalist politics under Slobodan Milosevic and the international reaction to the former Serbian regime, which generated a political, rather than an identity-based rift between Belgrade and Podgorica. In Georgia, the conflicts were triggered by the ethno-nationalism of the nascent Georgian republic, coupled with the legacy of Soviet federalism and the ensuing role of Russia in the South Caucasus since the early 1990s. Finally, in Israel–Palestine, the violation of rights and law cannot be understood without an appreciation of twentieth century European politics, ensuing Middle Eastern politics and external involvement during and since the end of the Cold War.

The five conflicts are also at different stages of evolution. Serbia and Montenegro is the only case in which a negotiated constitutional agreement has been reached. This occurred in 2001 and then evolved into the peaceful separation between the two republics in 2006. But the conflict never endured a stage of outright violence, and the 2001 Belgrade agreement can be viewed more as an instance of conflict prevention than of conflict settlement and resolution.

Conflicts such as those in Cyprus and Georgia are frequently referred to as 'frozen'. A 'frozen' conflict is one which has reached a fragile no-peace-no-war equilibrium, following the minority community's military 'victory' (with external support), whose independence however is not recognized and thus remains in violation of international law. Yet the 'frozen conflict' metaphor is a misnomer. In both cases, while peace processes have tended to be relatively frozen, dynamics on the ground have not. Furthermore, also in terms of peace efforts, these two conflict areas lie at very different points of the 'frozen conflict' spectrum. Cyprus has seen a far more active involvement of the international community, culminating in the comprehensive 'Annan Plan' proposed by the United Nations (UN) in 2002–04, which included a fully fledged constitution with thousands of pages of draft laws, agreements and treaties. The Georgia–Abkhazia and Georgia–South Ossetia conflicts are nowhere near peaceful resolution through mediated negotiations. Proposals by the conflict parties and by external actors are sporadic and have never delved beyond broad outlines and ideas. Moreover, in the rare instances in which external proposals have gained the tacit approval of the external mediators, such as UN Special Representative (UNSR) Dieter Boden's outline for Abkhazia in 2001, they have been rejected out-of-hand by either one party or the other.

In Israel–Palestine and Turkey, cyclical violence persists. In the former case, peace pipe-dreams generated by the Oslo process were shattered with the eruption of the second intifada in 2000. In the latter case, the illusion of an end of separatist violence following the 1999 capture of Abdullah Öcalan crumbled in 2004–5, with the resumption of hostilities, albeit at a lower scale compared with the 1980s and 1990s. Yet similarities in terms of the cyclical nature of political violence in Turkey and Israel–Palestine are not matched by a similar history of conflict resolution efforts. In Israel–Palestine, peace negotiations took the form of the Oslo process between 1993 and the failed summits at Camp David and Taba in 2000–1. By contrast, negotiations between the Turkish state and the secessionist Partiya Karkeran Kurdistan (PKK) have never taken place, not least because relative military victory allowed the Turkish state to pursue a unilateral process of peaceful reconciliation through human rights reforms, and to refuse negotiations with either the PKK or any other Kurdish representative.

The five conflicts also differ in terms of their attempted solutions. In Cyprus, Serbia–Montenegro, Abkhazia, and South Ossetia negotiations revolved around the contrasting principles of territorial integrity and self-determination. Negotiations thus considered different models of autonomy, federalism, confederalism or secession as a means to reconcile the metropolitan state's call for territorial integrity and the minority community's demand for self-determination. Yet in Cyprus and Georgia, the legitimacy of far-reaching federal or confederal solutions was paradoxically triggered by the military victory of the minority communities, rendering the re-incorporation of the secessionist minority within a unitary state structure a practical and political impossibility.[1] In Serbia–Montenegro instead, the international legitimacy of confederalism and secession was caused by the international delegitimization of the Milosevic regime in metropolitan state Serbia. In this respect, it is interesting to note how the Turkish Cypriots, the Abkhaz and the South Ossetians (like the Armenians in Nagorno Karabakh or the Transniestrians in Moldova) point to Montenegro and Kosovo when arguing in favour of their own secession.[2]

In Turkey, the metropolitan state's military victory against the secessionist PKK, coupled with the complex regional politics of the Kurdish question, invalidated proposals of Kurdish autonomy within a decentralized or federal Turkey, let alone the idea of an independent Kurdistan occupying part of Turkey. Discussions have revolved around the extension of individual, cultural or minority rights to Turkey's Kurdish citizens. The Israeli–Palestinian conflict instead is the only case in which – despite the international community's aversion to secession and the Palestinian theoretical acceptance of citizenship within a democratic Israel – all variants of a one-state solution have been shunned by metropolitan state Israel, in view of the Zionist goal of securing a Jewish state.

Finally, the five conflicts vary considerably in terms of their external involvement. In Cyprus and Georgia, the conflicts are marked by the politics of powerful protector states (Greece and Turkey in Cyprus, and Russia in Georgia–Abkhazia–Ossetia). These conflicts are characterized by a 'double minority' configuration. The local disputes between the larger Greek Cypriot and Georgian communities and the smaller Turkish Cypriot and Abkhaz or South Ossetian communities are set within the wider conflicts between the small Greek Cypriot and Georgian states and major powers Turkey and Russia in support of the local minorities. The fragile 'double minority' set-up has both shaped the outbreak and outcome of violent conflict as well as the ensuing 'frozen' equilibrium.

In Israel–Palestine, Turkey and Serbia–Montenegro, the eruption and evolution of conflict has also been influenced by regional and international politics. The Israeli–Palestinian conflict has been amongst the most internationalized of conflicts in the twentieth century. Particularly since the 1970s, it has witnessed muscular US mediation, as well as the constant interest of major European actors. The conflict also includes a pronounced regional dimension in view of the wider conflict and peace process between Israel and the Arab world, the dispersion of Palestinian refugees in Syria, Jordan and Lebanon, and the de facto political, military and economic role of Jordan and Egypt in the West Bank and Gaza Strip respectively. The regional politics of the war-torn Western Balkans has affected the politics of Serbia and Montenegro. In particular the progressive break-up of former Yugoslavia set the scene both for the 2002 Belgrade agreement, and for its ultimate termination through Montenegro's secession. The Kosovo question has also shaped the evolution of the State Union of Serbia and Montenegro. Turkey's Kurdish question has oscillated in response to the wider politics of the region, due to the dispersion of the Kurds between Turkey, Iraq, Iran and Syria. The re-eruption of Kurdish violence in 2004 is in fact closely linked to developments in Iraqi Kurdistan following the 2003 US invasion and occupation of Iraq, and the prospects of an independent Kurdistan there.

EU contractual relations with conflict parties

The five conflicts, however, have not been selected on the basis of their similarities or differences. The principal criterion for selection is rather the nature of the contractual ties that they enjoy with the Union.

The Cyprus conflict involves four principal parties. Two parties, i.e. Greece and the Greek Cypriot community, are full members of the Union since 1981 and 2004 respectively. The remaining two, i.e. Turkey and the Turkish Cypriot community, are either legally (in the case of Turkey) or practically (in the case of the Turkish Cypriots) excluded from it. In the case of Turkey, an accession process regulates relations with the EU. In the case of the Turkish Cypriot community, whereas Turkish Cypriot citizens can enjoy on an individual basis the benefits of EU membership, northern Cyprus is territorially excluded de facto (albeit not de jure) from the remit of the Union. In Cyprus, what has been the impact of the accession process, culminating in the full membership of the divided island, on the conflict parties and their intra- and inter-party dynamics? What has been the resultant effect on the conflict?

Turkey's Kurdish question involves EU candidate Turkey, which is already part of the EU customs union and has had long-standing association relations with the Union. Unlike Cyprus, however, Turkey's accession process is far more long-term and uncertain. What has been the impact, to date, of Ankara's protracted accession process on the evolution of the Kurdish question? In particular, what effect has the accession process had on intra-Turkish dynamics and the ensuing relationship between the Turkish state and its Kurdish citizens?

Serbia and Montenegro lie beyond the accession process and fall within the Stabilization and Association Process (SAP). However the EU has openly acknowledged that the SAP is intended to prepare the Western Balkans to the full accession process, and that the future of the region lies within the Union. In other words, Serbia and Montenegro are accepted as prospective EU candidates. What effect has the SAP and the expectation of future candidacy had on the constitutional and political dispute between Serbia and Montenegro? What impact has it had on the signature, evolution and ultimate break-up of the State Union between the two republics?

Israel and Palestine fall in the category of non-European, non-candidate (or prospective-candidate) countries. Yet this is not to say that contractual ties with the EU have been insignificant. Israel enjoys by far the most developed association agreement in the Euro-Mediterranean Partnership (EMP) and the Palestinian Authority (PA) has received key sums of EU financial (as well as technical) assistance from the Union. In addition, both Israel and the PA have been included in the European Neighbourhood Policy (ENP). What has been the impact of association, aid and the ENP on the internal and external dynamics of the Israeli–Palestinian conflict?

Finally, Georgia is a European non-candidate country, without concrete prospects of entering the accession process. Contractual ties have been conducted through the loose Partnership and Cooperation Agreement (PCA). In addition, Georgia, as well as the secessionist Abkhazia and South Ossetia have received modest sums EU assistance. In 2004 Georgia, together with Armenia and Azerbaijan, was included in the ENP. What effect, has the PCA and the ENP had on Georgia's conflicts with Abkhazia and South Ossetia?

The conflict case studies are thus selected on the basis of their different contractual relations with the Union. By selecting different types of contractual arrangements, this book tackles the following questions. How do the institutional, legal, economic and political frameworks underpinning EU contractual ties alter the structural features underpinning ethno-political conflicts? How do the incentives embedded in EU contractual arrangements and the manner in which they are mobilized by EU actors affect the behavioural dynamics of conflict parties and consequently relations between them? Most importantly, what are the determinants affecting the relative success or otherwise of these foreign policy instruments?

Structure of the book

In order to answer these questions, the book is structured as follows. Chapter 2 sets out an analytical framework to assess the impact of the EU's contractual relations on neighbourhood conflicts. It analyzes both the discernible trends on the ground within the conflicts, as well as the solutions advocated in principle by EU actors. It then turns to the possible mechanisms through which the Union could affect the conflicts in pursuit of its declared objectives through the mobilization of its contractual relations. Finally, it outlines the possible determinants of the success or failure of these EU mechanisms. The framework outlined in Chapter 2 is used to structure the following five case study chapters.

In all five cases, the book first explores the interests, objectives and solutions advocated by the Union. In doing so, the case study chapters focus on the EU's public declarations and documents, as well as on interviews conducted with EU officials. It does not assess these objectives from a normative perspective, but simply takes them at face value. These goals are then mapped against evolving trends on the ground within the conflict situations, in order to assess the extent to which developments have matched, approximated or distanced themselves from the EU's advocated solutions. While well aware that the evolution of these five conflicts could only be partly (if not marginally) affected by the EU, the case study chapters proceed to analyze the extent and manner in which the EU's contractual relations have been used (or misused) to pursue the EU's stated objectives. In particular, the case study chapters discern the factors determining the EU's effectiveness in contributing to the advancement of its peace-related aims in these conflict regions.

Chapters 8 and 9 conclude by assessing comparatively the case study results. Chapter 8 begins by analyzing the EU's impact on different factors fuelling the five conflicts. It does so in order to determine whether the Union has contributed to their resolution by operating on one or more of these factors. It then assesses comparatively the determinants of the EU's effectiveness in conducting contractual relations with the conflict parties at the service of its conflict resolution objectives. Finally, Chapter 8 casts these lessons in broader terms, analyzing both their implications for the EU's wider role in peacemaking and for the pursuit of other EU foreign policy goals.

2 The EU's role in conflict resolution: a framework of analysis

EU aims in neighbourhood conflicts and trends on the ground

In the 1991 Maastricht Treaty, the EU specified for the first time its foreign policy objectives. These included conflict resolution as well as strengthening international security, promoting regional cooperation, combating international crime, and promoting democracy, the rule of law and human rights (Article J.1). Since then, the EU has remained firm on its objectives. The draft Constitutional Treaty states that the Union's external action would aim at 'preserving peace, preventing conflicts and strengthening international security' (Art III-193(2c)), and in doing so, it would be 'guided by, and designed to advance in the wider world, the principles which have inspired its own creation, development and enlargement' (Article III-193(1)). These principles include democracy, human rights, fundamental freedoms and the rule of law (Article I-2 and I-3). The EU Security Strategy then pinpointed the neighbourhood as a key geographical priority of EU external action. It stated that the Union's task is to 'make a particular contribution to stability and good governance in our immediate neighbourhood (and) to promote a ring of well-governed countries to the east of the EU and on the borders of the Mediterranean with whom we can enjoy cooperative relations' (European Council 2003b). The ENP explicitly aims to promote the EU's values as a means to spread stability, security and prosperity in the southern and eastern neighbourhoods. It also aspires to strengthen the EU's contribution to the solution of regional conflicts (Commission 2004a: 6).

Inherent in the EU's approach is the link drawn between values such as human rights, democracy and the rule or law on the one hand, and the prevention and resolution of conflicts and regional cooperation on the other hand. The former values, while being viewed as ends in themselves, are also considered as instrumental to achieving the latter objectives. Ethno-political conflicts often emerge with, and subsequently manifest themselves through, the violation of rights and law. As such, EU institutions have explicitly acknowledged that human rights, the rule of law, a vibrant civil society, strong institutions and sound socio-economic management are key ingredients of conflict prevention and conflict resolution, as opposed to mere crisis management or conflict settlement (Commission 2001a; Kronenberger and Wouters 2005).

Beyond the EU's self-image as a normative power which promotes values abroad as ends in themselves, the EU also has discernible interests in promoting peace, democracy, rights and law in its near abroad (Manners 2002; Smith and Sjursen 2004). Irrespective of whether conflicts are frozen or violence persists, the absence of mutually agreed settlements threatens the stability and security of the EU due to their proximity and potential spillover effects (European Council 2003b: 4–5). Where active violence persists, the potential for instability is evident. The conflict between Israel and Palestine not only represents one of the key factors (by no means the only one) underlying political violence, radicalism and stagnant development in the Middle East; but it also fuels tensions within Europe, in particular in view of the presence of large Muslim communities in the continent. Other violent conflicts entail other risks and problems including uncontrolled asylum and refugee flows, accelerating migration, disrupted commercial flows and imperilled energy security. Where conflicts are seemingly frozen into a no-peace-no-war status quo, the absence of active violence creates the perception of stability. As such, international attention tends to be weak and sporadic. Yet frozen conflicts do not entail frozen dynamics on the ground. The inevitable evolution of the status quo through unilateral moves on the ground generates a latent potential for instability, ready to explode at any point in time. It was only as recently as 1998 that EU member state Greece and candidate Cyprus were on the brink of war with soon-to-be-candidate Turkey. Frozen conflicts and non-recognized states also frequently act as pockets for lawlessness and organized crime, whose effects spill into the rest of Europe. This has been the case in the Balkans and the Caucasus. Finally, ethno-political conflicts, whether active or frozen, can complicate or harm EU relations with interested and powerful third parties such as Russia in the Caucasus or the United States (US) in the Middle East.

Turning to the EU's preferred solutions in its neighbourhood conflicts, three broad categories can be identified. In most cases, the Union advocates federal and/or power-sharing solutions to secessionist conflicts. Autonomy, federal, consociational and, in rare cases, confederal models are viewed as the best recipes for the reconciliation of the metropolitan state's territorial integrity and its accompanying claims to property restitution and refugee return, with the minority community's calls for collective rights and self-determination. Hence, the Union's support for the Annan Plan in Cyprus, its mediation of the State Union of Serbia–Montenegro and its support for the federal proposals of the UN or the Organization for Security and Cooperation in Europe (OSCE) in Georgia's conflicts with Abkhazia and South Ossetia respectively.

In other cases, the Union supports the integration of the minority community through the extension and respect of individual, cultural and minority rights within multicultural unitary states. In the case of Turkey's Kurds, the Union has supported and pressed for the entrenchment of individual human rights, effective political participation and the extension of cultural and minority rights to Kurdish citizens, possibly also including elements of decentralized governance.

In very rare cases, the Union has supported secession. This was the case in former Yugoslavia and has become the accepted reality in Kosovo and Montenegro. It is certainly the case in Israel–Palestine, where the Union since the late 1990s has persistently called for a two-state solution along the 1967 borders. The EU's open support for a two-state solution to an ethno-political conflict is atypical. In line with the international community, the Union normally upholds the principle of territorial integrity and is reluctant to recognize secession both on normative and interest-based grounds. The Israeli–Palestinian conflict is a notable exception in this respect. This is because of the Union's support for both Israeli (Jewish) and Palestinian rights to self-determination through statehood, as well as its aim to act in unison with the US on the Middle East dossier.

Yet the de facto 'solutions' taking root on the ground point to very different directions (McGarry and O'Leary 1997). There, where the Union advocates federalism, developments move either towards the metropolitan state's domination and assimilation of the minority community or towards the minority's unrecognized secession without a lawful and negotiated solution. Without a negotiated agreement, trends thus see either the violation of the minority's collective rights or the grievance of the majority and the violation of its individual rights. With the rejection of the Annan Plan in Cyprus by the Greek Cypriot community in 2004, the island has oscillated between the 'Taiwanization' of northern Cyprus and the Greek Cypriot domination of the Turkish Cypriot community. In Serbia and Montenegro, the State Union was stillborn coming to a formal end after Montenegro's secession in 2006. In Georgia, attempts to promote federal solutions to the Abkhaz and South Ossetian conflicts are punctually truncated by the regimes in Sukhumi and Tskhinvali, who appear far more inclined to pursue integration with Russia if their recognized independence cannot be achieved.

In cases where the Union advocates the extension of individual and collective rights within a unitary state, progress remains well below expectations, entailing the permanent grievance of the minority and the constant threat (or reality) of violence against the majority. Despite Turkey's impressive reform process since 2002 and the entrenchment of individual human rights in the country, the Turkish establishment is still reluctant to accept Kurdish minority rights, effective political participation let alone minimal territorial autonomy. Its reticence to proceed along this path has grown in response to the re-eruption of PKK violence since 2004. The concept of assimilation as opposed to integration continues to retain the upper hand amongst key decision-makers in Ankara.

Finally, where the Union advocates a negotiated two-state solution, trends point towards the majority's hegemonic control and/or the risk of the minority's forced displacement. Hence, the persistant and aggravating violation of the minority's human and self-determination rights, and the frequent abuse of the majority through the minority's criminal acts of political violence. In the Middle East, the accelerating process of colonization of the occupied territories is making the accomplishment of a viable two-state solution increasingly unlikely, and places the accompanying respect of Israeli and Palestinian human rights increasingly under threat.

EU mechanisms to promote peace in the neighbourhood

In view of the frequent gap between EU objectives and developments on the ground, how could the Union positively influence its neighbourhood conflicts through the contractual ties it enjoys with the conflict parties? As pointed out by Hill (2001), an EU role in conflict resolution can be twofold. First, the EU framework of governance, law and policy can offer a conducive context for the settlement of ethno-political conflicts. Second, the Union can generate incentives for the settlement and ultimate resolution of conflicts through its policy instruments. The roles of the EU as a framework and as an actor are not unrelated, particularly in the neighbouring regions (Tocci 2004a). Most EU actions in the neighbourhood, such as the accession process, the SAP, the EMP and the ENP make use of, and are embedded in, EU institutional, legal and policy frameworks. But more precisely, how can the Union contribute to the resolution of ethno-political conflicts by welding conflict parties in its web of contractual relations and the institutional, legal, economic and political components they include? Through which mechanisms can EU actions, conducted through its contractual relations, alter the incentive structure underpinning conflicts?

Conditionality

Particularly over the last decade and in the process of the eastern enlargement, the EU has developed its policies of conditionality as a means to transform the governing structures, the economy and the civil society of the candidate countries. Generally, conditionality can be defined as a strategy whereby a reward is granted or withheld depending on the fulfilment of an attached condition. More specifically, 'political conditionality entails the linking, by a state or international organization, of perceived benefits to another state, to the fulfilment of conditions relating to the protection of human rights and the advancement of democratic principles' (Smith 1998: 256). Obligations can thus be political and economic, as well as technical, legal, institutional and related to the EU's *acquis communautaire*.

Conditionality can be positive or negative, ex ante or ex post. Positive conditionality entails the promise of a benefit, in return for the fulfilment of a predetermined condition. Both the promise and the obligation are specified in the contract. It is most frequently used in the delivery of economic assistance, as well as within the context of EU accession. Negative conditionality involves the infliction of a punishment in the event of the violation of a specified obligation. Diplomatic and economic sanctions on Serbia (1991–2000), Syria (1987–94), Libya (1987–92/1999–03) and Belarus (1998–9) are clear cases of negative conditionality.

While in principle positive and negative conditionality could have similar effects, in practice their impact is often very different. Positive conditionality may provide advantages to the donor as well as to the recipient. This can increase the credibility of the promise given the greater likelihood of its delivery. However it can also reduce the credibility of an attached condition, in view of the donor's desire to deliver the promised benefit irrespective of the recipient's behaviour. Negative conditionality, such as sanctions, can lose its credibility when the recipient party finds alternative suppliers. While positive incentives can be effective through unilateral action, sanctions often hinge on multilateral efforts, unless the recipient depends on a single supplier. Negative conditionality can also have counterproductive psychological effects, strengthening the recipient state's siege mentality and reducing its flexibility and receptiveness to compromise.

The fulfilment of obligations can be ex ante or ex post, i.e. either conditions are fulfilled before the contract is signed, or conditions specified in an agreement need to be respected, otherwise the contract may be lawfully suspended unilaterally (Zalewski 2004). In between these two extremes, conditionality can be exerted over time, and not exclusively at the time of, or following the delivery of, specified side payments. The case of the 1993 Copenhagen criteria is an example of ex ante conditionality, while the 'human rights clause' in the EU's association agreements is an example of ex post conditionality. Financial assistance instead lends itself to a constant exercise of conditionality over time, given the divisible nature of the benefit on offer. Ex post conditionality and inclusion have the advantage of building trust over time between the donor and the recipient. Ex ante conditionality and exclusion instead may be more credible, and can thus generate stronger incentives for conflict parties.

Positive and negative, ex ante and ex post conditionality have different strengths and weaknesses (Cortright 1997 and Dorussen 2001). However, irrespective of the pros and cons, in practice the Union has demonstrated its reluctance to engage in negative and ex post conditionality. Sanctions are used sparingly and often target small and far-away states (Smith 2004: 119). They are used against neighbours only in response to major security threats (e.g. Syria and Libya for state-sponsored terrorism, former Yugoslavia for war crimes and regional instability, and Belarus for the treatment of EU and OSCE diplomats). The only example of EU sanctions in response to a lack of cooperation in conflict resolution was the 2003 visa ban on the Transniestrian leadership. Sanctions in response to violations of peace, human rights, the rule of law and democracy are normally used further afield, often against former European colonies in Sub-Saharan Africa and Southeast Asia (Portela 2005).

The Union has also demonstrated its unwillingness to engage in ex post conditionality by unilaterally suspending signed agreements. With few exceptions (e.g. Belarus since 1997, Croatia in 1995–6 and Russia in 1995), the EU has never suspended any of its agreements in response to a state's conduct in conflict or its violations in the fields of human rights, democracy and the rule of law. The 'human rights clause' in EU association agreements has been used as a means to upgrade human rights and democracy into acceptable subjects of political dialogue, rather than a vehicle to exert ex post conditionality on third-party countries.

The EU has stated its preference for cooperation and engagement over punishments and coercion (Commission 2003c: 11, 2001b: 8–9). This is all the more so when it comes to major powers or EU neighbours. The Union's preference for positive and ex ante conditionality has several explanations. Politically, EU actors are well aware that conditional engagement represents a far milder challenge to a third country's sovereignty and is thus more acceptable and less likely to fuel antagonism and inflict harm on the local population. As such, the EU generally considers that retaining open political channels is a far more effective tool for exerting influence. Furthermore, the suspension of one association agreement could set a precedent justifying the suspension of many agreements, given that particularly when it comes to the EU's east and south, most countries are responsible for serious shortcomings in the fields of conflict, democracy or human rights. Yet several member states would object to the widespread use of suspension on the grounds of commercial, political and security interests.

Legally, EU actors highlight the difficulties involved in exerting negative or ex post conditionality. When it comes to embargoes and sanctions, EU approval is difficult to reach due to internal decision-making rules.[1] Legal constraints also discourage the use of ex post conditionality, given the stringent conditions that need to be met to justify the suspension of an agreement (Brandter and Rosas 1999). The violation of human rights could justify a partial or total suspension of an agreement only if it constitutes a material breach, i.e. a breach which impedes the accomplishment of the 'object and purpose' of an agreement (Riedel and Will 1999). But the 'object and purpose' of these agreements is not the promotion of human rights and democracy per se (although these are essential elements of the agreements). It is rather the promotion of free trade, political dialogue and the dialogue between societies. Hence, only if a human rights violation hinders these primary aims, ex post conditionality could represent an 'appropriate measure' of response (Rockwell and Shamas 2005). In addition, an appropriate measure is one which passes the legal tests of 'effectiveness' and 'proportionality'. Suspension is thus legally justified only if it constitutes an effective and proportional remedy to a material breach, which least disturbs the functioning of the agreement.

Within the context of the eastern enlargement, the EU refined its techniques of positive political conditionality. It developed two main steps in the process: namely gatekeeping, and benchmarking and monitoring (Grabbe 2001). Gatekeeping refers to the process whereby the depth and speed of a third country's domestic transformation determines when and whether EU institutions give the green light either to different stages along the accession process or to the delivery of other benefits. The stages which applied to the Central and Eastern European Countries (CEECs) were: privileged access to trade and aid, signing and implementing enhanced association agreements, opening accession negotiations, opening and closing 31 chapters of the *acquis*, signing the Accession Treaty, ratifying the Accession Treaty and finally entering the EU. Over the course of the accession process, EU institutions also benchmarked and monitored the progress of the candidate states. The two main instruments in doing so were the Accession Partnerships and the Commission Progress Reports. The Accession Partnerships set out a list of short- and medium-term recommendations that candidate states were expected to fulfil in order to satisfy the Copenhagen criteria. They were based on and revised annually according to the Progress Reports, which overviewed the developments within candidate countries in relation to the accession criteria.

The Union has made use of positive conditionality also in other types of contractual relations, which can be complementary or alternative to full accession. Complementary benefits include the SAP for the Western Balkan countries, expected to result in the full accession process, or the inclusion of Turkey in the EU customs union. Other benefits are viewed as alternatives to membership. These include the disbursement of financial assistance to the southern Mediterranean and the former Soviet countries, or the Euro-Mediterranean association agreements and the PCAs.

In principle, the major alternative benefit to membership is the ENP. Yet whether and how the ENP will make use of positive political conditionality remains uncertain. In its early stages, the ENP foresaw the conditional delivery of benefits in response to conduct in the fields of peacemaking, democracy, human rights and international law (as well as *acquis* compliance).[2] Being modelled on enlargement, the ENP adopted its same method. Hence, the ENP Action Plans were shaped on the Europe agreements and they were to be followed by annual ENP reports inspired by the Progress Reports (Kelley 2006). By 2004 this approach had been diluted significantly, primarily because of the appreciation that the ENP would not culminate with the delivery of the same benefit as the accession process, i.e. membership. If the incentives were of a categorically different nature, the accompanying demands could neither be as stringent nor as conditional. Hence, the balance in the ENP tilted towards the far more ambiguous notions of 'partnership' and 'common values' (Commission 2004a: 3). Although the Commission conceded that these values in practice were not perfectly shared, its policy shift hinted at the belief that strict forms of positive conditionality cannot or should not be applied to non-candidate countries (Commission 2004a: 12).

Turning back to the link between conditionality and peacemaking, how could positive conditionality affect conflict resolution? The impact on peace efforts could be direct and indirect. The delivery of EU benefits could be made directly conditional on peacemaking. The 1995 Stability Pact promoted by French Prime Minister Balladur was intended to diffuse minority and border tensions in the CEECs. Unless the candidates settled their most salient disputes, they would be prevented from opening accession negotiations. Although the Pact was a political and non-legally binding document, its inbuilt incentives promoted agreements between Slovakia and Hungary (1995) and later between Romania and Hungary (1996). It also entrusted the OSCE with a monitoring role and set the precedent for future initiatives such as the Royaumont Process or the Stability Pact for Southeastern Europe. In Cyprus, direct conditionality on the Greek Cypriot side was lifted, but was retained for the Turkish Cypriot side, given the EU's policy of non-recognition of the Turkish Republic of Northern Cyprus (TRNC). It was also exerted on Turkey particularly since 1999.

Conditionality could also have an indirect effect on conflicts by affecting policy fields linked to the conflict resolution agenda, which can affect the bargaining positions of the conflict parties. Commission requirements on trade policy vis-à-vis Serbia and Montenegro affected the positions of Serb and Montenegrin authorities towards each other and towards the State Union itself. EU demands on Turkey to extend language rights to its non-Turkish population affected the state's stance towards the Kurds. Likewise demands made on Ankara to normalize relations with the Republic of Cyprus have affected the evolution of the Cyprus conflict. Finally, the conditional disbursement of aid to the Palestinian Authority on the reform of the fiscal or the judicial sectors shaped positions and developments determining the nature of Palestinian governance.

But how does conditionality work its way into domestic dynamics (Börzel and Risse 2003)? Rational institutionalism argues that actors are rational, goal-oriented and purposeful. They engage in strategic bargaining using resources to maximize their utilities on the basis of ordered preferences. They weigh the costs and benefits of different strategies anticipating the other's behaviour. EU conditionality thus generates 'simple learning', i.e. strategies and tactics change, while underlying interests and preferences do not – 'institutions are a structure that actors run into, go 'ouch', and the recalculate how, in the presence of the structure, to achieve their interests' (Checkel 1999: 90).

EU conditionality can have either a direct effect by prescribing particular solutions and ruling out others, or an indirect effect by altering the domestic opportunity structure in conflicts (Knill and Lehmkuhl 1999). In the former case, conditionality can affect the range of feasible solutions in peace negotiations. If the EU categorically rejects the option of secession within a candidate state, the secessionist entity within that state may have to concentrate on other solutions if it is determined to integrate into the Union. For example, all European institutions opposed the separate accession of two states in Cyprus, as well as the accession of northern Cyprus together with Turkey. In so far as Turkey and northern Cyprus wanted to join the EU, their bargaining strategies in negotiations altered in 2004.

Yet given the EU's limited ability to categorically prescribe laws and policies beyond its borders, conditionality generates domestic change principally by altering the domestic opportunity structure within and between conflict parties. EU conditionality alters political opportunities by offering resources and legitimacy to some actors while constraining the ability of others to pursue their goals. The empowerment of some groups over others may occur indirectly by legitimizing and strengthening the positions advocated by particular groups (Risse *et al.* 2001: 11). For example, the discourse of Europe and Europeanization played an important role in empowering the moderate camp in Turkish Cypriot politics and the Justice and Development Party in Turkey in 2002–5. EU support can also be overt and direct, such as the financial and political support for specific parties or movements or sanctions on others. For example, EU funding has been made available to bi-communal groups in Cyprus, in the Middle East, in the Balkans and in the Caucasus. Technical, political and financial support has been provided also to the efforts of 'moderate' forces in conflict situations. In 2003, member states expressed their support for the Israeli–Palestinian Geneva accords, brokered by Palestinians and the Israeli centre-left opposition to Ariel Sharon. On the other side of the coin, the EU has punished specific groups within conflict parties. The 2003 visa ban against the Transiestrian leadership or the 2006 boycott of the Hamas government are clear cases in point.

The extent to which conditionality can generate domestic change also depends on the overlap between EU conditions and pre-existing domestic practices (Risse *et al.* 2001: 6–7). When the overlap is complete or entirely absent, conditionality is least likely to have effect. When instead some groups within the domestic political system are working towards change in a similar direction to that advocated by the Union, conditionality can strengthen these groups and influence resulting policies. The ousting of former Slovak Prime Minister Vladimir Meciar when, in 1997, the Union refused to open accession negotiations with Slovakia due to the country's human rights record, contributed to the victory of Dzurinda in the autumn of 1998. However, at times, domestic positions which are far removed from the EU's wishes may be reformulated and empowered by an EU discourse. The call in Cyprus for a 'European solution' is paradoxically used to legitimize hardline nationalist assimilationist positions in southern Cyprus.

Social learning

Contractual relations can affect conflict and conflict resolution also through more diffuse mechanisms of learning and persuasion, taking place through the institutional, political, economic and wider societal contact and dialogue between EU actors and conflict parties. As opposed to conditionality, which alters decision-makers' cost-benefit calculus, in the case of learning domestic change occurs through a transformation of perceived interests (and possibly identities), as domestic actors voluntarily internalize the norms and logic underpinning the EU system. Through participation in, or close contact with, the EU institutional framework, parties may come to alter their substantive beliefs, visions and purposes (e.g. changing views on human rights, identity, sovereignty or democracy). They may also alter their preferred strategies (i.e. negotiation, compromise and international law over unilateralism, brinkmanship and political violence). This is what Checkel has defined as a process of 'complex learning'. It occurs when 'agents, in the absence of obvious material incentives, acquire new values and interests; their behaviour in turn, comes to be governed by new logics of appropriateness' (Checkel 1999: 90). In other words, rather than acting through direct influence or coercion, learning occurs when domestic actors are faced with new institutional and discursive frameworks which induce the re-articulation of their identities, in a manner indirectly conducive to the resolution of ethno-political conflicts in the long term (Diez 2002: 6–7).

The social constructivist literature argues that through participation in common institutional structures, actors change their identities and therefore also their perceived interests and ensuing actions This can occur in a top-down fashion, where 'change agents' or 'norm entrepreneurs' in close contact with the EU international framework, persuade other domestic elites and the population to change their interests (Börzel and Risse 2003: 67). Bottom-up change is also possible. In this case, non-state actors unite in their support for international norms and mobilize to induce decision-makers to change their policies. Finally, transformation may take place through structural change, i.e. through institutional interaction over time. In all three cases, the density of institutional contact is of the essence. The more contact there is, the more likely is process of transformation through social learning.

The degree of pre-existing overlap between EU and domestic norms as well as the identification of the third party with the EU and its values are also important determinants of transformation through learning. The perceived quality and thus legitimacy and compatibility of EU norms with domestic norms affects the scope for learning. If EU norms do not resonate with the third party's historical, institutional, political, and socio-economic history, learning is less likely to occur. Equally problematic is when EU norms are distorted or misinterpreted, and the misinterpreted norms resonate and are accommodated domestically. For example, the manner in which EU membership was viewed as almost synonymous with membership of the North Atlantic Treaty Organization (NATO) by many Turkish elites highlighted their lack of understanding of what EU accession entailed, and their ensuing rejection of EU-demanded reforms in the spheres of democracy and human rights.

Another key determinant of the scope for social learning is the degree of popular dissatisfaction with the status quo. To the extent that the third country is generally dissatisfied with its leadership and policies, it is more likely to be receptive to domestic change. In these situations, when EU actors delegitimize a third country's leadership by juxtaposing its actions to EU values and the goal of integration, the Union can trigger domestic change by inducing a change in leadership. This was the case with Rauf Denktaş in northern Cyprus and partly with Milosevic's regime in Serbia.

But are mechanisms of change through conditionality and learning mutually exclusive or complementary? Important differences exist between these two analytical concepts. Change through conditionality may occur in the short and medium terms as actors, with unchanged identities and interests, simply alter their actions to account for a change in context. The more deep-rooted change that occurs through the transformation of identities and interests can only occur over the longer-term. However, one mechanism can give way to the other (Börzel and Risse 2000). Initially, a rational institutional account may capture better the mechanisms of change, as elites confronted with coercion or incentives may modify their positions and accept a negotiated settlement. Over time, and within the EU institutional framework, the institutional, economic, social and political contact that these relations entail can give rise to a deeper process of change. This may first manifest itself through a change in discourse, which is then assimilated through a change in beliefs and perceived interests. Over time, this may filter through different layers of society, leading to a deeper process of societal reconciliation (i.e. conflict transformation and resolution over and above conflict settlement).

This is not to say that conditionality automatically gives rise to endogenous processes of social change. If policies of conditionality are viewed as insufficiently legitimate, if existing domestic practice is uncontested, if EU norms are unrelated to domestic practice, or if institutional ties are weak, conditionality may either have no effect or it may generate perverse effects within third parties. A virtuous circle of absorption, assimilation and transformation can thus reverse into a vicious circle of retrenchment into the violation of rights, laws and democratic practice. Furthermore, conditionality can give rise to settlements that do not necessarily open the way to resolution. Conflict resolution occurs only if the induced settlements account for the parties' basic needs, creating a conducive environment for societal reconciliation. Otherwise, rather than a process of transformation, a settlement imposed through coercion and conditionality may trigger new waves of ethno-nationalism and political violence in future.

Passive enforcement

A third mechanism of EU impact is that of 'passive enforcement' or 'rule application' (Olsen 2002). Given the above-mentioned EU propensity to rely on constructive engagement and its reluctance to engage in ex post or negative conditionality, the Union can exert influence by relying on a system of 'passive enforcement' of its rules. Rather than highlighting the logic of punishment, which sets in when rules are violated, this EU mode of foreign policy-making hinges on a system of rule-bound cooperation, which is expected to work through its inbuilt incentives. While often confused with conditionality, passive enforcement is conceptually distinct from it. It does not attempt to alter incentives by altering the cost-benefit calculus through the offer of conditional carrots or the threat of sticks. The EU's delivery of benefits does not come as a recompense to a third country's concession. Obligations constitute the necessary rules which determine the overall framework that make mutually beneficial cooperation possible.

For passive enforcement to work, firstly there must be a clear set of legally defined and definable rules embedded in EU contracts. Passive enforcement cannot be easily used for conditions that the EU simply considers politically desirable, but which have no legal standing. Furthermore, this system of rules must either not be viewed by third parties as a cost, or it must be considered a necessary price that comes with EU engagement. In the case of third states whose policies oppose EU objectives (as is often the case in conflict cases), these rules will initially be viewed as costs, and probably as excessively high costs (i.e. the infringement on a state's sovereign capacity to pursue unconditionally its perceived interests). In these situations, the process of change embedded in passive enforcement requires that costs are viewed as obligatory. Effective passive enforcement also requires that the third party feels a sense of belonging with Europe and/or desires cooperation/integration with it, in order for it to accept the obligatory nature of the cost that comes with EU engagement. Without this, the third party will not willingly embark on the experience of respecting the rule, that could in time lead to its re-evaluation of its inherent value. When the rule comes to be viewed as a sine qua non by a third country, a far more subtle process of change is activated, compared with that of conditionality.

This process is related to the logic of social learning and can be viewed as a process of experimental learning. In the case of conditionality, the re-evaluation of attributed costs may occur through coercion (in the case of negative conditionality) or through a recalibrated cost-benefit calculus, altered by augmenting real or potential benefits. In the case of passive enforcement, the re-evaluation of attributed costs occurs endogenously, by internalizing the logic of the rule through the experience of respecting it. As opposed to the process of social learning, change does not occur through institutional contact, dialogue and exposure to and learning from others. It is rather based on a party's own experience of respecting a rule, and experiencing that its attributed cost is much lower than expected. Over time, the respect of the rule could also come to be viewed as a benefit.

The case of Turkey offers an interesting example in this respect. In order to open accession negotiations with the Union, EU institutions clarified that the abolition of the death penalty was essential for the launch of accession negotiations. The rule was reaffirmed over the years in successive Commission Progress Reports and Accession Partnership documents. Initially Turkey attributed excessive costs to the respect of this rule. In view of the securitized discourse surrounding the Kurdish question, the abolition of the death penalty was considered tantamount to catalyzing the country's territorial disintegration. Yet as the rule became viewed as an obligatory cost, the Turkish authorities ultimately accepted it and in 2002–3 passed the necessary constitutional and legal amendments to abolish capital punishment. Since then, evidence has demonstrated that the cost that Turkey had ascribed to the rule was excessive. The Turkish establishment thus began re-evaluating its attributed costs and may in time come to view the rule as a benefit. In the Turkish case, the authorities initially did not see the inherent value of abiding by the EU rule. Yet having internalized it as a necessary cost, they proceeded to respect it, only to discover that their attributed cost had been too high. The extent of the re-evaluation by the third party could also come as a surprise to EU actors. The Union may underestimate a third country's potential for experimental learning, and may thus be reluctant to impose a condition, fearing that the third party would respond by opting out of engagement.

The determinants of EU impact

EU contractual relations can thus influence ethno-political conflicts through three interrelated mechanisms. But what determines the effectiveness of these mechanisms? Which factors affect the extent and manner in which conditionality, social learning and passive enforcement can positively influence ethno-political conflicts in the European neighbourhood?

The value of the benefit

The effectiveness of conditionality, social learning and passive enforcement depends on the value of the benefits on offer and the costs of compliance with contractual obligations. Only if the potential gains relative to the costs are perceived to be sufficiently high, could the Union meaningfully exert influence on its neighbourhood conflicts. Value is determined by the objective nature of the contract as well as by the manner in which it is subjectively perceived by the third country to whom it is offered.

Objective value

Beginning with the objective elements in the EU contract, the first primary observation is that when full membership is an option, the EU's potential leverage is higher than in cases where relations are based on association, partnership or financial assistance. This begs the question of whether the EU can significantly influence third states that it cannot or does not wish to fully integrate. Indeed this is the core dilemma underlying the ENP. Precedents such as the European Economic Area (EEA) demonstrated that being included in 'all but institutions' proves ultimately unsatisfactory to neighbouring countries (Smith 2005). However, in a post-enlargement and post-constitutional crisis context, the question of the EU's final borders has become a principal strategic question on the European agenda. It has become increasingly clear that despite the success of enlargement, the EU cannot indefinitely rely on the same instrument as a means to positively induce transformation beyond its borders. Doing so would end up by making the Union unable to provide the very benefits that have inspired its neighbours to join it (Wallace 2003). Future enlargements may well see the entry of Turkey and the Western Balkan countries. However, the Union's relations with the remaining post-Soviet states (Ukraine, Moldova, Belarus, Georgia, Armenia and Azerbaijan and Russia itself) as well as with the entire southern Mediterranean basin and the Middle East require alternative policy instruments. Hence the challenge, undertaken by the ENP, of seeking new ways and means to act beyond the traditional accession/non-accession dichotomy (Lynch 2004).

When it comes to the EU's eastern neighbours such as Moldova and the Ukraine, it seems doubtful that the ENP will become sufficiently valuable. Denying the prospect of membership, while having the benefit of lowering external expectations, acts as a major disincentive in itself. This is all the more true given that the ENP denies this ultimate benefit while emulating the method and concept of enlargement. As such, no matter how valuable the ENP instruments are, to the extent that they are conceptualized as an alternative to membership, their value remains relatively low. In other words, the carrots on offer may be extremely appetizing; but some simply do not eat carrots. Yet even in the case of neighbours with no intention of joining the Union, the ENP may face the limits deriving from insufficiently valuable gains. Some countries, such as Israel, already enjoy many of the benefits on offer in the ENP. It remains doubtful that the additional benefits on offer in the ENP would be sufficiently valuable to grant the EU significantly more leverage on Israel. Other countries of the southern Mediterranean would value highly the liberalization of the four freedoms, and in particular agricultural liberalization and visa facilitation. Yet it seems unlikely that the Union will extend these freedoms to the south, particularly in a post-September 11 period, in which the fear of terrorism, organized crime and illegal migration has induced many Europeans to retrench to a 'fortress Europe' mentality when it comes to the south.

The carrots on offer also depend on the degree of proximity of the third country to the Union. The closer the EU is to a conflict – and thus the greater the
EU's potential interest in it – the more likely the Union is to engage in peacemaking through deep contractual relations. Hence, the EU's relative engagement
in the Western Balkans since the 1999 Kosovo war, compared with its relative
neglect of the South Caucasus. Proximity is also more likely to trigger a sense
of urgency to act in moments of crisis, given the greater visibility of a conflict and the more likely its spillover effects into the EU. This may induce a
greater EU effort to reach consensus on the forms and modalities of intervention
(Hill 2001).

The value of the benefit and, in particular, the distinction between membership
and non-membership also affects the potential for social learning. The key question here is whether learning can take place beyond the EU's borders, where EU
institutional, political, economic and social contact is limited and confined almost
exclusively to third country elites. Is the accession process and, less still, looser
forms of contractual relations sufficiently dense to generate a process of endogenous change through learning? If so, is learning possible beyond elite levels to
encompass the wider public and thus induce conflict transformation and resolution?
As opposed to reaching inter-elite settlements, conflict transformation and resolution calls for a deep-rooted change in the public's attitudes and positions, which
does not necessarily occur in response to the workings of elite-driven multilateral
institutions.

Finally, the objective value of contractual relations affects the prospects for
passive enforcement. As mentioned above, passive enforcement requires that rules
are legally defined and definable. As such, passive enforcement is more easily
applicable to the accession process than to looser forms of association. In the case
of accession, EU institutions have at their disposal thousands of pages of legally
binding *acquis*, which candidates are called upon to adopt and implement. Some
of the rules embedded in the accession process can have a direct or indirect effect
on conflict resolution efforts. In the case of looser forms of association instead,
the EU has much less 'material' at hand. It can rely on passive enforcement only
when these either have a basis in international law or relate to the existing legal
obligations of the third state (derived from its membership of the UN or the Council
of Europe for example).

Subjective value

Second and equally important is the importance of the subjective value of EU
benefits, i.e. the perceived value by the recipient. The more a third country identifies with 'Europe' or the more dependent it is upon the Union, the greater is
the EU's potential influence on it. Yet different domestic actors within a third
country may value EU benefits differently. Domestic actors have different aims,
strategies and tactics, which are driven by different historical, economic, and
political interests and understandings (Dorussen 2001). As such their assessment
of the Union differs. Although full membership is the most powerful foreign policy

instrument at the EU's disposal, it may be of little value to a nationalist aiming first and foremost to assert an ethnically based separate state. Hence, to the extent that nationalist forces enjoy the upper hand within a third country, EU benefits are unlikely to affect a conflict. Depending on the relative balance of different domestic actors and their interaction, the overall effect of EU conditionality can be positive, negative or nil.

In principle the subjective value of the benefit should be higher than the subjective cost of the obligation in order for EU policies to be effective (Schimmelfennig *et al.* 2002). Ineffectiveness may thus arise when the attributed cost of compliance with EU conditions/obligations is considered too high by the third party (either by the leadership or by the population). If the perceived cost of compliance is higher than the reward, then the third country may reject the conditions. This is frequently the case in conflict situations when EU conditions touch upon the most critical existential questions of a state or community. For example, a Turkish nationalist will reject EU conditions relating to Kurdish minority rights not only because of the insufficient value accorded to the goal of EU membership, but also because of the perceived costs of such a reform.

Compliance occurs either if EU benefits increase or are perceived to be more valuable, or if the attributed cost of EU conditions/obligations falls. This necessitates either a change in perceptions through social or experimental learning, or through empowerment of domestic actors with different attitudes towards compliance (e.g. through conditionality). However, when conditions and obligations do not resonate with existing domestic practices, learning may not take place. And often in ethno-political conflicts, the discourse is based on very different premises from those characterizing the EU framework. Notions of absolute sovereignty, exclusive identities, and indivisible territory feature prominently in these contexts and contrast sharply with EU notions of shared sovereignty, permeable borders and multiple identities.

In the ENP, the costs of compliance may well come to exceed the benefits on offer. The ENP offers a 'stake in the single market' to the neighbours. Yet, assuming it is granted, a stake in the single market entails costly harmonization with the thousands of pages of minute laws, rules and regulations of the *acquis*. In areas such as justice and home affairs, *acquis* harmonization could also be politically (as well as administratively and financially) costly, given that it may hinder the free access to kin-communities in neighbouring states. As such, without significant financial and technical EU support, it seems unlikely that neighbouring countries would have the capability and will to engage in this arduous legal and administrative revolution. Moreover, given that the prospect of accession is excluded, it remains unclear why the 'Europeanization' of the neighbourhood ought to take this precise 'EUization' form.

An inverse problem related to subjective value may also arise. EU engagement may trigger disincentives for conflict resolution when domestic actors value EU accession over and above conflict resolution. After years of failed attempts at stitching a state back together, the metropolitan state may abandon the search for a complex federal solution and focus its attention on unilateral

EU membership instead. Tendencies of this sort have been present in Serbia and Montenegro, in the Greek Cypriot Republic of Cyprus, as well as in Moldova. Some domestic actors may abandon the search for a constitutional solution and argue that by doing so they can progress faster to EU membership. Others may feel that entering the EU would strengthen their bargaining position, thereby securing a more favourable constitutional deal in the future.

Idiosyncrasies within the Union often exacerbate these trends. While the Council of Ministers and the European Council declare their support for conflict resolution and European integration, the Commission – focussing on the latter – may reinforce secessionist trends. Integrating a centralized unitary state is often easier than integrating a complex federation. Yet the solutions to most ethno-political conflicts often require finely tuned federal and confederal features (Lijphart 1977). Particularly in the short to medium term, these solutions may not necessarily go hand-in-hand with the objectives of establishing efficient states, capable of assuming the obligations of membership. As such, the requirements dictated by the Commission often generate disincentives against conflict resolution. Moreover, both secessionist forces and nationalist actors within the metropolitan state can legitimize their positions by using the very discourse of European integration. Precisely because the objective is that of EU accession, the search for *sui generis* federal settlements or decentralized governance is set aside (Hughes *et al.* 2004: 528).

Timing

Another determinant of value is that of timing. In the case of ex ante conditionality, particularly in the context of accession, expected reforms are demanded in the short and medium terms but the actual delivery of the benefit (membership) occurs in the long run. This generates two sets of problems. Long-term benefits are valued less than short-term ones. The unpredictability of the former reduces the value of the benefit and the potential incentives for reform. The time lag between the demand for reforms and the subsequent delivery of the benefit may also induce domestic policy-makers to delay reforms until the delivery of the benefit is closer and surer. This may be particularly true in conflict situations. The settlement of an ethno-political conflict is often viewed by the conflict parties as taking a step into the unknown. EU membership can be viewed as a means to hedge against risk in view of the security guarantees embedded in EU accession. As such, principal parties may be reluctant to reach an agreement until the prospects of membership are closer. This dilemma appears to characterize the Turkish position on Cyprus and the Kurdish question.

Furthermore, EU benefits such as membership suffer from their one-off nature. Grabbe (2001) identifies this problem as one of 'bluntness of gate-keeping'. Given the one-off nature of benefits in the context of the accession process, EU gate-keeping is often too blunt a measure to be used as an instrument for progressive domestic transformation. It cannot induce precise changes at precise moments in time over a long period. Gatekeeping was used successfully in 1997, when the

Union prevented Slovakia from opening accession negotiations due to its human rights record. It was successful in persuading Turkey to support the Annan Plan in 2004. But when carrots are eaten in one bite, it is difficult to use the incentive of a dangling carrot – no matter how appetizing it is – as a means to induce transformation over time. This is particularly true given that once a benefit is granted it is complicated to withdraw it.

Linked to this, benefits delivered before the fulfilment of their accompanying obligations (i.e. through ex post conditionality) suffer from the opposite problem of time inconsistency. When the benefit, such as the conclusion of an association agreement, is delivered in the short term, based on an understanding that the respect of its accompanying obligations will follow suit, its value is absorbed by the recipient party. This may induce third countries to avoid or postpone their respect of the obligations. EU benefits such as financial assistance or the ENP instruments could mitigate these time inconsistency problems. This is because their delivery can be graduated over time, in response to a third country's respect for EU conditions.

The credibility of the obligations

Effective conditionality, social learning and passive enforcement require valuable gains. But if gains are on one side of the equation, obligations are on the other. In other words, for an effective EU role conducted through contractual relations, it is imperative for the obligations/conditions to be credible. Credibility depends on the recipient's perception of the donor's capacity and willingness to carry out declared commitments. In the case of ex ante conditionality, credibility is related to the Union's track record in delivering its promised gains, when, and only when, the specified conditions are fulfilled. In the case of ex post conditionality, credibility is related to the EU's track record in withdrawing benefits in cases of consistent violations of specified obligations. Credibility in passive enforcement entails cooperating when and only when the rules governing engagement are respected by all parties. Credibility also impinges on the potential for learning, given that a particular norm is more likely to be assimilated when all parties engaged in contractual relations are steadfast in their respect of it.

The determinants of credibility

Some conditions/obligations are more credible than others in view of the object and purpose of the contract in question. The obligations falling within the scope of the Copenhagen criteria are more credible than the human rights and democracy demands made in the context of association or partnership and cooperation. In addition, in so far as the accession process anticipates the Union's incorporation of a third country, EU actors have greater interests in ensuring that candidates are peaceful, democratic and respectful of human rights and international law. A candidate state is aware of this, and knows that its scope for bending or evading an EU rule is circumscribed.

However, a contractual relationship foreseeing full membership suffers from a problem of sunk costs, which may hinder the credibility of conditionality as the process gathers momentum. Given the human, financial and political capital which needs to be invested in the accession process, it becomes increasingly unlikely that the EU will deny the ultimate carrot of membership in response to a candidate country's disrespect of an obligation. In the case of the eastern enlargement, after over a decade of assistance and negotiations, it was improbable if not politically impossible for the EU to deny entry on the basis of a candidate's flaws in compliance. In other words, as time passes, while the credibility of the promise increases, that of the threat decreases.

A third country's observation of the EU's interaction with peer states enjoying similar contractual relations also affects the credibility of EU obligations. When a third country observes that a peer state is absolved from its contractual obligations, it will not miss the opportunity to accuse the EU of double standards, thus weakening the Union's own bargaining stance towards it. The third country's attributed value of EU obligations also dissipates when it observes that EU actors are willing to renege on the obligations on the basis of other interests. They conclude from this that the Union does not ascribe sufficient value to its demanded conditions. It is interesting for example to note how Muslim countries in the southern Mediterranean carefully watch Muslim Turkey's accession process. To the extent that the Muslim world perceives the EU's reluctance to include Turkey to be driven by bias against Turkey's culture and religion, the Union's credibility in demanding liberal reforms in the southern Mediterranean is harmed.

The credibility of the EU's conditions and obligations also falls when the Union does not believe that a third country can, or will, respect a demanded rule, due to the excessive cost attributed to it. In such cases, the logic of passive enforcement gives way to a flawed logic of conditionality. EU actors tend to present a set of EU-related carrots to induce third countries to 'concede' on the respect of the rule. The rule thus becomes a condition that can be bargained on and possibly circumvented, rather than a sine qua non of cooperative engagement. The EU implicitly signals that the rule can be bent or avoided, and as such it undermines its credibility. This prevents the third country from engaging in experimental learning through respect of the obligation.

Finally, the EU's credibility is seriously damaged if third countries observe that the Union itself does not respect a condition or obligation demanded of it. If third states observe the disrespect of particular rules within the Union itself, this impairs the Union's own reputation as well as the prospects for social learning beyond its borders. Likewise, if EU policies are perceived as displaying double standards, favouring one side of a conflict, an inverse social learning effect may set in, inducing a social distancing from the Union and its proclaimed norms and values.

The problem of double standards is particularly acute in cases of secessionist conflicts where the EU does not play a direct mediating role. For fear of indirect recognition, the Union is often excessively cautious, refusing to have any official contact with the de facto authorities of a secessionist entity. This is the case across the EU neighbourhood, from Cyprus to the former Soviet space. Yet official ties with the metropolitan state and the snubbing of the unrecognized entity creates resentment within the latter, which may lead the secessionist entity to abandon the goal of European integration and discard the values that allegedly underpin the EU project.

The clarity of the obligations

EU credibility also requires clarity in the specification of conditions and obligations. In addition to its informational value, the clarity of a condition is key to credibility because it reduces the scope for the political management of a contractual relationship (Schimmelfennig and Sedelmeier 2004). It also raises the likelihood of social and experimental learning given the clear nature of the rule or obligation to be assimilated. When it comes to *acquis*-related obligations or rules grounded on clearly defined areas of international law, EU conditions can be specified clearly. This signals to the recipient both how it is expected to act as well as the importance attributed by the Union to the respect of that particular obligation. Conditions grounded on the obligations stemming from other organizations of which the third country is a member also raise their degree of clarity. For example, the recommendations of the Venice Commission in the judicial and constitutional domains, or the judgements of the European Court of Human Rights (ECtHR) can raise the clarity of EU obligations in these spheres when the third country in question is a Council of Europe member.

Yet often, when it comes to political questions, clarity is hard to obtain. When are human rights respected? When is a country fully democratic? Human rights violations and features of undemocratic practice, racism and xenophobia exist within the EU as well as outside it. The meeting of criteria is rarely clear-cut and often a question of degree. In addition, the Union does not have ready-made benchmarks to monitor precisely the implementation of political reforms, and often does not have specific models that provide a clear format for an expected reform.

In conflict cases, the question of clarity exacerbates when the Union does not specify the details of its advocated solutions, but calls for vague proposals in between the two extremes of the right to territorial integrity and that to self-determination. When the Union limits itself to supporting 'federalism', when it calls for 'peaceful and non-violent solutions' and when it advocates 'autonomy', 'effective political participation' and the 'right to enjoy one's culture', domestic elites in ethno-political conflicts can portray a very wide range of positions as falling within the scope of EU demands. Lack of clarity both signals the Union's relative lack of interest in the specifics of a conflict, and it allows domestic actors to pursue and legitimize initiatives which may be portrayed as fulfilling EU goals, while remaining in spirit and practice far removed from them.

Some EU conditions have inbuilt problems of clarity, linked to their lack of legal grounding. This is the case of minority rights, in principle one of the Copenhagen criteria for accession. When advocating minority rights, EU institutions draw their conditions from the norms of other pan-European organizations such as the Council of Europe and the OSCE (i.e. the Council of Europe's 1995 Framework Convention for the Protection of National Minorities, or the work of the OSCE's High Commissioner for National Minorities). However, Community law lacks the adequate instruments to assure the protection of these rights. On the contrary, the emphasis in EC law is on individual human rights, which in some instances may contrast with the protection of minorities. Article 6(1) of the Treaty of the EU (TEU), setting the principles on which the Union is founded (and thus presumably the conditions for entering it) only mentions the principles of liberty, democracy, human rights and fundamental freedoms and the rule of law. It excludes the protection of minorities, included instead in the Copenhagen criteria for entry (De Witte 2002). Within EU law, there is neither an attempt to define minority rights, nor a concrete mechanism to ensure their monitoring and protection (Hughes and Sasse 2003). EU law only calls for non-discrimination (Article 13 of the TEU) and affirms the value of preserving regional diversity (Article 151 of the TEU). Legally, the problem is not exclusive to the EU. It is part of the general problem in public international law of defining group rights as distinct from individual rights. In addition, the practice within EU member states varies widely and minority problems within the EU persist. The violation of these rights is often flagged by candidate countries, such as Turkey and the Baltic states, that aim to circumvent EU calls to extend minority rights there.

Political management

Rather than representing a determinant of EU effectiveness in its own right, political management frequently provides the underlying explanation of the above-mentioned shortcomings in the EU's role. It is often due to political imperatives, operating beyond the blueprint of a contract, that problems arise relating to the value of the benefits or the credibility of the obligations.

An effective EU contractual relationship would necessitate the automatic entitlement to rights when obligations are fulfilled and the automatic withdrawal or non-entitlement of benefits when they are not. Yet such automaticity is never present in practice. Beyond the contract lie the political imperatives of EU actors. Both the granting and the withdrawal of a benefit requires a consensus within the Union. For an association agreement or an accession treaty to come into force, there must be unanimity of the member governments, and the ratification of national parliaments and the European Parliament (EP). Such a consensus depends on the fulfilment of the contractual obligations of the third state. But it also depends on other factors, which are motivated by underlying political or economic imperatives.

The eastern enlargement occurred despite the fact that some conditions were not fulfilled. The importance of the fifth enlargement went way beyond the minutiae of compliance with the *acquis communautaire.* Hence, for example the design of the Progress Reports, which appeared driven by the desire to tell a cumulative success story (Sasse 2006). The same is true for the withdrawal of a benefit in the case of ex post conditionality. Suspending a Euro-Mediterranean association agreement would sever the contractual link between the EU and a southern Mediterranean country, and thus reduce the EU's potential influence on it. Equally problematic are situations in which a benefit is not granted, despite a third country's respect of ex ante conditionality. If for example the EU rejects Turkey's bid for membership despite Turkey's fulfilment of all the Copenhagen criteria, then the credibility of the EU will be seriously impaired. In other words, if the EU's ultimate judgement were to hinge on Turkey's size, location, culture, religion or level of economic development, i.e. on reasons that lie beyond the blueprint of the accession partnerships, the progress reports and the accession negotiations, then the effectiveness of its contractual relations with Turkey and other neighbours will diminish significantly.

The credibility of the EU's contractual relations depends critically on the structure of the wider relationship with the third country. When a third country is highly dependent on the EU, the latter is more likely to adhere to the formal and specified conditions included in the contract. When, however, the wider relationship is governed by ties of mutual dependence, then the third country can exert leverage on the EU to obtain the promised benefits without fulfilling its obligations.

Some degree of political management in determining when and whether conditions are met and when and whether benefits should be granted is inevitable. However, when blatant violations persist without consequences or when benefits are not granted despite the general fulfilment of contractual obligations, then the EU's own credibility is harmed. In other words, when other conditions unspecified in the contract govern the Union's relations with third states, then EU policy loses its effectiveness.

The five chapters that follow analyze the EU's impact on and effectiveness in five ethno-political conflicts in the EU's backyard. They assess how the accession process, the stabilization and association process, association, partnership and cooperation, financial assistance and the ENP have affected the incentives of conflict parties. The EU's impact on the five cases is examined by analyzing the effectiveness of the three mechanisms of EU influence analyzed in this chapter (conditionality, social learning and passive enforcement). The effectiveness of these mechanisms is tested through an analysis of their value, their credibility and their political management.

3   The missed opportunity to promote reunification in Cyprus

EU interests and objectives in the Cyprus conflict

EU interests in the Cyprus conflict are defined in relation to its wider concerns for peace and stability in the eastern Mediterranean. Peace and stability in the region are valued both because of the eastern Mediterranean's proximity to the Union, particularly since Greece's accession in 1981, and because of its closeness to the turbulent and strategic Middle East. A solution in Cyprus would also encourage peace between NATO ally and EU candidate Turkey and member state Greece.

Moving beyond these general interests, some member states have more specific concerns than others (Tocci 2004b: 32–8). Greece is the member state whose national interest has been most closely associated with the conflict. This is because of Greece's ties with its kin-Greek Cypriot community, its historical role in the conflict, and because of the salience of Cyprus in the wider Greek–Turkish dispute. While no longer advocating union with Cyprus (*enosis*), Greece has continued to support the Greek Cypriot cause. Taking the cue from the Greek Cypriot community since 1974, it has thus promoted the reunification of the island through a tight federal (or unitary) structure, significant territorial readjustments, the liberalization of rights and freedoms, and a much reduced (preferably absent) Turkish role in Cyprus' security arrangements. Greek support took different forms at different times. While in the late 1970s, Constantine Karamanlis' Nea Demokratia (ND) government retreated to the backstage on the Cyprus dossier, Andreas Papandreou's Pannelion Socialistikon Kinima (PASOK) in the 1980s and 1990s took a more hands-on approach. Particularly under PASOK rule, Greece contributed to the mobilization of the international community – including the EU – in support of the Greek Cypriot cause.

The United Kingdom (UK) is the second member state with close interests in Cyprus. British interests are motivated by its colonial past, by its two sovereign military bases on the island (of key importance given their proximity to the Middle East), by its post-1960 role as 'guarantor power', by its permanent seat on the UN Security Council (UNSC) and by its interests in close relations with Turkey. In addition, since the eruption of violence in Cyprus in 1963–4, and particularly in the aftermath of the 1974 partition, the UK has hosted large Greek Cypriot and Turkish Cypriot communities. Since 1974, the UK has supported the

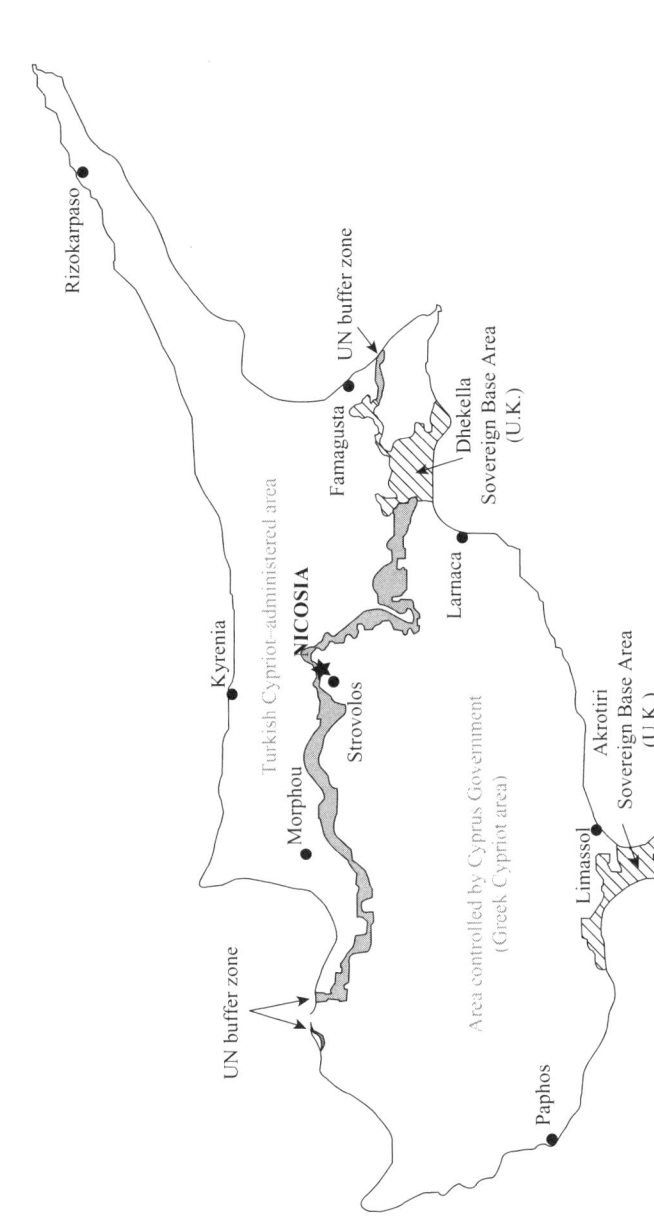

Map 1 The partition of Cyprus.
Source: The General Libraries, The University of Texas at Austin. http://www.lib.utexas.edu/maps/cyprus.html.

good offices of the UN Secretary General (UNSG) and its attempts to promote a bi-zonal and bi-communal federation. British interests in Cyprus have been pursued both through bilateral relations with the conflict parties (e.g. through the British Special Representative or the High Commissioner in Cyprus), or through the UN. While supporting Cyprus' EU accession, the UK has adamantly resisted an EU involvement in the conflict.

Other member states have paid sporadic attention to the conflict. France, as a permanent UNSC member, and Germany, in view of its strong ties to Turkey and large Turkish immigrant community, have paid occasional attention to the conflict. However, like the UK, when they turned to Cyprus they did so outside the confines of the EU. No other member state has ever pressed for an active EU involvement in the conflict. Some considered the conflict as an internal dispute between its two communities, which only called for the independent involvement of member states Greece and Britain. Others focussed on Turkey's prime role in the conflict, and considered that meddling in it would imperil relations with geostrategic partner Turkey. Moreover, neither did the seemingly frozen conflict pose serious and immediate threats to stability in the eastern Mediterranean, nor did the member states wish to jeopardize their relations with the parties by attempting to untie the Gordian knots bedevilling the island. Indeed, with the partial exception of European Political Cooperation's (EPC) attempts to encourage a ceasefire in July 1974, the EU has never developed a specific and independent policy towards the conflict. After 1974, the member states downgraded the conflict from the EPC agenda, limiting themselves to supporting the UNSG's good offices. A Council Working Group dealing with Cyprus was established, but the problem was never the subject of high-level political discussions.

In turn, the Union never proposed a solution to the conflict, and only supported the UNSC resolutions and the Secretary General's mediation efforts in Cyprus. Indeed, each and every EPC declaration on Cyprus merely affirmed the Community's commitment to the independence, sovereignty and territorial integrity of the island, and called for reunification in accordance with UN resolutions. The advent of Cyprus' accession process in the 1990s did not alter this fact. It only strengthened the EU's existing aversion to a two-state solution, which would have complicated the task of EU accession. The member states were keen to see a settlement prior to membership, given their reluctance to import a bitter ethno-political conflict into the Union. Furthermore, a settlement would have strengthened the EU's image as a community of peace and security. But while EU rhetoric emphasized the desirability of a solution and raised the expectation that the accession process would act as a catalyst for this purpose, EU actors did not articulate what kind of solution they had in mind, nor did they operationalize and implement this 'catalytic effect'. EU officials simply claimed that there was a 'division of labour' between the Commission and the UN. While the former negotiated accession, the latter mediated inter-communal negotiations.[1]

The EU's retreat to the backstage does not imply that the Union has no views on a solution in Cyprus. Precisely because of its commitment to UN mediation, the EU supported the increasingly precise plans for a federal settlement elaborated by the UNSG and endorsed by the Security Council. Hence in 1975, the Community backed UNSC resolution 367 proposing a solution based on an independent, sovereign, bi-communal and bi-zonal federation. In the late 1980s and early 1990s, the EC/EU supported UNSG Pérez de Cuéllar's and UNSG Boutros Ghali's good offices, which culminated in the 1992 'Set of Ideas', endorsed in UNSC resolution 750. The Union also strongly, unreservedly and unambiguously backed UNSG Annan's efforts to mediate a settlement prior to Cyprus' EU accession, which culminated in the successive versions of the comprehensive 'Annan Plan' (Council 2004b). The Union supported the Plan to the extent of being willing to accommodate its provisions (in some cases not fully compatible with the *acquis communautaire*) into Cyprus' Treaty of Accession. Since Cyprus entered the Union, partly because of the lack of new UN initiatives, and partly because of the EU's reluctance to interfere in the internal affairs of its member states, the Union has not expressed its views on the conflict, beyond sporadically expressing its desire to see the island reunified within the European fold.

The evolution of the Cyprus conflict

Turning to Cyprus itself, the following sections briefly review the emergence and evolution of the conflict, focussing on whether, when and how the decades-old conflict has neared resolution along the lines proposed by the UN and supported by the EU.

The emergence and consolidation of conflict

The potential for inter-communal conflict in Cyprus dates back to the period of Ottoman rule and the emergence of separate Greek-speaking Orthodox and Turkish-speaking Muslim communities on the island. Yet the seeds of the modern dispute were sown during the years of British colonial domination in the early twentieth century. In the 1920s, the Greek Cypriot community became increasingly dissatisfied with British rule. But unlike other twentieth century decolonization movements, desire for freedom did not imply a demand for independence. Instead, viewing themselves as one people with mainland Greeks, the Greek Cypriots called for *enosis,* or union with Greece. By the mid-1950s, the Greek Cypriot community (backed by Greece) launched an armed struggle against the British, conducted by the EOKA guerrilla movement (Ethniki Organosis Kyprion Agoniston). Initially, the British reacted through force and repression, and mobilized the Turkish Cypriot community (18 per cent of the population) and Turkey in support of its anti-*enosis* struggle. As Turkish and Turkish Cypriot resistance against *enosis* grew, their positions crystallized into the diametrically opposite claims to *taksim*, or partition of the island into Greek and Turkish Cypriot zones. Turkish Cypriot goals were also pursued by armed resistance, through the Türk Mukavemet Teşkilatı.

By the late 1950s, the parties were at loggerheads with each other, triggering a cycle of escalating violence. The path for compromise was cleared with a shift in the British position in support for Cyprus' independence. In 1959 and 1960,

Greece, Turkey and the UK, together with representatives from the two communities, reached agreements in Zurich and London, outlining the framework for a independent Republic of Cyprus (RoC). The treaties explicitly ruled out both *enosis* and *taksim*, provided for two sovereign British military bases, 950 Greek troops and 650 Turkish troops on the island, and entrusted guarantor status to Greece, Turkey and the UK in Cyprus.[2] The basic structure of the Republic was laid down in the 1960 Constitution, which established a bi-communal partnership state, i.e. a hybrid consociational set-up with elements of extra-territorial communal autonomy. Rather than through territorial separation, bi-communality was enshrined in community representation and power-sharing at the centre, and communal autonomy within the five largest municipalities.

Many Greek Cypriots expressed their dissatisfaction with these agreements from the outset, regarding them as a betrayal of the *enosis* cause. Most importantly, they contested what they believed to be the over-generous concessions granted to the Turkish Cypriot community relative to its size, which had been imposed on them by outside powers in view of Turkey's strategic significance. By November 1963, the first president of the Republic, Archbishop Makarios presented a proposal for amending the Constitution, amendments which in essence transformed the republic from a bi-communal partnership to a Greek Cypriot unitary state with Turkish Cypriot minority rights. The Turkish Cypriot leadership, backed by Ankara, rejected the proposal, triggering a collapse of the constitutional order (with the departure of all Turkish Cypriot officials from public institutions) and a renewed round of inter-communal fighting, which caused many deaths and the forced displacement of over 30,000 Turkish Cypriots into enclaves. The problem intensified with Greece's efforts to destabilize Makarios' government after the advent of military dictatorship in 1967. Greek interference in Cyprus culminated in the 15 July 1974 coup, which ousted the Archbishop's regime and extended the Greek military dictatorship to the island.

In response, Turkey invaded Cyprus on 20 July 1974, invoking its rights under the Treaty of Guarantee. The army initially took control of a narrow strip of coastline around Kyrenia, but after the failed attempt to broker a ceasefire, Turkey attacked a second time and occupied 37 per cent of the island's territory. Thereafter, Turkish troops remained in Cyprus and the 1960 constitutional order was not restored. A radically different order emerged instead. The military intervention and the ensuing 1975 Vienna agreements led to the displacement of 140–160,000 Greek Cypriots from the north and 60,000 Turkish Cypriots from the south. Both areas were almost entirely ethnically cleansed. Furthermore, Turkey encouraged mainland immigration to northern Cyprus (Hatay 2005). Property formerly belonging to Greek Cypriots was nationalized and distributed to Turkish Cypriots on the basis of properties lost in the south as well as to Turkish immigrants. The return and/or compensation of property and the fate of the Turkish 'settlers' became amongst the major sticking points on the conflict settlement agenda.

The island was thus divided into two zones, separated by the impenetrable 'green line'. In the north, the Turkish Cypriots first declared the Turkish Federated State of Cyprus in 1975, and in 1983 they unilaterally declared the Turkish Republic of

Northern Cyprus. The international community – excluding Turkey – condemned this as a secessionist act against the spirit of conflict resolution.[3] In the south, the Greek Cypriots retained the title of the RoC and since 1964 the international community has recognized the Republic as the only legitimate authority on the island despite the absence of Turkish Cypriots there. Human and political separation also had dire economic effects. While in the post-1974 era, the Greek Cypriot economy in the south underwent a vigorous recovery leading to economic prosperity, the Turkish Cypriot economy in the north stagnated. Tourism has been under-exploited mainly owing to the lack of international air links. Trade and investment have been hindered by restrictions largely caused by non-recognition,

Photo 1 Turkish soldiers parading in northern Cyprus. March 2000.

an uncompetitive environment and the uncertain legal status of land and property. The economy became dominated by an inefficient public sector, leading to serious fiscal imbalances. Dependence on Turkey also meant that northern Cyprus has inherited Turkey's macroeconomic ills, further hampering trade, investment and overall growth.

The history of negotiations and attempted solutions

Successive rounds of negotiations since 1974 have amounted to little more than a few superficial and inconsequential successes and a myriad of failures. The parties, at different times and to different degrees, rejected international proposals, refusing to alter their underlying negotiating positions. Yet at the same time, the UN became increasingly precise as to what the contours of a settlement could look like. Over time, proposals did not deviate significantly from one another, but rather built on each other and remained grounded on the principles underpinning the 1960 agreements.

The only concrete steps forward came shortly after partition. UNSC resolution 367 of 1975 proposed a solution based on an independent, sovereign, bi-communal and bi-zonal federation. A federation would take into account the post-1974 situation, while respecting the independence of Cyprus. Resolution 367 was essentially endorsed by the two communities and paved the way for the high-level agreements of 1977 between Rauf Denktaş and Archbishop Makarios and 1979 between Denktaş and Spyros Kyprianou. The agreements advocated the establishment of an independent, bi-communal and non-aligned federation, which included territorial readjustments between the Turkish Cypriot north and the Greek Cypriot south, and solutions to the refugee problem and to the liberalization of the 'three freedoms' of movement, settlement and property.

Yet once the parties entered discussions on what these general guidelines entailed, negotiations went through an unending series of failures. UNSR Hugo Gobbi mediated in Cyprus between 1980 and 1983, leaving office when the RoC secured UN General Assembly resolution 37/253 in favour of the immediate withdrawal of Turkish forces, and the Turkish Cypriots unilaterally declared independence, triggering a walkout of the Greek Cypriot negotiating team. Talks resumed in Vienna in 1984, and in 1986 UNSG Javier Pérez de Cuéllar drafted three proposals for a federation consisting of two provinces together with compromise arrangements on territory, the 'three freedoms', the withdrawal of Turkish troops, the resettlement of the former tourist resort town of Varosha and the reopening of the airport at Nicosia. The Turkish Cypriot side accepted the first and third draft agreements, but both Andreas Papandreou and Spyros Kyprianou rejected them.

There was a greater sense of optimism when talks were re-launched in 1988 between Denktaş and the newly elected and moderate Greek Cypriot president George Vassiliou. In 1989, Pérez de Cuellar presented his ideas for a settlement, based on the principles of political equality, bi-zonality and bi-communality. Negotiations on the basis of the UNSG's ideas ultimately failed when in 1990

Denktaş demanded the right of separate self-determination and was turned down by Vassiliou. The UN's efforts persisted unabated. In 1991, UNSC resolution 716 reaffirmed the principle of a single Cyprus based on the political equality of the two communities. In 1992, UNSG Boutros Boutros Ghali picked up the Cyprus dossier from where his predecessor had left it. The process culminated in the 'Set of Ideas', which fleshed out in greater detail previous UN proposals for a bi-zonal and bi-communal federation. Vassiliou accepted it as a basis for negotiation and Denktaş endorsed 91 points of the 100-point proposal. Yet the talks collapsed in November 1992 with Boutros Ghali concluding that the peace process suffered from a deep crisis of confidence.

Immediately afterwards, the positions of both parties hardened, reducing the prospects for an agreement (Tocci 2004b: 69–82). In 1993, Glafcos Clerides won over incumbent Vassiliou, running his presidential campaign on a nationalist pledge to significantly alter the Set of Ideas and upgrade Greek Cypriot defence policy. Internal political changes in Nicosia dovetailed with those in Athens, with the return to power of Andreas Papandreou. Papandreou immediately strengthened Greek ties with the RoC, most notably in the field of defence through the Joint Defence Doctrine. Greece and the Greek Cypriots also began exerting greater pressure in European legal forums for a condemnation of Turkey and the Turkish Cypriots. The first key case was the 1994 Anastasiou case in the European Court of Justice (ECJ), which ended preferential Turkish Cypriot exports to EU markets, damaging significantly the already weak and isolated northern Cypriot economy. The second critical case was that of Titina Loizidou in 1996 at the ECtHR, which opened the way to an unending string of Greek Cypriot cases against Turkey, aiming to secure the return of Greek Cypriot property in the north through arbitration rather than negotiation. The Turkish Cypriot side instead moved towards greater de facto integration of northern Cyprus into Turkey.

Unsurprisingly, when inter-communal negotiations were re-launched in Troutbeck and Glion in 1997 they had little chance of success. In that context, the UNSG tabled a proposal which, like the Set of Ideas, proposed a federal state with single sovereignty emanating equally from the two communities, with single international personality and citizenship, and composed of two federated states with identical powers. But the talks were short-lived and ended with a Turkish Cypriot walkout and Denktaş's refusal to participate in further negotiations. Thereafter, the Turkish Cypriot position hardened considerably. The Turkish Cypriots first demanded that future negotiations be conducted between two sovereign equals, and then called for the establishment of a confederation between two sovereign states. In southern Cyprus, nationalistic defence policies persisted, culminating in the incident, which almost triggered a Greek–Turkish war in 1997–8, over the Greek Cypriot acquisition of S-300 missiles from Russia which were to be stationed on the island.

In 1999, to break the impasse caused by Denktaş's preconditions, the UNSC called for proximity talks.[4] The talks made little headway towards opening direct negotiations, let alone a settlement, and were later defined by the UNSG as a process of 'procedural wrangling', 'verbal gymnastics' and 'shadow boxing'

(UNSG 2003a, paragraph 23). In December 2000 the Turkish Cypriot side unilaterally abandoned the talks, and the peace process once again plunged into deadlock. Alongside, Turkish–Turkish Cypriot efforts towards integration persisted, and were exacerbated by Turkish threats to annex northern Cyprus (Cyprus News 2001).

Direct negotiations were re-launched in early 2002, with a turn-around in the Turkish Cypriot position, and culminated in the publication of the first version of the 'Annan Plan' in November 2002. Constitutionally, the Plan adopted several aspects of the Swiss and Belgian federal constitutions, providing for the sharing of sovereignty between the two communities both in terms of representation and decision-making within the thin federal level, and between the two constituent states in northern and southern Cyprus respectively. The Plan foresaw a reduction of the northern zone to 28.5 per cent of the land. This would have allowed a majority of Greek Cypriot refugees to return to their properties under Greek Cypriot rule. The remaining refugees who wished to return, would be able to do so under specified rules and regulations that would ensure a continued Turkish Cypriot majority in the north. In terms of military security, in addition to the continuation of the Treaty of Guarantee, there would be an equal number of Greek and Turkish troops, which would be progressively scaled back to the levels stipulated in the original 1960 accords, with the objective of complete demilitarization.

Despite the publication of three successive versions of the Plan in late 2002 and early 2003, the parties failed to reach an agreement in December 2002 (at the Copenhagen European Council), in February and in March 2003. These failures were largely due to the Turkish and Turkish Cypriot rejection of the Annan Plan. Both Turkish and Turkish Cypriot politics at the time were in a state of deep upheaval, and in early 2003 the political changes underway had not consolidated yet into a policy shift in favour of a settlement. In Turkey, the November 2002 general elections saw the rise to power of the reformist Adalet ve Kalkınma Partisi (AKP). Yet, while immediately leading to a change of rhetoric on Cyprus, a substantive policy shift occurred gradually over the course of 2003 and 2004. In northern Cyprus, an even deeper political upheaval – verging on regime change – was under way. Beginning with the mass demonstrations in December 2002 and early 2003, the Turkish Cypriot centre-left and liberal camps, backed by large segments of civil society, mobilized to overturn the political system, dominated since 1974 by nationalist parties (in particular by Rauf Denktaş) together with nationalist and conservative circles in Ankara.

Real political change in Turkish Cypriot politics and policy began in late 2003. By then, the AKP had succeeded in altering Turkey's historical stance on the conflict (i.e. that a solution had been achieved in 1974), consolidating its support for the Annan Plan. In northern Cyprus, the December 2003 parliamentary elections saw the rise of the moderate Cumhuriyetçi Türk Partisi (CTP) and the nomination of its leader Mehmet Ali Talat as prime minister. Hence, while in 2002 and early 2003, the Turkish Cypriots rejected the Annan Plan, one year later they undertook the initiative to re-launch the peace process on the basis of the same Plan. Negotiations re-started in February 2004, leading to two further revisions of the

Plan and separate referenda in northern and southern Cyprus in April 2004. In the referendum in northern Cyprus, 64 per cent of the public accepted the Annan Plan.

Yet while Turkey and the Turkish Cypriots were shifting towards moderation in 2003–4, the Greek Cypriots turned to nationalism and intransigence. During the last years of Clerides' presidency in 2002, the former Greek Cypriot leader and his party Democraticos Synagermos (DISY) had displayed far greater moderation compared with his early years in office. When the Annan Plan was first presented, Clerides accepted it as a basis for negotiation and ultimately hinted at his willingness to accept the Plan if no agreed revisions to it were possible (UNSG 2003a). Eighty-three-year-old Clerides' decision in early January 2003 to stand for re-election with a limited mandate to conclude negotiations also indicated his willingness to seal a deal. Yet Clerides lost the elections to Tassos Papadopoulos in February 2003. In the early months of Papadopolous' presidency, there was no stark shift in the Greek Cypriot position, not least because Denktaş' rejection of the Annan Plan overshadowed all other obstacles to the peace process. The salience of the Greek Cypriot political shift emerged in full force in 2003–4, and most critically when following the re-launch of the peace process in February 2004, Papadopolous failed to negotiate in good faith and ultimately called his people to reject the Plan with a strong 'no' (UNSG 2004). In his rejection, the President was backed by his own party Democratico Komma (DIKO), by the socialist party Enie Democratiki Enosis Kyprou (EDEK), by the leftist Anorthotikon Komma Ergazomenou Laou (AKEL), as well as by large segments of civil society, the media and the Orthodox Church. The positions of the leadership were reflected in popular opinion. While a mere 24 per cent of the Greek Cypriots voted in favour of the Plan, an overwhelming 76 per cent rejected it.

The referenda earthquake did not trigger fundamental political changes in Cyprus. In northern Cyprus, the political turnover away from nationalism consolidated. The February 2005 parliamentary elections saw a further rise of the CTP, and the April 2005 presidential elections led to the replacement of Denktaş by Mehmet Ali Talat. However, the rise of the CTP came at the expense of the left and liberal camps, rather than the nationalists, leading to an unchanged overall balance between nationalist and moderate forces between 2003 and 2005. The only visible change in the north has been the end of the acute polarization of positions over the Annan Plan and the emergence of a middle 'neo-official position' (embodied by Talat himself), which, while favouring a solution based on the Annan Plan, also cultivates close relations with Ankara (Kaymak and Vüral 2006). In the south, day-to-day politics has taken precedence over the conflict and Papadopolous, backed by a majority of the population, has discarded the Annan Plan and focussed on other strategies to strengthen the Greek Cypriot position. This has shifted trends away from reunification on the basis of a loose federation and towards radically different orders, which are far removed from the EU's declared objectives.

One possible trend would see a solution along the revealed tenets held by the Greek Cypriot leadership. This would imply abandoning the basic philosophy and approach of the Annan Plan (and indeed of all negotiations since 1974) and seeking to rebuild an empowered central state in which majority decision-making would prevail and all Greek Cypriots would be able to return to the north, diluting if not eliminating the bi-zonal aspects of an agreement. Under this scenario, there would be a faster and more extensive withdrawal of Turkish troops and settlers, stronger international guarantees, and a weaker (or absent) Turkish role in Cyprus' security arrangements. To achieve this goal, the Greek Cypriot government has been fostering the conditions for the re-emergence of bi-communality in the south, or *osmosis*, as expressed by Papadopolous in his address at the UN General Assembly in September 2005. The RoC has in fact granted citizenship, jobs, education and healthcare services to individual Turkish Cypriots, without the accompanying political rights foreseen in the 1960 Constitution.

Turkey and the Turkish Cypriots are unlikely to bend to this solution. If they succeed in resisting it, an alternative solution, equally removed from the philosophy of the Annan Plan, is that of a creeping recognition of the TRNC. The Turkish Cypriots while remaining committed to a federal settlement, have clearly displayed their frustration with the peace process and their disillusionment with their Greek Cypriot neighbours. The results of an opinion poll conducted in the north two months after the referenda were striking.[5] The majority of respondents supported the promotion of the TRNC (70 per cent) and the lifting of its isolation (73 per cent). Only a minority backed a second Greek Cypriot referendum (25 per cent) and the renegotiation of the Annan Plan (14 per cent).

The position of the international community is far more complex. International perceptions of the Cyprus conflict have changed since April 2004. While between 1974 and 2004, the Turkish Cypriot side was viewed as the primary obstacle to a solution, justifying the continued recognition of the Greek Cypriot RoC, the referenda eroded this logic. The Greek Cypriots are now regarded as the intransigent side perpetuating the status quo. This does not entail necessarily a future international recognition of the TRNC. As far as the EU is concerned, the RoC government wields veto power, and the principle of intra-EU solidarity makes it very difficult for other member states to recognize the TRNC. However, even when official EU policy is determined by the interests of one member state, the bilateral dealings of individual members may take different forms.[6] Fewer restrictions apply to other countries, including the US. Moreover, even without formal recognition, a government can acquire most of the trappings of statehood (e.g. Taiwan).

Assessing EU impact on the Cyprus conflict

The 1990s witnessed a progressive distancing in the positions of the conflict parties, reducing the prospects of a federal settlement along the lines proposed by the UN. Between 2002 and 2004, there was a window of opportunity to reach an agreement on the basis of the Annan Plan. Yet by the time the Turkish and Turkish Cypriot sides converged to support the Plan, the Greek Cypriots had turned against it. Events since then have not been encouraging. Prospects for a federal agreement are withering away, overtaken by oscillating trends towards the diametrically opposite scenarios of Greek Cypriot domination and Turkish Cypriot secession.

The evolution of the Cyprus conflict has been largely determined by the actions of and developments within the parties involved. In the early and mid-1990s, the positions of the two leaderships hardened due to domestic developments. The replacement of Vassiliou by Clerides in 1993, coupled with the re-election of Papandreou in Greece, ushered in a rise in Greek Cypriot nationalism. The hardening of Turkish Cypriot positions in the late 1990s was fuelled by the persisting isolation of the north, and the mutually reinforcing nationalist positions of Denktaş in Nicosia and Bülent Ecevit in Ankara. Greek–Turkish brinkmanship, particularly in 1996–8 also hindered efforts to broker peace in Cyprus.

The window of opportunity in 2002–4 was opened by key developments in Cyprus, Turkey and Greece. The Greek–Turkish *rapprochement* over the course of 1999, institutionalized after the August/September earthquakes, provided a propitious atmosphere for reconciliation in Cyprus. In the north, the turnover in Turkish Cypriot politics since 2002 was generated by severe economic decline, exacerbated in 1999 by the International Monetary Fund (IMF) austerity package in Turkey and in 2001 by the financial crises there. The opening of the green line in April 2003 invalidated many of the dire consequences resulting from intercommunal contact which Turkish Cypriot nationalists had often warned about. In Turkey, the 2002 electoral results were largely explained by the public's disenchantment with the former political class, particularly in the wake of the 1999 earthquakes and the 2001 economic crisis.

These positive domestic and regional trends were overshadowed by opposite domestic trends in southern Cyprus. In view of Cyprus' colonial history and the humiliation of 1974, the Greek Cypriot 'Οχι' (No) to the Annan Plan was viewed as a courageous attempt to resist foreign control. The fact that almost every provision in the Plan had come from proposals made by local negotiators did not resonate amongst the public. This was not least because the idea of compromise had been denigrated for decades by local leaders (both in the south and in the north), backed by an uncritical education system and media. But, unlike northern Cyprus, in 2004 the Greek Cypriot public could (or felt they could) turn down a compromise agreement and wait for a better deal in future, particularly one which would account for their security concerns vis-à-vis Turkey (Lordos 2006). Hence in the words of UNSG Annan, many Greek Cypriots saw in the Plan 'very little to gain, and quite a lot of inconvenience and risk' (UNSG 2004, paragraph 85).

Notwithstanding the importance of these domestic factors, the EU has acted as a principal external determinant of the Cyprus conflict since it initiated and conducted its accession process with the RoC. The importance of the EU's role is precisely due to the way in which it has interacted with domestic and regional factors. The following sections assess the EU's impact on the conflict, drawing out the principal threads of these interactions.

The value of the EU benefit: accession...for whom and when?

The first key determinant of the EU's impact is the real and perceived value of EU relations with the conflict parties. In the case of Cyprus, the Union offered the most valuable benefit at its disposal, that of full membership. However, the manner and time gap with which this benefit was promised hindered its potential positive impact and generated unexpected disincentives.

The objective value of accession

The EU's potential to influence the Cyprus conflict grew considerably with the accession process, launched when the RoC applied for membership in 1990. This immediately upgraded the basis for contractual ties previously grounded on the 1972 association agreement. After 1993, Cyprus' accession course gathered steam. At the 1994 Corfu European Council, the Union decided to include Cyprus in its next round of enlargement. In 1995, the General Affairs Council decided to open accession negotiations with Cyprus six months after the completion of the 1996 Intergovernmental Conference (IGC). The sixteenth EU–Cyprus Association Council launched a structured dialogue for Cyprus' familiarization with the *acquis*, its inclusion in several Community programmes, and the disbursement of €136m in pre-accession aid. The December 1997 Luxembourg European Council decided to start accession talks. Negotiations began in March 1998 and ended at the December 2002 Copenhagen European Council, when Cyprus was invited to enter the Union. By the turn of the century, the rise in value that came with Cyprus' accession process and the clear EU preference for a solution prior to membership induced the former Greek Cypriot leadership to seek an agreement. In November 2000, proximity talks had ended, but not at the wish of the Greek Cypriots. When in December 2001, Denktaş invited Clerides for direct talks, the latter readily accepted, and throughout 2002 the Greek Cypriot team never hinted at abandoning the process. With the failure of the talks, the UNSG praised the Greek Cypriot team for its constructive positions (UNSG 2003a, paragraphs 35 and 136).

In the years 2000–2, the problem rested primarily on the other side, not least because of the EU's inability to offer sufficiently valuable benefits to the Turkish Cypriots and Turkey. Cyprus' accession process was launched and conducted by the Greek Cypriot RoC. The Turkish Cypriots were excluded from the process and did not witness any objective rise in value in their relations to the Union. Admittedly, before the launch of accession negotiations, the European Council persuaded Clerides to invite his counterpart Denktaş to the talks. But the terms of participation were not specified, providing the reluctant Turkish Cypriot leader with an argument (or excuse) to reject the proposal. Not only were the Turkish Cypriots excluded from the accession process, but even the benefits of association progressively disappeared. Whereas the 1977 first financial protocol accorded 20 per cent of its funds to the Turkish Cypriots, the 1984 protocol granted a mere 3 per cent to them, and in the fourth and fifth protocols, the only EU funds allocated to the north came from the bi-communal Nicosia master plan project (Biçak 1997). Moreover, EU institutions unwittingly harmed the Turkish Cypriots. The 1994 ECJ Anastasiou case is the most evident case in point. At the time of the ECJ judgement, 74 per cent of Turkish Cypriot exports were directed to the EU.

Two years later, Turkish Cypriot exports to the EU fell to 35 per cent because of the end of preferential treatment (Brewin 2000: 196–9).

Another key variable which reduced the value of EU ties for the Turkish Cypriots and Turkey was the late start and uncertainty of Turkey's own accession process. As opposed to Cyprus, Turkey's path to Europe has been long, tortuous and uncertain. Turkey applied for membership in 1987, but it was turned down by the Community in 1989. In 1995, EU–Turkey relations were upgraded through the customs union agreement. But this was hardly comparable to Cyprus–EU relations, which were concomitantly upgraded to the stage of accession negotiations. Moreover, while Cyprus' accession talks were opened, EU–Turkey ties plunged to their lowest ebb when the 1997 Luxembourg European Council denied Turkey EU candidacy.

A categorical shift in gear took place at the December 1999 European Council, i.e. almost a decade after the initiation of Cyprus' accession process. In Helsinki, the European Council recognized Turkey's candidacy. However, the Helsinki decision retained a gap between Turkey and the other candidates, including Cyprus. While all candidates launched or proceeded with accession negotiations, Turkey was kept in a category of its own because of its deficiencies in the field of human rights and democracy. Moreover, the Helsinki euphoria was short-lived, as new problems surfaced on the EU–Turkey political agenda, ranging from the French recognition of the Armenian genocide to the dispute concerning Turkey's participation in the European Security and Defence Policy (ESDP). Turkey's accession prospects became more tangible at, and after, the December 2002 Copenhagen European Council, when a rendezvous date was set to examine the possibility of opening Turkey's accession talks. Demonstrating the importance of the value of EU ties was that fact that only after the Copenhagen European Council, Turkey and the Turkish Cypriots began converging in support for the Annan Plan. All Turkish Cypriot and Turkish interlocutors agree that the mass mobilization in northern Cyprus and the policy shift in Ankara which took place between late 2002 and April 2004 would not have occurred without the rising momentum in Turkey's accession process in those years.[7]

Yet in December 2002, the European Council also invited a divided Cyprus to join the Union. Thereafter, all the necessary steps were taken to proceed with Cyprus' entry (the signature of the Accession Treaty in April 2003, and the process of ratification between then and May 2004). As Cyprus entered the Union and thus the EU benefit was delivered to the Greek Cypriot side, the EU's influence on the south dissipated. This occurred precisely when the value of EU–Turkey ties was rising, increasing considerably the appeal of membership also to the Turkish Cypriots, including the more nationalist and conservative segments of public opinion. In other words, the EU failure to offer the parties sufficiently valuable benefits in a coordinated fashion and at the same time reduced its scope to influence positively the conflict.

The EU's negative impact on the conflict increased after Cyprus' accession. The benefits of membership have been used by the Greek Cypriot side to strengthen its negotiating position at the expense of the Turkish Cypriots. The government has blocked all EU attempts to lift the economic isolation on the north through aid and in particular trade measures. It has attempted to re-formulate the conflict as one between the RoC and Turkey, hoping to exert leverage on Turkey within the EU context in order to obtain Turkey's recognition of the RoC. This would entail a coercive re-writing of the Turkish historical narrative of the conflict and its non-recognition of the northern Cypriot de facto state.[8] Greek Cypriot leverage was exerted most visibly in the run-up to the opening of Turkey's accession negotiations in October 2005, when it insisted that Turkey should normalize its relations with the RoC. The issue has remained on the agenda since then and has been associated with the question of the de jure and de facto extension of the EU–Turkey customs union to member state Cyprus. The RoC's strategy of 'osmosis' in the south and pressure on Turkey at EU level has distracted attention from inter-communal negotiations aimed at reaching a federal agreement through UN mediation.

Since Cyprus' EU entry, the Union has done little for the Turkish Cypriots. Despite its promise, on the eve of enlargement, to lift their isolation, the EU has failed to deliver. The Commission initially drafted two proposals. The first provided for the disbursement of €259m to the north and the second for re-establishing direct preferential trade between the north and the EU (halted since the 1994 ECJ judgement). These two draft directives, which were only modest steps to support Turkish Cypriot development, remain to a large extent unimplemented. The trade directive has been flatly turned down by member state Cyprus, arguing that it would entail an implicit recognition of the TRNC. €120m provided for in the aid directive were lost due to the time lag in the approval by the Council of Ministers. Although the remaining €139m were approved in February 2006, disputes persist on the modalities of disbursement.

There is also a distinct possibility that, far from supporting Turkish Cypriot development, EU actions may be hindering it further. In December 2004, upon Cyprus' insistence, the European Council demanded that Turkey sign the protocol extending its customs union with the EU to the new member states (including Cyprus) before its accession negotiations could begin. In the autumn of 2005, Turkey fulfilled this request, yet it refrained from implementing the protocol. At the insistence of the RoC, the implementation of the protocol was pinpointed as a priority in the 2005 Turkey Accession Partnership document, and EU pressure on Turkey on this question mounted in 2006 and 2007.

In the event that Turkey extends the customs union to southern Cyprus without an EU initiative to include northern Cyprus in the EU customs union, the psychological impact on the north could be harmful.[9] It would represent yet another instance of the Turkish Cypriots being left out of the loop of European integration. It is in this context that Turkey, through an 'Action Plan' presented to the UNSG in January 2006, called for the inclusion of the Turkish Cypriots in the EU customs union together with its implementation of the customs union protocol. Despite an initially warm reception by the Commission and member states Italy, Spain and the UK, the Turkish Action Plan has remained unimplemented, largely due to Greek Cypriot objections. In turn, the Union's unkept promises to the Turkish Cypriots and the unmaterialized value of EU ties for the Turkish Cypriots have fed public disillusionment in the north. Hence, Talat's shift towards the centre and the absence of new peace initiatives by the Turkish Cypriots and Turkey.[10]

The subjective value of accession

To fully understanding the significance of membership for all conflict parties in Cyprus, and thus its impact on the conflict, it is necessary to delve deeper into the perceptions and value of the Union in the region.

The Greek Cypriots came to value highly the prospects of membership. While initially reluctant to embark on the accession course, over the 1990s EU membership became the cornerstone and principal objective of Greek Cypriot foreign policy. This ambition was not unrelated to the conflict. On the contrary, both Greece and the Greek Cypriots valued Cyprus' accession precisely because of the effects they anticipated this to have on the conflict. By the late 1980s and early 1990s, the Greek Cypriot side felt disenchanted by the UN's approach, viewing it as powerless in influencing Turkey and willing to accommodate maximalist Turkish Cypriot demands. Pursuing EU membership was viewed as a means to reverse these trends. Accession would bolster the RoC's status as the only legitimate government on the island, discredit further the TRNC and provide the RoC with an additional forum in which to present its case. It would also increase Greek Cypriot leverage on Turkey in view of Turkey's own membership ambitions. EU accession would also bring critical security gains to the Greek Cypriots, because of the unlikelihood of a Turkish attack on an EU member state. Finally, Cyprus' membership would create a framework for the liberalization of the three freedoms with the implementation of the EU's *acquis.*

The value ascribed to the Union had contrasting effects on the Greek Cypriot political elite and public, which emerged in diametrically opposite ways over the years. Former President Clerides appeared far more open to compromise in 2002–3 than he had been in 1992–3, when he ran for and won his first presidency on a bid to reject the Set of Ideas. A key factor explaining this shift is the perceived value of EU accession. EU membership, which was increasingly within reach, imbued the Greek Cypriots with an enhanced sense of security and induced the former leadership to accept hitherto unthinkable concessions (such as Turkey's role in Cyprus' security).

Yet, as accession approached in 2003 (and was finally realized in 2004), the perceived value of EU membership served to harden the stance of the next Greek Cypriot leadership. This was because of its belief that a compromise agreement could be improved significantly post accession. So, as Papadopoulos put it, why should the Greek Cypriots 'do away with our internationally recognized state exactly at the very moment it strengthens its political weight, with its accession to the EU?' (UNSG 2004, paragraph 65). More precisely, Greek Cypriot nationalists/maximalists came to value EU accession over and above a loose federal settlement. As put by one interlocutor 'it is better to be in the EU without a settlement than to accept a bad settlement'.[11] To the extent that the Annan Plan was viewed as a 'bad' settlement, the leadership, backed by the public, concentrated on EU accession instead.

Turning to the Turkish Cypriots, the EU accession process was viewed as a threat up until late 2001. This was true both for the public at large and for the nationalist elites in power at the time. The main incentive offered by the EU to the Turkish Cypriots was economic (Bahceli 2001). But in a context of international isolation, economic incentives were branded a 'bribe' to lure the Turkish Cypriots into compromising on their collective security and identity.[12] Furthermore, until late 2001, the Turkish Cypriots believed (without being credibly rebuked by EU officials) that Cyprus' membership would necessitate a strongly centralized state, that it would eliminate bi-zonality through the application of the *acquis*, and that it would cut vital links to Ankara. Hence, many supported EU membership only after a settlement and/or after Turkey's accession. A loose federal settlement would mitigate the threats from EU accession, while Cypriot membership alongside that of Turkey would provide additional guarantees. To the most nationalist forces, the accession of a divided island was actually seen as a blessing in disguise, justifying a de jure settlement on the basis of partition. In other words, until late 2001 perceptions of the Union in northern Cyprus reduced Turkish Cypriot incentives to reach an agreement.

The U-turn in the Turkish Cypriot position in 2002–4 partly rests in their re-evaluation of EU membership. While former President Denktaş continued to dismiss EU economic incentives, the appeal of membership gained hold amongst the public, contributing to the overhaul in Turkish Cypriot politics. Economic gains rose in value because of the deterioration of the Turkish Cypriot economy since the mid-1990s and particularly since 2001. This generated Turkish Cypriot fears of the unsustainability of their status as a self-governing community in northern Cyprus. Another consequence of isolation was the increasing dependence on Turkey, which led to a growing sense among the Turkish Cypriots that, far from democratically governing themselves, they were being controlled by Ankara. By 2002 EU accession was no longer viewed as a threat, but rather as the necessary condition for Turkish Cypriot communal survival and prosperity.

The Turkish Cypriot shift was also critically linked to that in Ankara, which came when domestic political change led to a reassessment of the value of Turkey's own accession process. Under the former Turkish coalition government, Turkey's accession process failed to generate sufficient political will to support a federal settlement in Cyprus not least because accession was not genuinely supported by all the relevant forces within the Turkish establishment. For those who were sceptical of if not opposed to membership, stalemate in Cyprus was covertly viewed as a convenient excuse to block the accession process. This largely remained the case until the November 2002 elections. The election of the AKP, coupled with the approaching prospect of opening EU–Turkey accession negotiations, enhanced the collectively perceived value of EU accession. This was manifested both by an unprecedented commitment to pursuing democratic reforms and by the U-turn in Turkish policy towards Cyprus. By the time this occurred however, incentives on the Greek Cypriot side had turned against a federal agreement.

The credibility of the obligations

The time gap between the offer of membership to Cyprus and to Turkey goes far in explaining the EU's missed opportunity to reunify the conflict-ridden island. Yet this explanation needs to be complemented by an analysis of the obligations embedded (or not) in EU relations with the conflict parties.

The asymmetric use of conditionality

When the EU launched Cyprus' accession process, the understanding was that a settlement was a precondition of accession. The 1993 Commission's Opinion on Cyprus unequivocally stated that accession negotiations would begin 'as soon as the prospect of settlement is surer', and that 'Cyprus' integration with the community implies a peaceful, balanced and lasting settlement of the Cyprus question' (Commission 1993, paragraphs 48 and 47). Alone, this formulation would have presented a strong form of conditionality on the Greek Cypriot side (who had applied for membership), without an accompanying message to the Turkish Cypriots and Turkey (whose own accession process was not on the horizon at the time). Hence, the Opinion added that 'should this (a failure of inter-communal negotiations) eventuality arise, the Commission feels that the situation should be reassessed in view of the positions adopted by each party in the talks and that the question of Cyprus' accession to the Community should be reconsidered in January 1995' (Commission 1993, paragraph 51). In other words, if inter-communal negotiations failed due to Turkish Cypriot intransigence, accession negotiations without a settlement could take place.

The balance struck in 1993 was then progressively abandoned. On the one hand, conditionality on the Greek Cypriot side was dropped. The Commission's 1997 Agenda 2000 suggested that accession negotiations with Cyprus could begin without a settlement being a precondition. Two years later, the European Council in Helsinki concluded that a settlement would not be a condition for Cyprus' actual accession. To this, the European Council – adamant not to give the impression that Cyprus' accession was automatic – added that it would 'take into account all relevant factors' (European Council 1999b, paragraph 9b). But the persisting conflict was not viewed as a sufficiently 'relevant factor' when in 2002 the European Council in Copenhagen invited Cyprus to enter the Union, when in 2003 the RoC signed the Accession Treaty, or when in 2004 the divided island became an EU member state.

On the other hand, conditionality on Turkey was strengthened after the launch of Turkey's accession process. Turkey's 2001 Accession Partnership stated that Turkey should '...strongly support the UN Secretary General's efforts to bring to a successful conclusion the process of finding a comprehensive settlement of the Cyprus problem...' (Council 2001b: 13). Moreover, EU institutions waved their stick at Ankara by lifting conditionality on the Greek Cypriot side and thus opening the prospect of Cyprus' accession as a divided island. The problems entailed by this were made painfully explicit by the Commission in 2003, when it stated that the conflict posed a 'serious obstacle' to Turkey's accession path (Commission 2003d: 16).

The abandonment of conditionality on the Greek Cypriot side did not reduce the incentives of the former Greek Cypriot leadership to clinch an agreement. Up until late 2002, the Clerides leadership never considered accession as being automatic (at least at the level of public discourse).[13] Even when Cyprus was invited to enter the Union, the former President appeared committed to reach an agreement. The approaching deadline of accession and the awareness that the international momentum generated in 2002–4 would have dissipated thereafter raised Clerides' incentives to reach an early agreement. However, lifting conditionality on the Greek Cypriots eliminated all constraints from the next Greek Cypriot leadership to bluntly turn down the Annan Plan by the time the referendum was held. Having secured EU membership, Papadopolous felt unconstrained in rejecting the Annan Plan despite the strong criticisms and accusations of his EU partners. In other words, once accession was guaranteed, the potential effectiveness of conditionality came to an end, and the conflict party was once again free to pursue its interests as it saw fit.

Turning to Turkey, the progressive strengthening of conditionality on Ankara began having its desired effects after 2002. Until late 2001, the Turkish establishment simply did not believe (or did not want to believe) that the EU would accept a divided island into its fold. Turkey failed to understand why the Union would accept a problematic conflict-ridden island and 'give up' Turkey 'for the sake of' Cyprus. Many in Ankara failed to appreciate that, by 1999, the European choice was not between Turkey and Cyprus, but rather between Turkey and the fifth enlargement, the importance of which went way beyond Cyprus and Turkey combined. By the autumn of 2001, the Turkish establishment understood that Cyprus' EU accession had become inevitable. This was indeed a key factor motivating the re-launch of direct talks in January 2002. But some of those who did appreciate the credibility of EU conditionality were not motivated to find a settlement both because they viewed Cyprus as an imperative national security issue and because of their lack of commitment to Turkey's EU accession. It was only when the AKP government genuinely prioritized Turkey's accession course, and was backed by the liberal media, academia and key actors within different institutions, that the credibility of EU conditionality contributed to the Turkish U-turn on Cyprus.

The unexpected twists in the mechanisms of passive enforcement

The reasons underlying the EU's missed opportunity in Cyprus are also linked to the perverse impact of passive enforcement in a context in which the Union had not spelt out its conditions and obligations regarding a settlement.

When the 1993 Commission Opinion formulated its approach towards Cyprus, the logic on which it rested was that of passive enforcement rather than political conditionality. The Commission stated that the rights and freedoms embedded in the *acquis* 'would have to be guaranteed as part of a comprehensive settlement...'

(Commission 1993, paragraph 10). This statement was used to justify the need for a settlement prior to accession. As put by the Opinion, in the absence of a settlement, Cyprus would be unable to 'participate normally in the decision-making process of the EC...' and ensure '...the correct application of Community law throughout the island' (Commission 1993, paragraph 47). EU institutions thus rested on the bedrock of EU law when justifying the imperative of a settlement in Cyprus before accession.

As conditionality was lifted on the Greek Cypriot side, these same mechanisms of passive enforcement had a perverse effect. They provided the Greek Cypriot side a strong argument to oppose UN proposals, which provided for a limited liberalization of the three freedoms. Whereas in the past uncompromising positions were couched in the language of human rights and majoritarian democracy, the accession process allowed the far more specific and binding language of the *acquis* to legitimize Greek Cypriot inflexibility. Hence, in October 2000, the RoC House of Representatives rebuked UNSG Annan's first proposals on the grounds that 'it is a basic and fundamental principle of the talks that any proposals or ideas should be fully in line with the *acquis communautaire*' (Republic of Cyprus 2000). After 2002, the proposed restrictions to the three freedoms in the Annan Plan were rejected by the Greek Cypriot side because they entailed derogations to the EU *acquis* (Friends of Cyprus 2003: 3). The *acquis* also became a principal argument used by the former Turkish Cypriot leadership to oppose a settlement within the EU. Even following the change of leadership in the north, the Turkish Cypriots remained concerned with the implications of the *acquis.* Their fear was that the restrictions to the full application of the *acquis* provided for in the Annan Plan would be undermined by individual Greek Cypriot cases brought to the ECJ and the ECtHR.

The EU, with its laws as well as its realities, could have accommodated the terms of a settlement providing for some restrictions to the full liberalization of the three freedoms. This is often the case in both old and new member states (Tocci 2004b: 157–9). However, the lack of clarity on what kind of solution the EU supported in Cyprus allowed the most intransigent voices on both sides to use EU mechanisms of passive enforcement to hinder an agreement. Until mid-2001, EU statements did nothing to alter the view that accession would have set the guidelines for a settlement in favour of the Greek Cypriot side. Only at the June 2002 Seville European Council the Union officially mentioned the possibility of exemptions from the *acquis* in Cyprus.[14] But the vagueness of these statements together with their late arrival failed to mitigate the damage done by the discourse of the *acquis* over the decade-long process of Cyprus' accession.

The scope for social learning

The impact of the accession process through conditionality and passive enforcement on the Cyprus conflict has been largely negative. Yet in the long term, social learning could support the reunification of the island, so long as alternative trends of domination or secession have not consolidated instead.

Greece is the most evident case of a conflict party influenced by social learning inherent in contact with (and participation in) the EU. Since Greece acceded to the Community in 1981, it has changed significantly both as a state and as a polity, and in its pursued policies (Tsakaloyannis 1996). EU membership has induced much of this transformation, particularly under the PASOK governments, both in terms of discourse and mode of operation (e.g. increasingly moderating its positions and accepting multilateral decision-making), as well in terms of interest formulation. Through participation and learning, the EU has affected Greece's stance on the conflict as well as on Turkey, by raising the Greek sense of security, which gradually enabled Greek policy-makers to reassess the country's interests and reformulate its strategies.[15]

As Greek governments appreciated the economic and security gains inherent in EU membership, they began lobbying for Cyprus' inclusion in the bloc. Greek Cypriot security concerns could be resolved within the European security community, just like Greece itself was experiencing. So the PASOK governments assiduously worked first to persuade the Greek Cypriot government to apply for membership in 1988–90, and then to sway its sceptical European partners to accept Cyprus' EU accession.

Moreover, Greek foreign policy towards Turkey performed a radical U-turn in 1999. From epitomizing in the 1980s the most critical obstacle to closer EC–Turkey ties, Greece, under the PASOK government of Costas Simitis became the most vocal advocate of Ankara's European cause two decades later. EU membership allowed Greece to gradually understand that a 'European Turkey' would represent Greece's strongest security guarantee. In this context, the pending conflict in Cyprus represented a Damoclean sword hanging over both Turkey's EU accession and its rapprochement with Greece. This goes far in explaining the support of the Simitis government for the Annan Plan.

Greece's transformation coupled with Cyprus' own accession process also had a moderating impact on the former Greek Cypriot leadership. The transformation of Greek foreign policy altered the meaning of what Greek Cypriot nationalism entailed. Clerides had campaigned in 1993 on an overtly Greek Cypriot nationalist platform. He continued to flag his ties to kin-state Greece throughout his two presidencies, for example by pursuing the Joint Defence Doctrine. Yet this did not prevent him from moderating his views in 2002–3. On the contrary, the Greek government's support for the Annan Plan allowed Clerides to endorse the Plan while maintaining a degree of ideological continuity. Contact with EU institutions also led to a growing appreciation by the Clerides leadership of the security assets entailed in membership. This persuaded the former president to pursue more actively a settlement within the EU. It is perhaps not surprising that the most adamant supporters of the Annan Plan in the south were Clerides – president in 1993–2003 – and George Vassiliou – former president and Cyprus' chief EU negotiator, i.e. precisely those who led Cyprus into the EU in the 1990s and who had had most contact with the institutions.

This is not to say that the change of Greek foreign policy and less still that of Cyprus is unanimous or complete. In Greece, the shift owes much to the previous government and in particular to former Foreign Minister George Papandreou. The ND government elected in March 2003 has been far more cautious. The rapprochement with Turkey persists but has made few steps forward. Support for Turkey's accession also continues, but it has been far weaker and more conditional compared to that of the former government. Moreover, the government's attitudes towards Cyprus are considerably more detached. In the context of Papadopolous' rise to power, this has meant a publicly uncritical support for the rejectionist stance of the RoC government.

Less still has contact with the EU had a moderating impact on the current RoC government, or indeed on the wider public. The RoC government, much like Greece in the 1980s, has viewed the Union as a platform from which to exert pressure on Turkey and the Turkish Cypriots. There is a distinct difference between learning, which entails a genuine transformation of perceived interests and strategies, and the (ab)use of an EU discourse to legitimize unchanged (if not hardened) positions. The pleas of the Greek Cypriot leadership for a 'European solution' in accordance with EU values and the *acquis*, appear simply to use a new and more appealing language to persuade the international community and fellow member states of the desirability of its (unchanged) preferred solution (Richmond 2006: 157).

In northern Cyprus, there has been a profound transformation of the political system and polity. But this is predominantly due to domestic changes coupled with the hard-nosed messages of EU conditionality, rather than through a voluntary process of EU-induced learning. An interesting example of this is the Turkish Cypriot response to the ECtHR cases, compliance with which has been a key EU condition on Turkey (Gürel and Özersay 2006). Initially Turkey and the Turkish Cypriots flatly rejected the ECtHR's judgements on the return of Greek Cypriot property in the north. Yet, in view of mounting EU pressure on Turkey, of Ankara's ultimate compliance in paying the hefty fine to Ms Loizidou, and of the string of cases mounting at the ECtHR, the Turkish Cypriots modified their response. They did so aiming to account for the substantive objections raised by the ECtHR to their legal defence. In August 2003 the Turkish Cypriots established an 'Appraisal and Compensation Board' to which Greek Cypriots could turn to prior to the ECtHR. The Board was not recognized by the ECtHR as an effective domestic remedy in the April 2005 Arestis-Xenidis case. This was mainly because of its denied option of return and restitution. In response, in December 2005 the Turkish Cypriots revised their property board, providing for a (limited) element of reinstatement. It remains to be seen whether the ECtHR will accept the revised board as an effective domestic remedy.

Learning processes have thus taken place in northern Cyprus but through pressure and punishment rather than through institutional contact and 'socialization'. This is because of the extremely limited contact between EU actors and the Turkish Cypriots, in view of the unrecognized status of the TRNC. Given the EU's non-involvement in mediation, the Union has been excessively cautious in dealing with Turkish Cypriot authorities, for fear that this could constitute or be interpreted as an act of recognition. This has eliminated all scope for change through learning in northern Cyprus. Indeed, throughout the accession process, Turkish Cypriot civil servants bitterly complained about the absence of adequate information from EU officials, which led to the manipulation of the accession process by those unwilling to see an agreement.[16] The Commission did establish contact with Turkish Cypriot civil society and with the Chamber of Commerce in particular in 2002–4. This influenced profoundly the Chamber, in terms of its views on a settlement and EU accession. However, the exclusive focus on non-governmental organizations (NGOs) also polarized Turkish Cypriot society, and was denigrated by the former leadership as an imperial 'divide and rule' tactic.

Paradoxically, post-accession the scope for social learning in the north has reduced further. Turkish Cypriot individuals with RoC citizenship can travel and live freely throughout the Union and are thus exposed to and influenced by such contact. However, institutional contact with Turkish Cypriot authorities has diminished. The Commission delegation in Cyprus is now run by that member state's officials, i.e. by Greek Cypriots. Furthermore, while the Commission Enlargement Directorate General (DG) has retained a small unit dealing with northern Cyprus, contact is impeded by the objections raised by member state Cyprus.

Finally, a slow process of learning is under way in Turkey, particularly as its own accession course has gathered steam. The shift in the AKP government's Cyprus policy was crucially linked to the EU's increasingly stringent conditionality coupled with a more credible accession process. However, many policy-makers appear to have genuinely revised their strategies towards Cyprus. This is not to say that the change is unanimously held; less still that it is irreversible. But there does appears to be a narrow majority in Turkey who since 2004 has come to believe that aside from conditionality, a Cyprus settlement within the EU is in Turkey's best interests. In this respect, observing how Greece's membership became an asset for Turkey's EU bid, has partly altered Turkish views on the desirability of a reunited Cyprus in the Union.

The political management of Cyprus' EU accession

The Copenhagen criteria for EU entry include the stability of institutions and the respect for democracy, rights and law, as well as good neighbourly relations. Yet a divided Cyprus – where UN peacekeepers have been stationed since 1964, and where the recognized government violates its constitution, does not represent a quarter of the population, does not control a third of the territory, and is in open conflict with one neighbour – has been accepted into the Union. How did this occur? Behind an empty rhetoric, Cyprus' accession process was politically driven by EU interests that had little to do with the aim of reunifying the island within the Union.

Greece was the only member state with strong and clear interests in Cyprus. To pursue its aims, Greece was helped by the success of the RoC in pursing accession and portraying itself as the compromising party, as well as by the internationally condemned intransigence of the former Turkish Cypriot leader. However, Greece was primarily successful because it raised its arguments in EU forums

Table 1 The Cyprus conflict and EU–Cyprus relations

Population (2006)	RoC 835,000 and TRNC 264,000
Key Historical Dates	1571 Cyprus becomes part of the Ottoman Empire
	1878 Cyprus becomes part of the British Empire
	1960 The independent Republic of Cyprus is established
	1963 The bi-communal RoC collapses and fighting re-erupts
	1967 Military coup in Greece
	1974 Greek coup in Cyprus. Turkish invasion and partition
	1977 1st high level agreement sets the principles for a bi-zonal and bi-communal federation (BBF)
	1979 2nd high-level agreement spells out the principles for a BBF
	1983 The Turkish Cypriots declare the TRNC
	1986 The UNSG presents the Draft Framework Agreement
	1992 The UNSG presents the 'Set of Ideas'
	1996 Imia/Kardak crisis and clashes on the 'green line' in Cyprus
	1997 Inter-communal talks fail in Troutbeck and Glion
	1999 Greek–Turkish rapprochement. Cyprus proximity talks
	2002 Following two years of impasse direct negotiations re-start
	2003 Rauf Denktaş rejects the Annan Plan in The Hague
	2004 In separate referendums, Greek Cypriots reject and Turkish Cypriots accept the Annan Plan
EU Relations	1972 EC–Cyprus association agreement
	1981 Greece enters the EC
	1990 The RoC applies for EC membership
	1993 Commission Opinion accepts Cyprus' application
	1994 The Corfu European Council includes Cyprus in the fifth enlargement. The ECJ bans exports from the TRNC
	1995 The Council agrees to the customs union with Turkey and accession negotiations with Cyprus
	1997 The Luxembourg European Council sets a date for accession negotiations with Cyprus and denies candidacy to Turkey
	1998 EU–Cyprus accession negotiations begin
	1999 The Helsinki European Council grants Turkey candidacy and lifts conditionality on the RoC
	2002 The Copenhagen European Council invites Cyprus to enter the EU and extends a conditional date for Turkey's accession negotiations
	2003 The RoC signs the Treaty of Accession
	2004 Cyprus enters the EU as a divided island
EU Financial Assistance	In the four financial protocols disbursed under the EU–Cyprus association agreement (1978–99), Cyprus received an annual average of €10m in loans, grants and risk capital. While under the first protocol, Turkish Cypriots were allocated 20% of the funds, under the remaining three protocols, northern Cyprus received funding only for bi-communal projects (e.g. the Nicosia sewage system). In 2000–4, the RoC received an annual average of €11.4m in pre-accession aid. No funds reached the north. In 2004, the EU planned to disburse €259m to northern Cyprus. By 2006, €139m were approved by the Council

in conjunction with its applied pressure that touched on unrelated EU interests. At times, as during the March 1995 General Affairs Council or the December 1999 Helsinki European Council, Greece made its consent to deepened ties with Turkey (through the customs union in 1995 and EU candidacy in 1999) conditional on the progressive lifting of conditionality on the Greek Cypriots. At other times it threatened to veto enlargement (to the north in 1994 and to the east in 1997–2004) lest Cyprus be excluded from the Union. In other words, Greece relied on other EU interests to persuade the member states to include Cyprus in the EU.

The UK, was the only other member state with strong interests in Cyprus. Yet it accepted the island's unconditional entry in the EU. Allegedly this was because it believed that Cyprus' accession process would create new incentives for a solution. However, the UK supported accession also because of the RoC government's agreement that this would not jeopardize the status of the British bases on the island. Indeed, when in 2004 Cyprus entered the Union, the two military bases remained extra-EU territory.

The other member states only paid sporadic attention to Cyprus over the course of the accession process. Without strong interests and an accompanying strategy to settle the conflict through accession, they gradually accepted Greek demands. Particularly when other interests such as the success of the eastern enlargement were at stake, Cyprus, divided or not, paled into insignificance for most member states and EU institutions. The member states' ambivalent attitudes towards Turkey also played an important role. On the one hand, the imperative to seek strong ties with Turkey, advocated also by the US, was successfully used by Greece to obtain the progressive lifting of conditionality on the RoC. On the other hand, the pending conflict in Cyprus provided a convenient shield for the reluctance of some member states to proceed with Turkey's accession. Just as member states in the 1980s and 1990s hid behind Greece when keeping Turkey at arm's length, several member states, particularly since 2004, have raised Cyprus as a reason to re-evaluate Turkey's EU accession course.

Despite the potential of the accession process to catalyze a settlement in Cyprus, the political management of both Cyprus' and Turkey's accession course impeded the much acclaimed catalytic effect from working in practice. It can only be hoped that, as Turkey proceeds with accession, as the Union finds ways to lift the isolation of the Turkish Cypriots and as the Greek Cypriots come to reassess their interests much as Greece did over the course its membership, EU accession may nonetheless contribute to the reunification of Cyprus in the years to come.

4 Ebbs and flows in the Europeanization of Turkey's Kurdish question

EU interests and objectives in Turkey's Kurdish question

The EU's interests in Turkey's Kurdish question are driven first and foremost by Turkey's geostrategic importance. Turkey has always been pivotal to European security interests, both during the Cold War, when it stood as a bulwark against Soviet expansionism; and thereafter, as it lies as a potential beacon of westernized democracy, peace and stability in the midst of the turbulent Middle East and Eurasia. As such, EU actors have had a long-standing interest in Turkey's democracy and human rights, its internal stability and its foreign policy orientation, i.e. all issues which have been influenced by the Kurdish question. The EU's specific concern with Turkey's Kurds has also been fed by the Kurdish Diaspora in Europe, which since the 1990s has activated itself to put the Kurdish question on the European agenda. Fears of rising Kurdish and Turkish immigration further magnified EU interests in a peaceful stabilization of the Kurdish question. Finally and most recently, EU interests have resurfaced with the resumption of PKK violence in Turkey, the war in Iraq, the demography and status of the oil-rich city of Kirkuk, and the role of the Iraqi Kurds in the survival or dissolution of the country.

This is not to say that the Union has spelled out its preferred solution to Turkey's Kurdish question. In fact, the Union has not had a Kurdish policy as such. Although the European Parliament in a 1990 resolution called for an autonomous Kurdish region in southeast Turkey, these prescriptions have been the exception rather than the rule (European Parliament 1990). Beginning with the 1998 Progress Report on Turkey, the Commission has called for 'a political and non-military solution to the problem of the southeast', without specifying what such a solution entailed – it simply stated that 'a civil solution could include the recognition of certain forms of Kurdish cultural identity and greater tolerance of the ways of expressing that identity, provided it does not advocate separatism or terrorism' (Commission 1998b: 20). The 2004 and 2005 Reports went a tentative step further, discussing the Kurdish question in the context of minority rights and recommending that 'the normalization of the situation of the southeast should be pursued through the return of displaced persons, a strategy for socio-economic development and

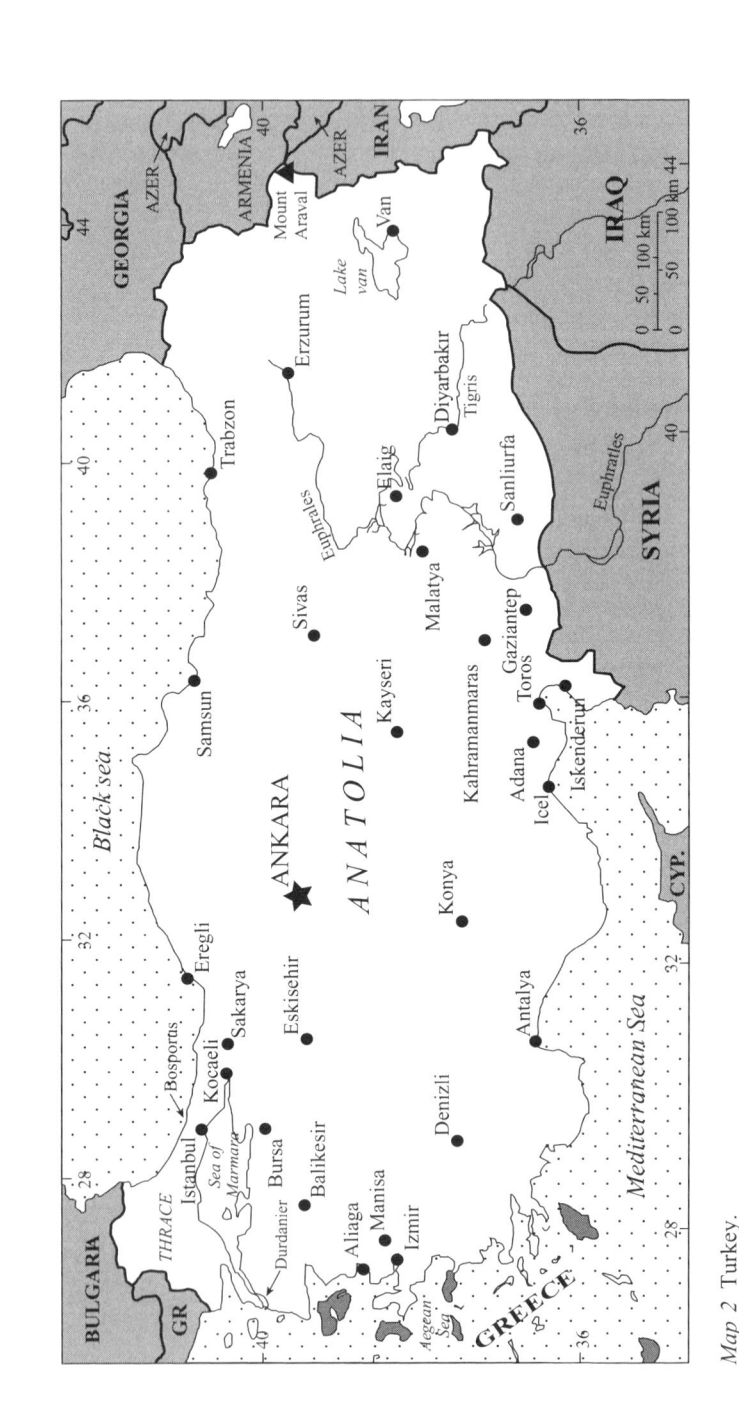

Map 2 Turkey.
Source: The World Fact Book. https://www.cia.gov/cia/publications/factbook/geos/mj.html.

the establishment of conditions for the full enjoyment of rights and freedoms by the Kurds' (Commission 2004b: 167).

Despite its vagueness on the Kurdish question, the Union has spelled out far more precise guidelines on issues that are directly or indirectly relevant to Turkey's Kurds. On top of the EU's wish list has been the imperative of respecting individual human rights. The EU's successive Progress Reports and Accession Partnership documents for Turkey have repeatedly stressed the need to guarantee non-discrimination, and the freedoms of thought, expression, association, peaceful assembly and religion. The EU has called for the abolition of the death penalty (including the revocation of Abdullah Öcalan's death sentence), the eradication of torture and the respect for rights and standards in trials and detention periods. Several recommendations on individual human rights have been specifically tailored to the Kurds. The Union has condemned the destruction of villages and the displacement of persons, it has called for an end of emergency rule and for the dissolution of the village guard system in the southeast, and it has advocated the return of internally displaced persons (IDPs).[1] It has also called for bridging regional disparities through a socio-economic development plan which would improve health, education, infrastructure and water facilities in the Kurdish-populated southeast.

Beyond individual human rights, the Commission has made specific demands on governance, cultural and minority rights, affecting principally (albeit not exclusively) the Kurds. It has called upon Turkey to ensure effective, transparent and participatory local government. It has demanded the right to use Kurdish names in Turkey, and the right to Kurdish broadcasting and education. The Commission has also called for effective Kurdish political participation. It has frowned upon the closure of pro-Kurdish parties and criticized the highly restrictive 10 per cent electoral threshold (which prevents parliamentary representation of pro-Kurdish parties concentrated in the southeast).

The evolution of the Kurdish question

Taking a step back to the region, let us assess whether, how and to what extent the evolution of Turkey's Kurdish question has been moving in line with the EU's interests and its recommendations.

From the establishment of the republic to political violence and repression

Before analyzing recent trends, it is important to recall the roots of the Kurdish question; roots which can be traced back to the establishment of the Turkish nation-state. Built on the ashes of the Ottoman Empire, the modern Turkish Republic aspired to create a civic nation in which all individuals within the confines of the new state would enjoy equal rights. The founders of the Republic, and Mustafa Kemal Atatürk in particular, linked the fall of the Empire with the centrifugal forces of contrasting ethnic nationalisms. As such, with the exception of three

(Greek, Armenian and Jewish) religious minorities recognized in the 1923 Treaty of Lausanne, all citizens, irrespective of their ethnic origin or branch of Islam were conflated into one community. The new nation would emerge from the melting pot of the Anatolian mosaic.

The choice of adopting a civic conception of the nation was not problematic in itself. The problem arose when in practice Turkish nationalism acquired clear ethnic undertones. This led to a double effect. On the one hand, the three recognized non-Muslim minorities entered into an unspoken pact with the state: i.e. the recognition of their minority rights in exchange for the non-recognition of their equal citizenship rights. On the other hand, all other minorities, first and foremost the Kurds, were recognized as equal citizens, so long as they abandoned their minority identities (Kurban 2005). State attitudes towards the Kurds hardened in the early decades of the Republic, in line with the intellectual evolution of Turkish nationalism and in response to the Kurdish rebellions of the 1920s and 1930s. In 1922, the Turkish authorities reneged on their promises of local Kurdish autonomy set out in the 1921 Basic Organization Law. In 1923–4, they violated Article 39 of the Treaty of Lausanne, which protected the use of the Kurdish language. In 1925, the Law for the Reestablishment of Order legalized repressive measures to crush the Kurdish rebellions. In 1934, the Resettlement Law was designed to dilute the Kurdish presence in the southeast and the Law on Surname banned the use of Kurdish names. People were thus resettled, place names were changed, Kurdish names and costumes were banned, the use of language was restricted, and the very existence of a Kurdish identity was denied. Kurds were simply Turks who as a consequence of their isolated lifestyle in the Anatolian hinterlands had developed separate dialects and needed to be re-educated about their 'Turkishness'. Equal treatment was assured for Kurds who assimilated within Turkish society, and indeed some of those who did, reached top government positions – but those who expressed a separate identity were punished.

Since the 1950s, the mass industrialization of western Turkey at the expense of the neglected and agricultural southeast accentuated regional inequalities, caused by the harsh climate, geographical isolation and the tribal social structure in the southeast. This fuelled the alienation and disenfranchisement of the Kurds. Increasing regional disparities led to further population movements, from the rural southeast to shantytowns (gecekondular) in the urban centres of Istanbul, Adana, Ankara and Izmir.

The mounting frustration felt by the Kurds took different political expressions over the decades. The Kurdish cause was first advocated by Kurdish and leftist movements in the 1970s, including the Turkish Workers Party (Türkiye İşçi Partisi), trade unions, youth revolutionary movements (Dev Genç) and cultural clubs, and in particular the Revolutionary Eastern Cultural Hearths (Devrimci Doğu Kültür Ocakları). These movements mobilized around the banner of 'eastism' (doğuculuk), which argued that the Turkish state internally colonized the southeast and its inhabitants. In pursuing their political platform, these groups increasingly clashed with extreme right-wing and nationalist movements, leading to a period of profound instability which culminated in the 1980 military coup.

The first answer of the Turkish state to the Kurdish challenge was to focus on its symptoms, tackling these through military force and political repression. The logic behind this approach was the negation of the Kurdish question as an identity, political or economic problem. The problem was one of terrorism and violence that could only be overcome by force. Indeed, following the 1980 coup, the 1982 Constitution circumscribed political and cultural rights in the country. The Constitution's preamble stated that 'no protection shall be afforded to thoughts or opinions contrary to Turkish national interests, the principles of the indivisibility of Turkey as a state and territory, Turkish historical and moral values, or the nationalism, principles, and reforms of Atatürk and his embracement of values of modern civilization...'. Article 14 prohibited any political activity based on class, sect, language or race. Article 125 of the penal code foresaw the death penalty for those who acted against the state's integrity. The legal system also banned the use of languages other than Turkish. By 1986, 2,842 out of 3,524 villages in the southeast had been renamed with Turkish names.

Yet repression fed the flames of radical Kurdish nationalism. The post-1980 period witnessed the most extreme expression of the Kurdish cause, both in terms of its objectives and of its strategies. The ostensible promoter of the Kurdish cause was the Kurdistan Workers Party PKK, whose declared aim was to establish, through violent means, a pan-Kurdish state based on Marxist-Leninist principles. The PKK, led by Abdullah Öcalan launched its first attack on the Turkish armed forces in August 1984, and progressively used all the instruments at its disposal, including terrorism (against the Turkish state, civilian dissidents, feudal lords, and rival Kurdish and left-wing groups). By the mid-1990s the PKK had approximately 8,000 militants operating inside Turkey and controlling large swathes of the southeastern countryside. The movement also exploited its foreign connections, using Syria and Lebanon in the 1980s and then northern Iraq since 1990–1 as training grounds and launching pads for attacks against Turkish targets. In the 1990s, the PKK also mobilized the Kurdish Diaspora in Western Europe to extend its struggle beyond the region.[2] It made effective use of the media and communication technology to forge a sense of nationhood amongst Diaspora Kurds.

Mounting PKK violence did not lead to the Turkish state's questioning of its methods. On the contrary, the number of Turkish troops in the southeast steadily increased, and the state recruited village guards to fight the PKK. Military forces used all licit and illicit means in their war, including the evacuation of villages, the displacement of persons, extrajudicial killings and disappearances, detentions, intimidation and torture. In July 1987, the state imposed emergency rule (Olağanüstü Hal – OHAL) in ten provinces of the southeast, which lasted until 2002. OHAL implied the appointment of provincial governors with broad powers to restrict civilian rights and freedoms, thus giving rise to a dual system of law in the country (Kurban 2003: 190). In 1991, a new Anti-Terrorism Law provided an extremely broad definition of terrorism and legalized a wide set of measures to combat it. The Turkish military also intervened regularly in Iraq after the 1991 Gulf war. Indeed rather than incursions, there was a regular Turkish military presence in northern Iraq to fight the PKK, which ranged between 1,000 and 30,000 troops.

The legal system was also used to ban pro-Kurdish political parties (Barkey 1998). In 1993, the People's Labour Party (Halkın Emek Partisi – HEP) was closed for allegedly basing itself on racial grounds. It was succeeded by the more radical Democratic Labour Party (Demokrasi Emek Partisi – DEP), but in 1994 the Constitutional Court both lifted parliamentary immunity of several of its deputies and then banned the party itself. The same fate awaited two of its successors, the People's Democratic Party (Halkın Demokrasi Partisi – HADEP), closed in 2003, and the Democratic People's Party (Democratik Halk Partisi – DEHAP), which dissolved itself in 2005. DEHAP was replaced by the Democratic Society Movement (Demokratik Toplum HarekeTi – DTH), founded in 2004 by former DEP members released from jail. In all court proceedings and rulings, the main accusations against these parties were their links with the PKK and their attempts to challenge the unitary nature of the Republic. The alleged links between pro-Kurdish parties and the PKK, if proved, may have been cause for legal action. Some of the actions by these parties were at the very least politically naïve and ambiguous in their attitudes towards the PKK.[3] However the lifting of parliamentary immunities and the banning of parties precluded the resolution of the Kurdish question within the democratic system. As stated by Koğacioğlu (2003: 273): '...the boundaries of the Turkish political domain are juridically marked in a way that to a large extent prevents substantial social concerns and aspirations from being translated into forms of legitimate political action'.

The state, while pursuing force and repression, accepted the socio-economic dimension of the Kurdish question by the late 1980s. This was not least because of the deteriorating underdevelopment of the southeast over the years of PKK insurgency. The economic solution was embodied in the monumental South East Anatolian Project (Güneydoğu Anadolu Projesi – GAP), intended to use the Tigris and Euphrates rivers to fuel the agricultural and industrial development of the country. The project included the construction of 22 dams and 19 hydroelectric power plants, irrigating 1.7 million hectares and generating $30bn worth of electrical energy. To date, the partial implementation of GAP (through the Atatürk dam on the Euphrates) has provided water and electricity to most villages of the region. However, the implementation of the plan has focussed far more on irrigation than on electricity, benefiting the industrial west more than the underdeveloped southeast. Furthermore, GAP has failed act upon the specific realities of the southeast, where land distribution is highly unequal, illiteracy is widespread and investment is almost non-existent. Indeed, GAP notwithstanding, in the 1994–2004 period, the southeast consistently ranked amongst the last in terms of literacy and health indicators, receiving on average a mere 3.2 per cent of public investment on education and 4.8 per cent on healthcare (Beleli 2005: 7). In addition, the Atatürk dam has displaced 50,000 villagers and the planned Ilısu dam to be built on the Tigris is set to displace a further 20,000, as well as to create ecological and cultural damage. GAP (as well as the presence of PKK camps in Syria and the Lebanese Beka'a valley) also complicated Turkey's geopolitical standing, bringing Turkey and Syria to the brink of war in 1998 when Turkey deployed 10,000 troops on the Syrian border.

Photo 2 Children on the streets of Diyarbakır, Turkey. August 2001.

The shift towards a rights-based approach to the Kurdish question

During the 1980s, the predominant approach to the Kurdish question was through violence. Violence was exerted by both sides to attain on the one hand Kurdish secession, and on the other hand Turkish suppression and denial of the very existence of a Kurdish problem. While force has remained a cardinal element of the Kurdish question, a rights-based approach to its solution began to emerge in the late 1990s.

The Kurdish shift towards a rights-based approach

By the early 1990s, when the PKK was at the peak of its strength and support, it began shifting its objectives, embracing greater pragmatism. It first abandoned the goal of a pan-Kurdish state, opting for the establishment of a separate state in Turkey's southeast. It then started advocating federalism or autonomy within the borders of the Turkish republic.[4] But the PKK's articulation of a federal solution never went beyond the level of general rhetoric and changed in response to political contingencies. With the 2003 war in Iraq and the drift of the Iraqi Kurds towards quasi-independence, Öcalan called for the establishment of a 'stateless confedera-tion' or a Kurdish Democratic Federation. But again, precious little evidence was provided as to what such a solution entailed.

Solutions centred around federalism, autonomy and decentralization were also advocated by the successive pro-Kurdish parties. In the mid-1990s, HADEP called for the establishment of a second legislative chamber representing an assembly of provinces. In 2004, a group of Kurdish politicians and intellectuals called upon Turkey to grant to the Kurds the same status as enjoyed by the Basques, Catalans, Scots, Lapps, South Tyroleans and Walloons (BIA News Center 2004). Kurdish public opinion also appeared to favour territorial solutions within the confines of the Republic, rather than the establishment of an independent Kurdistan. A 1995 study showed that a majority of respondents in the southeast favoured a solution within the confines of the Republic, with 36 per cent supporting a federation, 17 per cent supporting decentralization and 11 per cent supporting autonomy (Ergil 1995). But while the propositions of Kurdish parties and associations were specified in somewhat greater detail than the PKK's federal ideas, they have hardly represented coherent and comprehensive political platforms. Ergil's 1995 study also showed that Kurdish public opinion had little knowledge of what federal or autonomy-based solutions entailed.

In its mildest and most articulate form, which developed at the turn of the century, the Kurdish challenge is about the respect for individual and collective rights in Turkey. While Kurds have rarely openly called for minority rights, this is largely because of the negative connotations attached to this term in Turkey.[5] From a Kurdish perspective, the 'rights-based' solution has been articulated in terms of:[6]

- The freedom to publish and broadcast (radio and television) in Kurdish.
- Kurdish education. This could be achieved in stages beginning with private courses, followed by the teaching of Kurdish as a second language in public schools and universities, and ultimately the establishment of bilingual schools and universities.
- The freedom to establish and operate freely Kurdish NGOs, freedom of assembly and freedom of expressing non-violent political opinions.
- Freedom from torture and access to fair trial. The abolition of State Security Courts and of the death penalty.
- Compensation and return of IDPs.
- Lifting OHAL in law and practice and abolishing the village guard system. A general amnesty for all militants.
- Freedom to establish and operate parties and a reduction of the 10 per cent electoral threshold.

- The reduction of regional disparities and promotion of socio-economic development, including through some degree of local autonomy.

The 'democratic Turkey' solution was ostensibly advocated by the PKK between 1999 and 2005 (Öcalan 1999: 18). However, unlike its previous shift towards federalism in the early 1990s, this change appeared to be the tactical response to the PKK's weakening particularly with the capture of its leader. Indeed in 2005, the PKK shifted back to its support for a pan-Kurdish federal or confederal solution. While often linked to the PKK, the rights-based platform of pro-Kurdish parties and NGOs appeared far more genuine. HADEP, for example, argued in favour of a phased approach to the Kurdish question, beginning with the full implementation of human rights and then engaging in a debate on multiculturalism in Turkey. DEHAP attempted to disassociate itself from an exclusively Kurdish cause, standing for human rights of all minorities. DEHAP's successor, the DTH, however appears to have moved a step backwards, calling for extensive territorial autonomy and failing to distance itself fully from the PKK.

The Turkish shift towards a rights-based approach

Key actors within the Turkish establishment also progressively warmed to the concept of a rights-based solution, making this the only route to reconciliation between the Kurdish cause and the Turkish republican project.[7] However, unlike Kurdish and pro-Kurdish voices, most Turks who support a rights-based approach focus on the respect of individual and not of collective rights. It is through the exercise of individual rights that citizens would be free to express their communal identity while remaining committed to Kemalist values. Collective rights are viewed by many both as a form of discrimination and as a trigger for the territorial disintegration of the country.

The first tentative steps towards a rights-based approach were taken in 1991, during Turgut Özal's presidency. At the level of rhetoric, the centre-left Social Democratic Populist Party (Sosysaldemokrat Halkçi Parti – SHP) published a report calling for the recognition of Kurdish cultural rights. Mesut Yılmaz (from Özal's Motherland Party Anavatan Partisi – ANAP) toyed with the idea of upgrading Kurdish into Turkey's second language. In April 1991, after the bloodshed during Kurdish New Year, Özal aired the idea of legalizing the PKK. Some limited steps followed suit. Later that year, a bill was passed legalizing Kurdish in speech, music, records and videotapes and a partial amnesty law was passed. However, following Özal's death in 1993 and the end of a short PKK unilateral ceasefire, the state reverted to a military approach. The next steps were taken in 1995, when the Turkish parliament modified Article 8 of the Anti-Terrorism Law which made separatist propaganda a criminal offence. While retaining the essence of the Law, offences were defined more narrowly and penalties were reduced.

The tide seemed to turn in the early twenty-first century. The cessation of large-scale violence in the region saw an end to the destruction of villages, to the evacuation of civilians, to mystery killings and to widespread torture.

Moreover, Turkish authorities undertook fundamental constitutional and legal reforms, many of which benefited (albeit not exclusively) the Kurdish. In October 2001, parliament adopted 34 constitutional amendments, followed by seven 'harmonization packages' passed between 2001 and 2003, a further set of constitutional amendments in May 2004 and an accompanying eighth package in June 2004. In November 2004, a new Law on Associations entered into force and in March 2005 a new Penal Code was introduced. The government also established mechanisms to ensure reform implementation. These included human rights boards in major towns and cities to handle complaints; a Reform Monitoring Group to monitor compliance and overcome bureaucratic inertia; a parliamentary Human Rights Investigation Committee, and a Human Rights Presidency entrusted with raising awareness.

The principal area of democratic change was in the sphere of individual civil, political, social and cultural rights. First, freedom of expression was enhanced. The amendments of Articles 26 and 28 of the Constitution removed restrictions on the use of 'any language prohibited by law' in the expression and dissemination of thought. The harmonization packages amended the Anti-Terrorism Law (Articles 7 and 8) and introduced a new Penal Code. Collectively, these reforms reduced the criminalization of opinions allegedly threatening territorial integrity, manipulating ethnic, social or religious differences, or supporting terrorism. However, the amendments left untouched restrictions attached to the exercise of these rights for the purposes of safeguarding 'the indivisible integrity of the state'. In turn, at the level of implementation, there has been a strong tendency within the judiciary either to rely on other provisions left untouched in the Constitution or to use the amended laws to restrict the freedom of expression. Although most of these ongoing prosecutions have resulted in acquittals, cases continue to be brought forward. In 2005–6 the trial against novelist Orhan Pamuk and the probe against Member of the European Parliament (MEP) Joost Lagendijk, on the basis of statements on the Kurds, the Armenians and the Turkish military, are notable cases in point.

Second, the reforms enhanced the right to fair trial and abolished the death penalty and State Security Courts. The amended Article 36 of the Constitution reinforced the right to a fair trial. The third harmonization package bolstered by the second set of constitutional amendments and the eighth harmonization package abolished capital punishment and State Security Courts. The new Penal Code allowed for the presence of interpreters in courts, enhancing the right to fair trial to non-Turkish speaking citizens. The third and fifth packages provided for retrial of cases that have been found to be in violation of the European Convention on Human Rights (ECHR). The most well-known beneficiaries of these reforms were former DEP deputies (Selim Sadak, Leyla Zana, Hatıp Dicle and Orhan Doğan), whose cases have been re-tried and who were released from detention in June 2004. In May 2005, the ECtHR ruled on the unfairness of Öcalan's trial. Beyond the certainty that Öcalan will not receive capital punishment, it remains to be seen whether and how the Turkish judiciary will allow for his retrial, especially considering that the legal reforms only provide for retrial of cases pending after February 2003 (i.e. excluding Öcalan's case).

Third, freedom of association was strengthened, with an effective overhaul of the Law on Associations, which *inter alia*, opened the legal space for associations founded by and/or that seek to serve Kurdish citizens. The fourth harmonization package enabled associations to use any language in their non-official correspondence. However, the Law retains its restrictive character particularly vis-à-vis associations advocating Kurdish rights. In addition, a March 2005 regulation stated that associations that promote a particular cultural or religious identity cannot be legally registered. Indeed in May 2005, the Court of Cassation ruled to close the teachers union (Eğtim Sen) because of its calls for education in languages other than Turkish. The freedom of assembly has also been strengthened by amending the Law on Public Meetings and Demonstration Marches. However, the Law continues to grant governors broad authority to postpone meetings on the grounds of national security, which is often widely construed.

Fourth, the reforms alleviated restrictions on political parties. The amendment of Article 69 of the Constitution, followed by changes to the Law on Political Parties, stated that parties could be deprived of state aids as an alternative sanction to dissolution. The fourth harmonization package increased further the difficulty of dissolving a party by stating that dissolution required a three-fifths majority in the Constitutional Court. However, what was not altered were the substantive legal grounds for sanctioning a party (i.e. an alleged threatened violation of the state's indivisible integrity). Linked to this, the Political Parties Law continues to restrict the use of languages other than Turkish in official meetings and programmes. A further omission was the failure to lower the 10 per cent electoral threshold. More problematic still have been the decisions of the Constitutional Court after these amendments. They illustrate the link between the two sets of omissions indicated above. In March 2003, the Constitutional Court ruled to permanently dissolve HADEP, due to its threat to the state's indivisible integrity. The choice of dissolution rather than financial sanctions was motivated by the fact that HADEP had not reached the 10 per cent threshold required to benefit from state funding.

Fifth, cultural rights were extended. An amendment to the Civil Registry Law removed the restriction on parents' freedom to name their children with names deemed 'politically offensive'. However, a September 2003 circular restricted the scope of the amended law to names containing letters of the Turkish alphabet only (thus banning names involving the letters of q, w and x, commonly used in Kurdish). Amendments to the Cinema, Video and Music Works Law narrowed the scope for banning art works. However, as in the above-mentioned reforms, the legal grounds for bans remained the alleged violation of the state's indivisible integrity. Local police has often used this justification to prevent concerts, cultural events and conferences in Kurdish. On most occasions, events ultimately took place only through the intervention of the upper echelons in the administration or the judiciary.

Moving to the far more controversial subject of collective rights, it is imperative to note that despite the marginal steps made on this front, these were arguably the most significant features of the reform process. This is not because of their concrete impact on the Kurds (as well as other communities). To date, the Constitution continues to deem Turkish as the only 'mother tongue' in the republic and the only 'language of the State'. As such, it provides for the exclusive protection of and financial support for the Turkish language, history and culture. Yet the significance of these reforms stems from their impact on the nature and evolution of the Turkish republican project. The debate on collective rights has only just begun. An interesting example of this was the publication in November 2004 of a 'minorities report' by the Human Rights Advisory Board set up by the Prime Minister's Office (Republic of Turkey 2004). The report, calling for the respect of Article 39 of the Lausanne Treaty as well as for the signature of the Framework Convention on National Minorities, created much disdain within conservative circles, and was ultimately disowned by the government itself. But the very fact that such a report was published says much about the process of change which is ongoing in Turkey.

Within these strict legal confines, reforms entrusted linguistic minorities broadcasting and education rights. The broadcasting law was amended to allow radio and television broadcasting 'in different languages and dialects Turkish citizens traditionally use in their daily lives', including broadcasting on private stations. State broadcasting in Kurdish began in June 2004 and the first two regional channels broadcasting in Kurdish were approved by the radio and broadcasting board in March 2006. However, broadcasting rights were heavily restricted by prohibiting broadcasts that allegedly contradict republican principles. Once again, this restriction was problematic in view of its expansive interpretation. In addition, the administrative regulations accompanying the revised broadcasting law limit regional or local broadcasts, oblige state authorization and control over content, and restrict the nature and timing of the programmes.

The harmonization packages also amended the Law on the Teaching of Foreign Languages, allowing for private courses teaching Kurdish. These education rights do not approximate the rights of recognized minorities. No public education in Kurdish is allowed. In addition, these rights do not amount to the same opportunities available for education in foreign languages in Turkey. Most critically, the amendments only allow education *of* Kurdish, rather than *in* Kurdish. In addition, the amendments have faced important hurdles in implementation, by precluding state funding and specifying strict conditions on the curricula, the appointment of teachers, timetables and student requirements (i.e. the completion of primary education). Hence, by August 2005, the few Kurdish private schools which had opened were closed due to financial difficulties that derived from the strict conditions under which they were operating.

Turning more specifically to the southeast, since late 2002, the state of emergency has gradually been lifted in all provinces. In an effort to remedy the legacy of the OHAL regime, the parliament approved a set of measures, including a Return to Villages and Rehabilitation Programme, a Law on Integration in Society (essentially a partial amnesty for former militants) and a Law on Compensation of Losses arising from Acts of Terror and the Measures taken to Fight against Terror in July 2004. However, implementation has proceeded at a slow and uneven pace.

Regarding compensation, cases are only considered after 1987 (despite PKK violence having started in 1984), no compensation for pain and suffering is contemplated, the burden of proof is high, the threshold for maximum compensation is low, the compensation commissions include only civil servants, and there is limited capacity to process claims and provide legal support for applicants. Regarding return, several factors have hindered implementation. Procedures are not transparent and decisions to allow return rest with the governorships. Resettlement often takes place in newly built rural villages rather than in places and properties of origin. Health facilities and infrastructure is poor and little effort has been put in recreating employment opportunities. Finally, security risks dissuading IDP return persist not least because of the continuing presence of armed village guards. By the summer of 2005, just over one third of the IDPs (125,500 out of approximately 356,000) had returned (TESEV 2005). There has also been a lack of government cooperation with the ECtHR concerning IDP cases.

Finally, the first steps were made in the field of governance reform. A Framework Law on Public Administration was adopted in 2004, but was subsequently vetoed by the president. Notwithstanding this, the Turkish parliament approved a Law on Municipalities, a Law on Special Provincial Administrations, a Law on Association of Local Governments and a Law on Metropolitan Municipalities aimed at redistributing competences, rationalizing the administration and raising transparency and accountability. Turkey has also established 26 new regions and is working on new legislation for the establishment of Regional Development Agencies (Ertuğal 2005). However, much remains to be done, as little progress has been made in the establishment of Regional Development Agencies and powers remain concentrated in the central State Planning Organization.

Between 2002 and 2005, it seemed that Turkey had embarked on a slow yet unprecedented process of rights-based reform, which could have offered a much-sought solution to its national dilemmas, first and foremost that of the Kurds. Yet a set of domestic and international developments have caused a lull and in some respects a reversal in the reform process since 2005. First, the ruling elite appears to have turned its attention to other sectors of its electorate, whose priorities are not linked to EU membership. This is particularly relevant in view of the 2007 general elections. Second, the absence of a sufficiently large cadre of professionals below the top echelons of government has hampered the process of reform implementation and institutionalization. Third, there has been an alarming rise of nationalism across society, partly due to rising insecurities stemming from events in neighbouring Iraq and partly due to high unemployment rates and the adjustment costs of structural reforms (Sak 2005). The assassination of Turkish–Armenian journalist Hrant Dink in January 2007 has been one of the most alarming signals of rampant nationalism in the country.

On the Kurdish side, notwithstanding a much-weakened capability compared to the 1990s, the PKK followed the instructions of its imprisoned leader to renew violence against the Turkish state in June 2004. The decision was driven by several factors, including the fading prospects of Öcalan's release, the loosening grip over the Kurdish national movement and the opportunities presented by the war in Iraq.[8]

The decision created a further fragmentation of the PKK; as key elements within it (including Öcalan's brother Ösman) broke away from its formal structures. Yet a weakened structure did not make PKK violence and its consequences any less dangerous. Rather than focussing on rural insurgency, the post-2004 PKK violence targeted urban, economic and tourist targets, particularly in the summer of 2005.

As in the 1980s and 1990s, the Turkish establishment responded with force, reframed the Kurdish question national security terms, and thus allowed the re-empowerment of the 'deep state'[9] (*derim devlet*). Linked to this, tensions rose to new heights in November 2005 with the bombing of a Kurdish bookstore in the southeastern town of Sedimli by members of the Turkish gendarmerie intelligence organization. A wave of violence then swept across the southeast and the Kurdish-populated suburbs of Istanbul in the spring of 2006. In turn, the region witnessed renewed militarization with the deployment of Turkish military units along the Iraqi border and the reinstatement of roadblocks and checkpoints. The Turkish parliament also discussed a new draft Law for the Fight against Terrorism, which threatens to curtail some of the progress made in the reform packages.

Assessing EU impact on Turkey's Kurdish question

A rights-based approach offers the only feasible means to reconcile the (nonetheless diverging) positions of moderate Kurdish actors and the Turkish state. As and when the Turkish state engaged in human rights and democracy reforms, Kurdish public opinion became more sympathetic to a rights-based solution.[10] A rights-based approach also approximates most the EU's recommendations. Between late 2001 and 2005, the Turkish establishment moved towards meeting the EU's recommendations as well as the wishes of the Kurds. It sought a political solution by extending the protection of individual human rights, by enhancing the rule of law (abolishing State Security Courts and the death penalty and assuring the right to fair trial), by allowing the use of Kurdish names and legalizing Kurdish broadcasting and private education, and finally by lifting the infamous OHAL regime. Particularly under the AKP government, Turkey moved a long way towards recognizing the Kurdish question as such, and openly advocating a political and democratic solution to it.[11]

When cross-checked with the EU's recommendations, the most visible omissions relate to the need for an effective socio-economic development strategy in the southeast, concrete steps towards decentralization, the need to abolish village guards and to ensure IDP return and/or compensation. The question of development, village guards and IDP return are closely interlinked – without the former it is unrealistic to achieve the latter. While all IDPs should be offered the choice of return (and compensation), until and unless southeastern villages offer adequate socio-economic prospects, the full integration of (particularly young) IDPs into metropolitan centres will remain the most realistic and desirable prospect. Also, in the case of the village guards, disarming militias and taking them off the state's payroll only has a realistic chance of success if alternative employment prospects exist. In this respect, the renewed wave of PKK violence and the

Turkish state's response will exacerbate the vicious circle besieging the triple tasks of development, IDP return and enhanced civilian security.

Equally important is the need to encourage Kurdish political participation, not least by lowering the 10 per cent threshold and by inducing governance reform. The difficulty in fostering participation should not be underestimated. There is plenty of evidence hinting at the links between successive pro-Kurdish parties and the PKK. Several observers have gone as far as viewing Kurdish parties as the legal wing of the PKK.[12] Part of the explanation lies in the monopolizing, hierarchical and intimidating character of the PKK itself. For example, following the renewed wave of violence in the southeast since 2004, the PKK has also targeted political activists who were not part of the PKK as part of an intimidation campaign against possible Kurdish dissidents. However, much of the explanation lies in the Turkish state's stifling of any alternative Kurdish voice. This has prevented the emancipation of the Kurdish cause from the PKK, which has raised further the reluctance of the Turkish establishment to allow greater political participation by Kurdish actors for example by lowering the electoral threshold. Yet the need to encourage an alternative leadership through democratic participation remains one of the key challenges for the peaceful resolution of the Kurdish question. Much of the answer could come from the sphere of governance. If and as the Turkish state embraces decentralization, this could foster a professional and responsible Kurdish political elite at the local and regional levels.

Turning instead to the actual reforms passed, two sets of problems remain pending and risk being exacerbated in the post-2004 climate of political tension and violence. First, several omissions in the amended laws preserved important constraints on the exercise of these rights. Second, the tensions inherent in some of the new laws render the legal system susceptible to abuse in implementation. Indeed, many of the legislative reforms, particularly in the area language rights, were followed by restrictive implementing regulations adopted by the executive and the administration. The object and purpose of the new laws has also been hindered by overly activist prosecutors who have taken advantage of gaps in the legal framework.

With this analysis in mind, let us turn to the role of the EU. How, and to what extent, has the EU encouraged Turkey's reforms process as well as contributed to its pending gaps and renewed problems? It is of course important to clarify that the EU has not and could not act as the principal, let alone the only determinant of the Kurdish question. Domestic factors have represented the key determinants of change and lack thereof. More specifically, the end of large-scale violence in the southeast with the capture of Öcalan in 1999 both set the context and provided the momentum to embark on a non-military solution to the Kurdish question. Had the war not ended, the reforms would not have been possible.[13] The ongoing self-reassessment within the Turkish military, following four military coups in the republic's history is another key factor. The November 2002 election of the AKP with a wide parliamentary majority meant that for the first time since the Özal years in the 1980s, Turkey has had a strong government, which was also motivated to embark on a radical reform agenda. The ensuing strengthening of civil society as a result of the reforms also added to the reform momentum. On the negative side, the remaining tensions between progressive and conservative forces in Turkey, the relative re-empowerment of the deep state, the 2003 war in Iraq, the 2004 resurgence of PKK violence, and the beginning of electoral politics in Turkey in 2006, all explain the limits of Turkey's democratic transformation. Based on these premises, the following sections assess the EU's influence on Turkey's Kurdish question by interacting with the domestic and international factors which have shaped its evolution.

The value of the EU benefit: from association to uncertain accession

A first determinant of the EU's impact on Turkey's Kurdish question is the actual and subjectively perceived value of the contractual relationship on offer.

The importance of the jump from association to accession

Since its 1963 association agreement with the then EC, Turkey has had the prospect of enjoying the most valuable form of contractual engagement with the EU – that of full membership. Yet up until when membership was a remote possibility, the EU's influence on the Kurdish question was effectively nil, if not negative.

Between Turkey's 1987 application to membership and the 1999 Helsinki European Council granting Turkey EU candidacy, EU actors refrained from giving the green lights to Turkey's accession course. The nadir of EU–Turkey ties came at, and after, the 1997 Luxembourg European Council, in which the Union opened accession negotiations with the CEECs, Cyprus and Malta, while not recognizing Turkey as a candidate for membership. In that period, in view of the mounting violence in the southeast, EU institutions became increasingly vocal on the Kurdish question. Yet EU calls largely fell on deaf ears. As put by then Foreign Minister Murat Karayalçin 'Turkey will not accept any preconditions on democratization, human rights…Turkey will not democratize because it is ordered by its European friends' (Republic of Turkey 1995: 37). For example, in the run-up to the 1996 customs union agreement, the EP delayed ratification of the agreement in response to Turkey's arrest of the DEP deputies (Krauss 2000). Yet the Turkish government refused to release the Kurdish parliamentarians in response to European pressure. The Turkish parliament did approve an amendment to the Anti-Terrorism Law in October 1995, which proved sufficient to ensure the EP's ratification. But in practice the amendments were superficial and fell way below the EU's expectations. The absence of genuine reform was largely due to the instability of Turkish governing coalitions, at the time coupled with the ongoing PKK violence. However, equally important in explaining the EU's limited impact was the fact that the customs union, confined to the economic sphere, was not viewed by the Turkish establishment as a sufficiently valuable prize for Turkey to engage in difficult reforms.

Again, in the run-up to the 1999 Helsinki European Council, in its bid to secure candidacy, the Turkish parliament amended Article 143 of the Constitution, removing military personnel from State Security Courts. It also allowed Council of Europe monitoring of Abdullah Öcalan's detention and trial and agreed to respect the ECtHR's calls for a stay on his execution. Aside from the quest for candidacy, these first tentative steps in reform were possible because of the capture of Öcalan and the rise to power of a coalition government supporting a moderately reformist platform. However these changes, while adding to the momentum in favour of Turkey's candidacy, did not alter significantly the status and situation of the Kurds.

The change in Turkey's approach since it was accorded EU candidacy in December 1999 has been far clearer. The precise timing in the acceleration of Turkey's reforms is explained by domestic developments. In 2000, the overall attitude of Bülent Ecevit's cabinet towards reform became increasingly prudent due to the dynamics within the coalition. By mid-2002, the mounting divisions in the governing coalition were pivotal in accelerating the reform drive by triggering the extensive August 2002 harmonization package and in leading the country to early elections in November. The ensuing landslide victory of the AKP propelled the reform process into a higher gear. This was partly due to the creation of a stable single party government and largely due to the fact that the AKP based its political platform (aimed at demonstrating its emancipation from its Islamist past) on the goals of modernization and democratization. Another domestic factor was the economy, which collapsed in the aftermath of the 2000–1 financial crises, triggering a national debate on the illnesses of Turkey's political economy and generating a consensus on the need for structural reform. But while the precise timing of the reforms (in late 2001–2 rather than early 2000) was due to domestic factors, the jump from association to accession acted as a key external determinant of the reform process. Indeed the reforms were undertaken with the stated intention of fulfilling the EU's Copenhagen political criteria, necessary to open accession negotiations.

The importance of the jump from association to accession was not purely objective in nature. It is also, and indeed primarily, due to the subjective value ascribed by Turkey to it. Turkey has long viewed EU accession as the natural corollary of the Kemalist project. As stated by Chief of General Staff Büyükanıt: '...the EU is the geopolitical and geostrategic ultimate condition for the realization of the target of modernization which Mustafa Kemal Atatürk chose for the Turkish nation' (Kirişçi 2005: 62). In turn, it is hardly surprising that for the sake of accession, the authorities have been willing to go the extra mile in terms of the reforms undertaken.

This willingness is primarily generated by the sense of security embedded in the EU, which explains the key difference between association and customs union on the one hand and accession on the other. When EU actors called on Turkey to undertake reforms in the 1990s, the Turkish authorities rebuffed these calls, viewing them as too risky for the country's security. The 'Sèvres syndrome' exacerbated these views. The 1920 Treaty of Sèvres, imposed by the Western victors of World War I, allowed for Kurdish secession. Since then, Turkish policy-makers have often considered foreign proposals in favour of the Kurds as an attempt – within the legacy of Sèvres – to dismember Turkey. At different points in time, the perception that the EU would pose a threat to Turkey's territorial integrity was also widespread amongst the public (Öktem 2006). What made matters worse was the use made by the PKK of the rights and freedoms enjoyed in Western Europe to stage demonstrations, and establish media outlets (e.g. MED-TV, Media-TV, Roj-TV) and the Kurdistan Parliament in Exile. As and when 'Europe' made the qualitative choice to include Turkey in its club, it signaled its increased willingness to share the burden of Turkish security, reducing Turkish suspicions of it.

Equally important is the prime value accorded to EU accession by Turkey's Kurds, for reasons linked to the expectation of greater political rights and freedoms as well as of socio-economic development. A public manifesto, signed by over 200 Kurdish politicians and intellectuals in December 2004 stated that 'the European process offers both Turks and Kurds new and promising prospects, and gives them a chance for reconciliation on the basis of a peaceful resolution of the Kurdish question, with due respect for existing borders' (BIA News Center 2004). Kurdish public opinion conveys a similar message. While up until 2005 support for accession has tended to be over 70 per cent on average in Turkey, the highest peaks of support have consistently come from the southeast.[14]

The limits in the value of the EU promise

Turning to an explanation of the remaining gaps in the reforms as well as the lull in the reform process since 2005, it is important to note that some key actors in the establishment have only paid lip-service to the goal of membership. More accurately, their support was high until membership became a more realistic goal. As and when the accession process began, their effective support rapidly dwindled because of their reluctance to engage in comprehensive domestic transformation. Indeed the tensions within the Ecevit government were largely due to disagreements over the EU-induced reform process.

The accession process coupled with the rise to power of the AKP contributed to the relative weakening of the conservative/nationalist camp in 2002–5. But other developments both within the country and outside it cast a permanent shadow over the peaceful and democratic resolution of the Kurdish question. The slowdown in Turkey's reform drive in terms of implementation and new reforms is linked to electoral politics, the flaws in the administration, the war in Iraq, the rise in nationalism and the resumption of PKK violence and the state's reaction to it. But coupled with these domestic explanations, the mounting uncertainties in Turkey's accession process following the December 2004 European Council's decision to open accession negotiations have also contributed to the reform lull by reducing the value given to the accession process.

The fact that the 2004 European Council emphasized the 'open-ended' nature of negotiations and the need to account for the 'absorption capacity' of the Union, the impact of the RoC's EU membership on the EU's stance on the Cyprus conflict, the French decision to hold a referendum on Turkey's future membership, and the possibility of permanent derogations in key areas such as free movement of persons, structural funds and agriculture, have diluted the value of Turkey's accession drive. Turkey's accession process is also plagued with a problem of timing. Despite the launch of negotiations in October 2005, membership itself is expected to occur at least a decade later. The uncertainty of the process due to its timeframe affects negatively Turkey's incentives to engage in reforms in the short and medium terms. The freezing of accession negotiations on eight chapters in December 2006 has further reduced the predictability of Turkey's accession process. This dovetails dangerously with the nationalist tide that has swept across Turkey since 2005; nationalism which has been tainted by strong anti-imperialist and anti-European rhetoric. Nationalism and virulent accusations against Europe's 'Christian club', validated by the Union's cold feet on Turkey's accession, has damaged the impressive steps forward made in the previous three years and reduced the value of the accession process in Turkish eyes. This partly explains the sharp drop in support for EU accession from 72 per cent to 58 per cent in 2005–6 (Ülgen 2006).

The credibility of EU obligations

Turning from EU benefits to obligations, a first key observation is that even in this respect, the jump from association to accession was of key importance.

The rise in credibility through the accession process

The 1963 association agreement did not include any conditionality related to democracy and human rights, which could have been used by the Community to exert leverage on the Kurdish question. As discussed above, the EP did attempt to attach political conditions related to the Kurds in 1995, but largely failed in its intent. The political influence of EU actors through learning and persuasion was also extremely limited in that period. Contact between Turkish and EU bureaucrats and politicians, let alone civil society was circumscribed and occasional. The meetings of the Association Council and the Joint Parliamentary Committee were insufficient to trigger a meaningful process of learning in which Turkish actors willingly assimilated EU norms and recommendations. In addition, following the Luxembourg European Council's fiasco, Turkey froze its political dialogue with the Union. The Association Council did not meet between 1997 and 2000, and Turkey refused to participate in the European Conferences held on the margins of European Council meetings after 1997.

As Turkey entered the accession process, EU obligations became more credible. More specifically, the ex ante conditionality embedded in the accession process acquired the virtues of passive enforcement, given that conditions could no longer be viewed as a matter for political bargaining, but rather as the *sine qua non* for entering the EU club. The accession process also raised the credibility of conditionality stemming from other pan-European and international organizations, such as the Council of Europe, the OSCE, the UN, as well as the International Financial Institutions (IFI). In the post 1999 period, Turkey has taken far more seriously the judgements of the ECtHR (compliance with which is an EU condition)

(Betul Çelik 2005). It has responded more favourably to UN resolutions (particularly with respect to Cyprus), and it has shown unprecedented diligence in following the IMF's macroeconomic guidelines.

The most important period of EU leverage was between 1999 and 2004. The Helsinki European Council accorded Turkey candidacy, but refrained from opening accession talks because of Turkey's non-compliance with the Copenhagen political criteria. Given the generality of these criteria, the Commission's Progress Reports on Turkey became far more detailed after 1999, assessing the progress or lack thereof in the country's alignment with EU requirements. Beginning in 2001, the Union has also published Accession Partnership documents, pinpointing the short and medium term priorities that Turkey should address in its bid to fulfil the Copenhagen criteria. Since 1999, the European Council has regularly voiced its views on Turkey. Until late 2001, the slow pace of Turkey's reforms meant that no additional expectations were raised. Yet as and when the reform process accelerated, the tune of the European Council changed. The December 2001 Laeken Council concluded that recent developments had 'brought forward the prospect of opening accession negotiations with Turkey' (European Council 2001, paragraph 12). The December 2002 Copenhagen European Council introduced a rendezvous date (in December 2004) to decide on the opening of accession talks. The December 2004 European Council deemed that negotiations could begin on 3 October 2005 given Turkey's 'sufficient' fulfilment of the Copenhagen political criteria. In short, EU institutions displayed overall consistency in their political message to Turkey, which paid-off in terms of Turkey's reform process.

Turkey's accession process also raised the scope for social learning. Contacts between Turkish and EU officials increased significantly under the Association Council, the Joint Parliamentary Committee, the Joint Consultative Committee with the Economic and Social Committee, eight sub-committees reviewing progress in meeting the Accession Partnership's priorities; as well as through working groups, technical assistance seminars and twinning projects. Increased funding for Turkish NGOs on the one hand, and Turkish (and Kurdish) civil society's rising interest in EU accession on the other hand has triggered a social learning effect beyond elite officials. Important problems persist regarding the access of EU funds to NGOs in the southeast (due to the lack of training and expertise to compete for EU tenders). However, an increased openness of Turkish civil society to its European counterparts has already had a positive effect on their views and perceptions. If and when this extends to other regions in Turkey, it could enhance dialogue between Turkish and Kurdish civil society.[15] Broadening further still, the accession process has provided an alternative discourse, which legitimized what were previously considered as taboo subjects in Turkey. This has opened a political space both for suppressed Kurdish demands to come to the fore and for these to be discussed (albeit not necessarily accepted) within the more liberal segments of the establishment. As put by one interlocutor, 'the EU has sparked a debate in the region; it has provided moderate Turks and Kurds with a new language, which could facilitate debate both within the two groups and between them'.[16] As evidence of the degree of societal consensus around EU norms, the AKP government has repeatedly labelled the Copenhagen criteria as the 'Ankara criteria'.[17]

The launch of accession talks opens a new chapter in EU–Turkey relations. This adds credibility to EU conditionality on *acquis*-related matters. In fact, accession negotiations are not negotiations at all, but rather the candidate country's progressive adoption of EU laws and regulations. Passive enforcement rather than conditionality captures more accurately the nature of these 'negotiations'.

However, EU effectiveness in exerting sustained influence over Turkey's political reforms is far more doubtful. Turkey's Accession Negotiation Framework specified that 'the pace (of negotiations) will depend on Turkey's progress in meeting the requirements of membership' (European Council 2005b, paragraph 1), and called upon Turkey to consolidate and broaden its legislation and implementation in the fight against torture, the extension of minority rights, and the freedoms of expression and religion. The Framework stated that in the event of Turkey's serious and persistent breach of the political criteria, accession talks would be suspended and benchmarks would be specified for their re-opening.

Yet it is unclear how the Union would exert positive political conditionality over the years of negotiations. The Framework stated that the Union would strengthen its monitoring role in Turkey. But little information was provided as to how this would be done. The Framework also stated that the European Council would lay down benchmarks for the opening and provisional closure of each chapter. But the benchmarks relate to the negotiation chapter in question, and with the exception of Chapter 23 on the judiciary and fundamental rights, these are not strictly related to political reforms. Since the opening of the negotiation process, the Commission's Turkey Unit has reorganized itself according to the different chapters of the *acquis*, entailing a reduced level of attention to political issues. At the same time, when MEPs, observing the slowdown of Turkey's political reforms, hinted at the attachment of political conditions to the opening of the first chapter of negotiations in June 2006, this created an uproar in Turkey, given the mismatch between the substance of the negotiation chapter and the proposed political benchmarks for its opening.[18]

Accession negotiations do however raise the potential for social learning. The Framework specified that parallel to negotiations, the EU and Turkey would deepen their civil society dialogue. While the primary purpose of this dialogue would be that of shifting European public opinion on the question of Turkey's accession, a possible by-product may be the rise in social learning within Turkish (and possibly Kurdish) civil society.

The clarity of conditions

The credibility of the obligations also hinges on the clarity with which they are spelled-out. With respects to Turkey, individual human rights conditions have been defined relatively clearly, and increasingly so since the beginning of the accession process. The EU's reliance on the standards set by the Council of Europe and the OSCE has also raised the clarity of EU conditions. This also explains why individual rights and democracy standards have been the areas of political reform area where most progress has been achieved.

But the same cannot be said of the clarity of conditions regarding specifically the Kurds, the southeast and decentralization. These have been the areas in which reform has proceeded at a slower pace. In the sphere of governance, the Union has been extremely vague in its recommendations. The 2005 Progress Report only hinted that Turkey 'may consider' devolving responsibilities to sectoral ministries or to new regional structures (Commission 2005c: 103). This is not least because Chapter 21 of the *acquis* on regional policy only consists in general framework and implementing regulations, which are neither clear nor legally binding. Regarding the Kurds and the southeast, Turkey's Accession Partnerships, while calling for broadcasting and education in languages other than Turkish, and referring to regional disparities and the return of IDPs, never even mentioned the word 'Kurd', let alone called for Kurdish minority rights. Only the 2004 and 2005 Progress Reports, referred to the Kurds as a community when discussing minority rights, without however following through with specific recommendations on it. The question of minority rights raises additional problems in the clarity of conditions (see Chapter 2). The result is not simply ineffective (or non-existent) conditionality on group rights. It is also the reduced likelihood of a Turkish social learning effect on these questions given the absence of a homogenous minority rights model to observe, learn from and emulate. As far as IDPs are concerned instead, the problem has been that EU conditions have focussed exclusively on the return aspects of the problem, rather than on the pressing need to tackle the urban problems and provide employment and education opportunities to those IDPs who have not and will not return to their places of origin.

This vagueness and incompleteness has had the merit of not antagonizing Turkey on questions that are viewed as highly sensitive. It has also entrusted the protagonists involved with the task of defining and pursuing the precise means to accomplish peaceful reconciliation. This has been the case, as Turkey proceeded on its own account with the legalization of Kurdish broadcasting and private education without specific EU conditions on these matters. Moreover, the internal Turkish–Kurdish debate has far from ended, as Turks and Kurds are immersed in discussion on the reform process and its evolution. In other words, EU recommendations have simply provided the first necessary impetus for a much needed domestic debate. Yet the outcomes of this debate will be determined by the domestic actors themselves.

However, the vagueness and incompleteness of EU conditions has generated serious problems of assessment. Without a detailed specification of expected reforms, minimum standards and benchmarks, Turkish authorities could (and have) claimed that all conditions are met, while EU institutions could (and have) come up with new requirements over the years (Zalewski 2004). The result is often miscommunication, which eroded trust between the parties.

The political management of EU–Turkey relations

The ebbs and flows in the Europeanization of Turkey's Kurdish question are largely explained by the political imperatives underpinning EU–Turkey ties. This has two distinct components to it.

First, compared to other minority issues in Europe, EU actors have only paid sporadic attention to the Kurds, turning to the issue when the problem became acute. While in the case of the CEECs, minority issues were viewed as a security question for Western Europe itself, this has not been the case with Turkey's Kurds.[19] EU actors have tended to focus on the Kurds only when the question has threatened Turkey's stability and/or triggered flows of immigration and asylum-seekers into Western Europe. In addition, and particularly with the resumption of PKK violence and the EU's greater sensitivity towards the problem of global terrorism, EU actors have become far less outspoken on Kurdish rights.[20]

Second, the EU's political influence on Turkey is bedevilled by the Turkish suspicion, often corroborated by EU actions, of Europe's reluctance to include Turkey in its club. Until 2002–3, EU scepticism was rarely voiced in the open. With a few notable exceptions, European declarations normally focussed on Turkey's shortcomings in the areas of democracy and human rights. Yet Turkey's suspicions were motivated by hard facts. When the 1997 Luxembourg European Council denied Turkey candidacy while opening accession talks with the CEECs, Cyprus and Malta, Turks interpreted the decision as clear evidence of European double standards. As Turkey's reform process gained ground, other – non-Copenhagen criteria-related reservations – came to the fore. Key personalities in France have feared that Turkey's entry would dilute the EU's loosely defined 'esprit communautaire'. Actors in Germany, France, Holland and Austria, have argued that Turkey's economic development would entail high levels of redistribution of EU funds to Anatolia, it would bankrupt the Common Agricultural Policy and it would lead to an invasion of 'Turkish plumbers' into the Union. Greece and more recently Cyprus have mobilized EU conditionality to win bargaining points in their bilateral disputes with Turkey, threatening to block Turkey's accession negotiations lest Turkey recognize the RoC. Least noble of all, high-level personalities have been reluctant to embrace a country with an allegedly 'different' culture and religion.[21] Last, but not least, Turkey's geopolitical location has been used as an argument against Turkey's 'Europeanness' and in favour of retaining Anatolia as a buffer between the EU and its turbulent southeast. In this context, when EU actors raised political and human rights questions before the actual start of accession negotiations, this was viewed as yet another sign of discrimination and double standards against Turkey. In other words, wider EU doubts about Turkey's accession process reduced the legitimacy of EU political conditionality on Turkey.

Table 2 Turkey's Kurdish question and EU–Turkey relations

Population (2006)		73m of whom approximately 14–15m Kurdish citizens of Turkey
Key Historical Dates	1920	Treaty of Sèvres allows for the possibility of a Kurdish state
	1921	Basic Organization Law grants Kurdish autonomy
	1923	Treaty of Lausanne establishes the Republic of Turkey
	1924	Turkey violates Article 39 of the Lausanne Treaty granting Kurdish language rights
	1925	The Law for the Reestablishment of Order helps crush Kurdish rebellions in the southeast
	1934	The Resettlement Law dilutes Kurdish presence in the southeast and the Law on Surname bans Kurdish names
	1960	First military coup in Turkey
	1971	Second military coup in Turkey
	1980	Third military coup in Turkey
	1982	The new Constitution circumscribes human rights in Turkey
	1984	The PKK launches its attack against the Turkish state
	1987	Emergency rule is imposed in ten provinces of the southeast
	1991	The Iraq war erupts and Iraqi Kurds flee to southeast Turkey
	1993	The Turkish Constitutional Court bans HEP
	1994	The Turkish Constitutional Court bans DEP
	1995	The Turkish parliament modifies the Anti-Terror Law
	1998	Turkey deploys 10,000 troops on the Syrian border
	1999	Turkey captures PKK leader Abdullah Öcalan
	2001	The Turkish parliament passes 34 constitutional amendments. These are followed by eight legal harmonization packages in 2002–5 extending human rights in Turkey
	2003	The Turkish Constitutional Court bans HADEP. The US invades Iraq
	2004	The PKK ends its unilateral ceasefire
EU Relations	1963	EC–Turkey association agreement
	1970	EC–Turkey additional protocol to the association agreement
	1987	Turkey applies for EC membership
	1989	The Commission rejects Turkey's application
	1996	Turkey enters the EU customs union
	1997	The Luxembourg European Council rejects Turkey's candidacy, offering a 'European strategy' instead
	1999	The Helsinki European Council accepts Turkey's candidacy
	2002	The Copenhagen European Council sets a rendezvous date to decide on the opening of accession negotiations with Turkey
	2004	The European Council decides to open accession negotiations with Turkey in October 2005
	2005	Turkey begins the screening process of the accession talks
	2006	The EU freezes negotiations on eight chapters of the acquis in view of Turkey's non-implementation of the customs union protocol to the RoC
EU Financial Assistance	1996–9	Annual average €90m
	2000–2	Annual average €177m
	2005	€300m
	2006	Budgetary allocation €500m

This does not indicate that the Union has secretly decided against Turkey's membership. On the contrary, accession talks were formally launched in October 2005. However, what should have acted as a powerful antidote against Turkish suspicions, bolstering EU credibility, failed to match its potential because of the strings attached to the European Council's decision. In addition, the fact that until 3 October 2005 the European Council considered mentioning a 'privileged partnership' as an alternative endpoint of the negotiations demonstrated how EU–Turkey relations could easily turn sour.

More widely, the very existence of a debate on the desirability of Turkey's membership had two spin-off effects. On the positive side, it meant that EU institutions have been relatively strict in their observance of Turkey's progress in meeting the Copenhagen criteria, adding to the credibility of the Union's calls for reform. On the negative side, the absence of a strong European commitment to Turkey's membership fuelled Turkey's insecurity, bolstering nationalist and conservative views, which argue that Turkey should be cautious in passing reforms given that 'Europe' will never accept Turkey into its club. At each and every instance in which EU decisions are (or are perceived) as evidence of rejection or double standards, Turkish eurosceptics are bolstered by a 'we told you so' effect. In other words, the more EU–Turkey ties are politically managed, oscillating with the changing domestic politics of EU member states, the less will the EU's impact be on a peaceful and democratic resolution of the Kurdish question.

5 Mixed signals to Serbia and Montenegro

EU interests and objectives in Serbia and Montenegro

The EU has key interests in peace, stability and development in the Western Balkans. Lying at the heart of Europe, instability in the Balkans entails dangerous spillover effects into the Union in terms of lawlessness and organized crime, refugee flows and migratory pressures. Furthermore, in view of the EU's acknowledged failure to deal with the unfolding tragedy of the disintegrating Yugoslavia in the early and mid-1990s, the Union is also resolute to contributing to the region's stabilization. In the words of Enlargement Commissioner Olli Rehn (2006): 'Too often in the 1990s, Brussels fiddled while the Balkans burned. We must not risk this happening again'. To many, success in the Western Balkans is viewed as the quintessential litmus test for the effectiveness of EU foreign policy (International Commission on the Balkans 2005). Were the Union to fail again, the credibility of its foreign policy ambitions could be irredeemably shattered.

The EU also has a set of corollary interests in the region. Having unanimously concurred that the stability of the Balkans necessitates the region's progressive integration into the Union, EU actors are concerned with the region's compliance with EU norms, rules and regulations. This means the fulfilment of the Copenhagen criteria. Yet as opposed to the accession process, the SAP has been specifically designed for the Western Balkans, and includes additional conditions to induce the triple process of post-communist transition, post-war reconstruction and reconciliation, and EU integration. These include full cooperation with the International Criminal Tribunal for Yugoslavia (ICTY), the return of refugees, efforts in combating organized crime, regional cooperation, and the full respect and implementation of peace agreements (European Council 2003a, paragraph 5).

The last and most controversial EU interest and objective in the Balkans is that of preventing the further break-up of former Yugoslavia. In view of the EU's legal prerequisite to integrate states and not quasi-states or protectorates, as well as the greater inconvenience to absorb a greater rather than smaller number of new members (particularly if these are small or micro states), the EU repeatedly argued against further secessionism in the region (Batt 2004).

As far as Serbia and Montenegro are concerned, the EU's general interests translated into a set of specific recommendations. In 2000–6 the EU was adamant

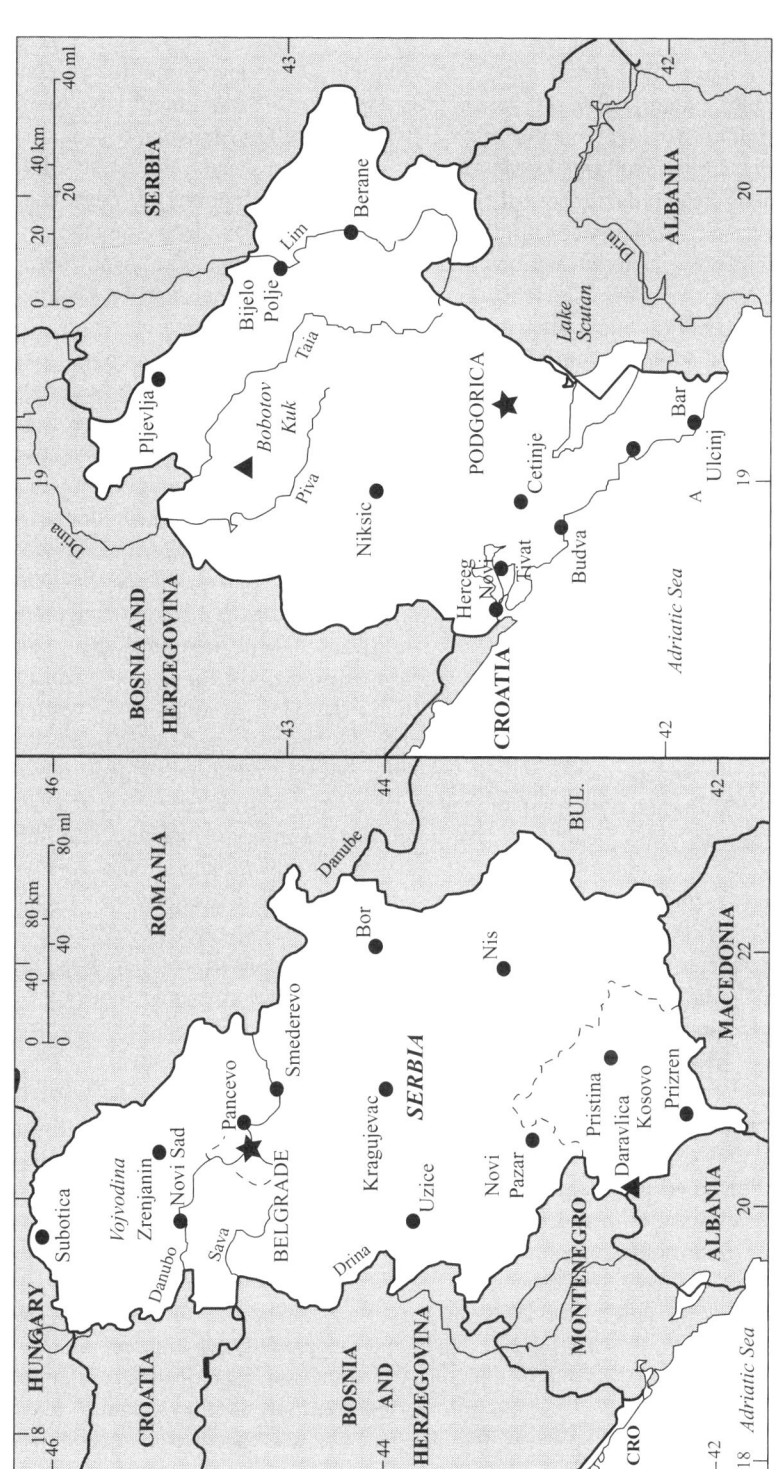

Map 3 Serbia and Montenegro.
Source: The World Fact Book. https://www.cia.gov/cia/publications/factbook/geos/mj.html.

to retain a constitutional link between Serbia and Montenegro, and thus to conclude a single Stabilization and Association Agreement (SAA) and ultimately see the accession of a single member state. Between the fall of Slobodan Milosevic's regime in October 2000 and the March 2002 Belgrade agreement, EU actors, while acknowledging the dysfunctional nature of the Former Republic of Yugoslavia (FRY), insisted that a new constitutional formula had to be found, ensuring the continued unity between its two entities. Hence, the mantra: 'a democratic Montenegro within a democratic Yugoslavia' (Council 2001a). The EU emphasized the need to resolve the constitutional stalemate 'through constructive cooperation in a restructured functional federal state' (Commission 2002: 18). EU institutions appreciated that Montenegro, after five years of de facto independence, could not be reintegrated into the over ten times more populous Serbia. However, the Commission in particular stressed the need to pursue economic harmonization between the two entities as well as an integrated visa and border management system.

A 'functional federal state' was viewed as an imperative to pursue domestic reforms, resolve mounting internal political problems and proceed with European integration. Moreover, federal unity was viewed as a sine qua non to hedge against several risks (ICG 2002). First, separation was viewed as potentially dangerous given it could have deepened the existing political divisions in Montenegro on the question of independence. Second, the EU was preoccupied about the viability of a Montenegrin microstate, particularly in view of its penetration by corruption, smuggling and organized crime. Third, the Union feared that recognizing Montenegro's independence would have prematurely catalyzed a decision on Kosovo's status, at a time when the international community had not yet reached a consensus on how to deal with the problem. On the contrary, a new federal state could have (optimistically) provided a framework for the reintegration of Kosovo into the FRY. Fourth, Montenegro's secession could have radicalized Serbian politics at an early stage of post-Milosevic transition. Within Serbia, it could have also fuelled irredentism and instability amongst the Hungarians in Vojvodina and the Bosniaks in the Sandzak (straddling the border between Serbia and Montenegro). Finally, in the wider region, Montenegro's secession could have generated irredentism in Republika Srupska (Bosnia) and amongst the Albanians in Macedonia. In other words in 2000–2, the EU feared that the disintegration of the Western Balkans had not yet reached the smallest Russian doll and that further fragmentation could have triggered renewed violence and instability in the war-torn region.

Many disputed these arguments at the time, claiming that whereas constitutional uncertainty hindered stabilization, settling for partition would not have done so. On the contrary, achieving a mutually agreed separation between Serbia and Montenegro could have been the most effective means to achieve stability and reform in the region (ICG 2001). But setting aside the possible validity of this counter-argument, in what follows this chapter assesses to what extent and how EU policies were deployed in the pursuit of EU interests and objectives as defined by EU actors themselves. Suffice it to say that not only is it important to question these interests and objectives. Particularly in view of the ultimate secession of Montenegro in 2006, it is also pertinent to assess whether the fulfilment of the EU's objectives was the most effective means to pursue the EU's stated interests. If the EU's interests lie in conflict resolution, stabilization, reform, regional cooperation and European integration, was a federal state between Serbia and Montenegro the best means to pursue these goals?

Notwithstanding these open questions, EU institutions were firm, up until the spring of 2006, on their preference for a single state between Serbia and Montenegro. Following the March 2002 Belgrade agreement establishing the new State Union of Serbia and Montenegro, the EU High Representative, the Council of Ministers and the Commission repeatedly and consistently emphasized the priority to pursue, develop and implement the new constitutional edifice. In particular in 2002–6, through its regular reports, complemented by the first European Integration Partnership for Serbia and Montenegro in June 2004, the EU stated clear priorities for the development of the State Union (Commission 2003b, 2004c, 2005d, 2005e).

In terms of legal, constitutional and institutional requirements, the Commission repeatedly mentioned the need to implement the 2003 Constitutional Charter, including the establishment of a State Union court and parliament (through agreed electoral rules), the revision of the two republics' constitutions, and the creation of appropriate mechanisms to ensure the financial sustainability of the federal level. It emphasized the need to strengthen State Union administrative capacity, particularly in terms of institutions dealing with EU integration. Until 2004, the Union recurrently called for a single State Union interlocutor dealing with and coordinating the SAP.

In terms of policy competences, the Commission called upon the State Union to pursue army reform through the adoption of a new security strategy and military doctrine, to ensure refugee return, and to develop a unified visa and asylum policy. Until 2004, the Commission emphasized the imperative to coordinate and harmonize the two republics' fiscal and transport policies, and most importantly their trade and customs regimes (through the implementation of the June 2003 internal market action plan). The Commission also called for the clarification of competence distribution in the fields of intellectual property, standards, visa and asylum, migration and border management.

The emergence and development of dispute

Before assessing whether, when and how these EU interests and objectives were met, let us take a step back to the Balkans, briefly reviewing its recent history, and then focussing on developments in Serbia and Montenegro since the fall of Milosevic.

The origins and evolution of the political dispute

The dispute between Serbia and Montenegro cannot be defined as an ethnic conflict, whereby the parties' perceived identities and ensuing subject positions are articulated in essentialist and mutually incompatible ways.[1] Perhaps most indicative of the political rather than ethnic nature of the conflict are trends in the self-identification of the peoples. While in a 1991 census, a mere 9 per cent of Montenegro's population defined itself as Serbian, in 2003 with the increased prospects of Montenegrin independence, the self-proclaimed Serbs in Montenegro had risen to over 30 per cent.[2] This wide variation in a relatively short timespan is possible not least because of the similarities between Serbs and Montenegrins. The two not only share the same religion (Orthodox Christianity) and language (with different dialects), but in 1863 they even voluntarily signed an agreement on political union. Furthermore, in view of Montenegro's size and topography, Montenegrins have a long history of migration in Serbia, and today there are more Montenegrins in Serbia than in Montenegro itself.

The two peoples' histories have been tightly interwoven (ICG 2005). It is precisely in these interconnected histories that the seeds of their political dispute were sown. Montenegro's history of independence predates that of Serbia and is linked to its ability to resist Ottoman rule in the Balkans (with the exception of a brief interlude in the late fifteenth century). Between 1637 and 1852, the Orthodox Church in Montenegro acquired secular, in addition to ecclesiastical, power, and regularly allied itself with European states against the Ottoman Empire. Montenegro was recognized as an independent principality at the 1878 Congress of Berlin, when Serbia was also first recognized as an independent country. In 1910, Montenegro upgraded its status to that of a kingdom and expanded its frontiers (approximately to today's borders) during the 1912 Balkan war. Both during the first and second Balkan wars as well as during World War I, Montenegro allied itself with Serbia. In view of this alliance, Montenegro was occupied first by Austria–Hungary and then by Serbia in 1918. In this period, the first sources of Montenegrin grievance against Serbia emerged, given the refusal of Serbian crown prince Karadjordjevic to allow the Montenegrin king to return from exile. Tensions with Serbia generated a political split in Montenegro itself. Differences emerged between the 'white Montenegrins' concentrated in the inland border regions with Serbia who supported Belgrade's policies, and the 'green Montenegrins' on the coast, who were adamant to retain their independence. In different forms, this split persists to this day.

After World War II, Montenegro was included in Tito's Yugoslavia. But in view of the country's former independence, it was given the status of a republic. Furthermore, under the 1974 Constitution, the Yugoslav republics were granted a high degree of autonomy, allowing Montenegro to reopen its foreign ministry in 1979. In those years, political tensions between Belgrade and Podgorica subsided. They re-emerged in full force with the rise to power of Milosevic, and his ousting of the Montenegrin government in 1989. It is in this context that Montenegro participated together with Serbia in the wars against Bosnia and Croatia, and then joined the FRY in 1992, a decision ratified by popular vote. Political trends turned when in 1996 Milo Djukanovic took control of the largest Montenegrin party, the Democratic Party of Socialists (Demoktatska Partija Socialista Crna Gore – DPS), and defeating the pro-Milosevic candidate in the 1997 presidential elections. As of 1998, Djukanovic's Montenegro increasingly severed its ties with Belgrade.

The West's sanctions on Serbia and its generous assistance to Montenegro provided Djukanovic with additional incentives to distance Montenegro from Belgrade. Unreserved Western financial and political support, however, did little to halt the already rampant corruption, smuggling and organized crime in Montenegro. Tensions came to a head when Podgorica sided with NATO in the 1999 Kosovo war, opening its borders to the Serbian opposition and to over 70,000 Kosovar refugees. In retaliation, Milosevic mobilized FRY's seventh batallion to desta-bilize Djukanovic's regime, and overrode all Montenegrin appointments at the federal level, leaving the pro-Milosevic Socialist People's Party (Socijalisticka Narodna Partija – SNP) as the only Montenegrin representative in Belgrade. This only augmented Montenegro's de facto independence, as Djukanovic unilaterally adopted the German mark in 1999, followed by the euro in 2002.

Risks of violent confrontation faded when the Democratic Opposition of Serbia (Demokratska Opozicija Srbije – DOS), a coalition of 18 parties led by Voijslav Kostunica, first won the September 2000 presidential elections in Serbia, and then overthrew Milosevic in October 2000 with the help of large segments of civil society and the population at large. But while the risk of violence eclipsed, the Montenegrin decision to boycott the 2000 Serbian elections, thus failing to con-tribute to DOS's overthrow of Milosevic, was resented both by the international community and by Serbian democrats (Whyte 2006). At this stage, Montenegro had the option either of seeking new formulas to reintegrate into Serbia or of con-tinuing its path to independence. The unquestioned preference of the international community, first and foremost of the EU, was that of reconstituting a new federal state. While, well aware that the FRY was an empty shell in urgent need of an overhaul, the West was intent to prevent its further disintegration. Yet Djukanovic, appealing to the 1991 Badinter Commission's recognition of Montenegro's right to self-determination,[3] impeded by the exclusive presence of the SNP in Belgrade, and having enjoyed three years of self-rule with Western support, was irrevocably bent on the course of independence.

However, the April 2001 Montenegrin parliamentary elections, while reaffirm-ing the majority of the pro-independence parties (the DPS, together with the smaller Social Democratic Party and the Liberal Union of Montenegro), saw a strong show-ing by the pro-Yugoslav opposition (the SNP, together with the People's Party, and the Serbian People's Party). The almost equal divide between the pro- and anti-independence camps complicated the pursuit of secession through a referen-dum (ICG 2001). Not only did the elections indicate that the referendum results would have been far from predictable but also the bargaining strength of the pro-Yugoslav parties allowed them to threaten a boycott of an eventual referendum and to insist on a substantial modification of the February 2001 referendum law.[4] The deadlock deepened as Djukanovic persisted in pushing for a referendum but was unable to call for one, given the opposition's strength.

By the autumn of 2001, a possible path to compromise was cleared by the growing willingness in Belgrade to allow a referendum in Montenegro. After one year of transition, important segments in DOS felt increasingly frustrated by the deepening constitutional stalemate and by the unwieldy alliance between DOS and the SNP in the federal parliament (which collapsed when Milosevic was extradited to The Hague in June 2001), which prevented Serbia from pursuing reforms. Some felt that any solution, including Montenegrin independence, was preferable to the status quo. These views gained a growing hold amongst the public. In a poll conducted in March 2002, 65 per cent expressed support for an independent Serbia (ICG 2003: 15).

The birth of the State Union of Serbia and Montenegro...

An agreement between Belgrade and Podgorica on a referendum in Montenegro could have served many of the EU's priorities. It could have ended the constitutional stalemate and political deadlock in Serbia, contributing to the stabilization of the region; it could have allowed the parties to proceed with their domestic reforms; and it could have expedited cooperation with the ICTY. Yet it ran counter to another EU objective, namely that of retaining federal unity between the parties. Without such unity, EU actors believed that other essential interests would be at stake.

Hence, at this juncture EU High Representative Javier Solana stepped in, intent on demonstrating that Europe would not watch helplessly while the region disintegrated further. Between December 2001 and March 2002, Solana personally invested much political capital in brokering an agreement between the parties. In what was viewed as one of the first major successes of EU foreign policy, Solana mediated the 'Belgrade agreement' on 14 March 2002, which gave birth to the State Union of Serbia and Montenegro. The agreement satisfied the EU, the Serbian government and the Montenegrin opposition's desire to retain a constitutional link between the parties. In its substance however, it reflected Djukanovic's prerogative to retain Montenegro's self-rule and to ensure that the State Union would provide political equality between the larger and the smaller republic. Furthermore, by allowing for a referendum in either or both republics after three years of establishment of the State Union, it both gave the Montenegrin president a way out of the referendum deadlock and it allowed all parties three more years to discuss their future relationship. By definition however, it did not put an end to the constitutional debate on Montenegro's status.

The Belgrade agreement established an extremely loose federal level of governance. The State Union would have a unicameral parliament, a president elected by parliament, a court, a council of five ministers and a common army led by the three presidents (of the two republics and of the State Union). There would be a system of rotation between representatives of the two republics within the federal executive (including foreign representation). The five ministers would be respectively responsible for foreign affairs, defence, human and minority rights, international economic policy and internal economic policy. All other competences rested with the two republics, including economic and monetary policy (hence the retention of separate currencies), trade and customs, policing, visas, asylum and border management. The agreement did, however, specify the importance of internal harmonization, particularly in the economic realm, claiming that this would be achieved through EU integration. It is for this purpose that the Belgrade agreement mandated the Union (and the Commission in particular) with a monitoring role to ensure implementation.

However, the role of the Union would not be restricted to monitoring. Another characteristic of the Belgrade agreement was its extreme brevity and vagueness; arguably the price to be paid to square the circle between the parties' irreconcilable claims. Hence, the Union would continue mediating between the two republics to reach subsequent agreements on the nuts and bolts of the newly established State Union. It is at this stage that Solana's initial success started to be marred by failure.

...And its demise...

Failure took four forms. First, it meant an increased difficulty in reaching further agreements, leading to delays and deadlocks in decision-making and implementation, and thus to a slow-down in reform. The Belgrade agreement called the parties to agree on a Constitutional Charter by June 2002, a legal prerequisite to give constitutional life to the State Union. However, an agreement was reached (after much debate and discord) with an eight-month delay in February 2003, and again it required the essential brokering of the EU High Representative. Hence for one year, the specific division of competences between the State Union and the republics was ill-defined, causing policy vacuums and overlaps. Even after the Constitutional Charter agreement, discord on competence allocation persisted in the fields of intellectual property, standards, visa, asylum, migration, border management and minorities. In addition, rotation in State Union positions often did not take place, as Montenegro retained many of the competences supposedly allocated to the centre. Delay over the Constitutional Charter also delayed membership of the Council of Europe by one year and the revision of the two republics' constitutions in line with the Charter never took place. More generally, constitutional and legal uncertainty hindered the entrenchment of the rule of law, necessary to consolidate democracy and human rights and to fight corruption, smuggling and organized crime.

Furthermore, several State Union institutions were either late in coming and/or dysfunctional. The State Union court was established only in 2004, and its functioning was hindered by the unclear scope of its judicial powers. Administrative capacity at State Union level was weak given the lack of adequate budgetary resources and of relevant civil service legislation. The high-level Serbia–Montenegro Council for European Integration established in 2003 only met sporadically; while the State Union European Integration Office lacked resources, a formal status and clear competences. This hindered the State Union's fulfilment of the priorities indicated in the EU's 2004 European Partnership document.

The case of the State Union parliament is perhaps the most critical illustration of institutional dysfunctionality. After much debate, which caused a near collapse of the Belgrade agreement and severe delays in the adoption of the Constitutional Charter, the parties agreed on the parliament's electoral laws in November 2002. These provided for indirect elections (through the delegation of parliamentarians from the two republics) for the first two years (after the adoption of the Charter) to be followed by direct elections. In view of its indirect mandate, the parliament was never particularly effective, causing problems in key areas such as army reform. The problem exacerbated when the date for direct elections (February 2005) expired, leaving the parliament without a legal mandate and causing further backlog in the legislative process. The issue was resolved through a revision of the Charter in April 2005 (again with Solana's intervention), providing for State Union elections to take place concomitantly with those of the two republics.

Second, the Belgrade agreement and the Constitutional Charter did not create what the European Commission would define as a 'functional federal state'. At most, the Belgrade agreement could have opened the way to a quasi-confederal construct, whereby the primary function of the State Union would have been that of coordinating the separate policies of the two republics.[5] Yet the EU, and the Commission in particular, opposed this concept from the outset. The Commission insisted that the State Union had to become a functional federation and not simply a 'letterbox' (Commission 2005e: 35). It insisted on policy harmonization in key areas, ranging from visa and asylum, border management and refugees, to customs and trade.

The Constitutional Charter and ensuing political developments entrenched the differences between the two republics. Nowhere was this more evident than in the realm of economics and trade. The Belgrade agreement, while accepting that economic policy, customs and trade would remain in the remit of the two republics, called for the harmonization of the two economies. In turn, the republics, with the aid of the Commission, were entrusted with the task of negotiating an 'Action Plan on an Internal Market'. Yet the differences between the parties revealed to be insuperable. Serbia as a large, industrial economy had high tariffs (12.5 per cent on average) to protect its socialist-inherited industry (principally metals and textiles). Montenegro as a small, service-based and open economy had considerably lower tariffs (3.5 per cent on average). Serbia claimed that in view of its relative size, Montenegro should raise its tariffs to Serbian levels. Montenegro asserted that as both republics had to harmonize with the EU (as stated in the Belgrade agreement), Serbia should lower its tariffs at least to EU levels. The Action Plan was agreed in July 2003 after many months of wrangling and EU cajoling. Yet while agreeing on a common tariff, the Action Plan was largely an agreement to disagree. It included key exceptions and transition periods on the most sensitive products. The economic harmonization saga thus continued, ultimately leading an exasperated EU External Relations Commissioner to admit failure in September 2004 and to suggest a revision in the Union's policy towards the State Union (Patten 2004). Chris Patten's suggestion was ultimately adopted by the Council in October 2004. In what became a public admission that economic harmonization would not take place, the EU accepted reality and agreed to conduct negotiations on an SAA through a twin-track approach, i.e. each level of government would separately negotiate with the EU in their respective spheres of competence.

Third, the State Union failed to garner domestic support and legitimacy in both republics. Solana attempted to square the circle between Serbian desires to reconstitute federal unity and Montenegrin prerogatives to retain self-rule. To many, the resulting agreement failed to do both, causing a lack of enthusiasm and political will to develop the new state. Hence, much of the explanation of the ineffectiveness and inefficiency of the State Union, which further eroded trust and support for it.

In Montenegro, the Belgrade agreement triggered an acute government crisis. The Liberal Union strongly committed to independence and ill-disposed towards its coalition partner the DPS, left government, triggering early elections in October 2002. In the election campaign, the Liberal Union allied itself with the SNP (despite their diametrically opposed views on secession), leading Djukanovic to form a government with Filip Vujanovic's Social Democrats in January 2003. Moreover, much to the grievance of both the Montenegrin opposition and the Serbian DOS, the three-year referendum clause provided Djukanovic with few incentives to make the State Union work.[6] As put by one SNP politician, 'if Djukanovic is seriously and exclusively concerned with the harmful economic effects of raising Montenegrin tariff levels, why hasn't he circumvented these by speedily concluding free trade agreements with all Balkans states in the context of regional cooperation initiatives?'[7] Others argued that given the internal divisions within Montenegro and the international community's reluctance to accept its secession, the Belgrade agreement provided Djukanovic with an alternative strategy to achieve his unwavering goal of independence.[8] The Belgrade agreement raised Montenegro's potential to act as a 'nuisance' to Serbia, which could have induced the latter to secede. This would have left the international community with little choice but to bless the velvet divorce between the two republics.

Indeed, from the outset the Belgrade agreement was criticized by many federalists and pragmatists in Serbia as well (ICG 2003). They claimed that the State Union entrenched in law Montenegro's de facto independence, granted it disproportionate powers relative to its size, and complicated federal decision-making thus hindering reform. The State Union was dubbed by many as an 'economic Frankenstein' (ICG 2002: 10). Resentment mounted over time, particularly amongst those who in 2002 had been most adamant to pursue a tight federation.[9] Hence, to the glee of Montenegro's independists, there was growing support in Serbia for the idea of separation. The Serbian public – bearing the burden of a triple transition from communism, war and EU integration, and being constantly reminded by its leaders of the dysfunctionality of the State Union – became increasingly impatient with it. To articulate these public feelings, a political movement emerged in 2003 – G17 Plus – under the leadership of Mladjan Dinkic and Miroljub Labus. G17 Plus argued that the State Union hampered the process of economic development and reform. Hence, either it transformed into a 'real federation', or Serbia should secede from Montenegro, conclude a historic agreement with Kosovo and proceed with its much-needed domestic reforms (G17 Plus 2003).

Finally, there have been worrying political trends in Serbia since 2003, which have both threatened to overturn Serbia's democratization and accelerated

Montenegro's independence drive. In March 2003, the reformist Prime Minister Djindjic, was assassinated, tragically reminding Europe that Milosevic's legacy was far from overcome. Even more worryingly, the December 2003 parliamentary elections in Serbia saw the phenomenal rise of the Serbian Radical Party led by ICTY indictee Vojislav Seselj and running on a nationalist 'Greater Serbia' platform. In view of the split within DOS and the imperative to keep the Radical Party out of government, Kostunica's Democratic Party of Serbia (Demoktatska Stranka Srbije – DSS) formed an unwieldy minority government with G17 Plus and the monarchist Serbia Renewal Party, which required the parliamentary backing of Milosevic's socialist party.

By 2005, trends inexorably pointed towards a referendum in Montenegro, to be held soon after the expiry of the three-year deadline (February 2006). Djukanovic had run and won the 2002 elections on a pledge to hold the referendum before the end of his mandate, and Serbian resistance to Montenegro's independence was dissipating. Furthermore, the Constitutional Charter was revised in 2005 to ensure that an eventual referendum would comply with the guidelines of the Council of Europe's Venice Commission (European Commission of Democracy through Law), an essential perquisite for it to gain international legitimacy. Initially, Montenegro's referendum law stipulated that a vote in favour of secession required a 50 per cent +1 majority and a 50 per cent eligible voter turnout. The Montenegrin unionists opposed the law, threatening a referendum boycott (that could have prevented the 50 per cent quorum to be reached). The EU again stepped in, through Solana's Special Representative Miroslav Lajack, to resolve the referendum law quagmire. Solana's prerequisite was that of achieving a solution through the participation of both Montenegrin camps. Lajack's proposed compromise was that of a 50 per cent +1 voter turnout and a 55 per cent majority in favour of independence. Having gained the approval of both camps on these requirements, the EU – under another Solana appointee, Frantisek Lipka – supervised the formation of the Montenegrin Referendum Commission.

The referendum took place on the 21 May 2006 with a 86.5 per cent voter turnout and a sufficient albeit extremely narrow 55.5 per cent majority in favour of independence. With it, the prospects of the EU's much desired and pursued federal unity were ultimately foreclosed. However, this did not entail an enhanced danger of conflict in the region (ICG 2006b). Intra-Montenegrin divisions persist, as shown by the referendum results. But this does not threaten to translate into deep instability, let alone political violence. Indeed the EU praised the conduct of Montenegro's referendum and recognized its outcome (Council 2006b). The threat of instability and nationalism in Serbia also continues, and may have been strengthened by the Montenegrin vote. The results of the January 2007 elections indeed confirmed the 2003 strong showing of the Serbian Radical Party as the largest single party obtaining 29% the vote. But Serbian nationalism in the twenty-first century has been fuelled more by the unsolved question of Serbia's final borders (with Kosovo and Montenegro), than by the loss of Montenegro per se (Batt 2005). In this respect Montenegro's secession, having provided a clear answer to one of these questions, could help Serbia resolve its national question.

Assessing EU impact on Serbia and Montenegro

The EU, and most notably the High Representative and the Commission, played a key role in the establishment and evolution of the State Union. But what exactly has the impact of the EU been? The successes and failures in Serbia and Montenegro have been largely due to the parties themselves. Serbia, in 2002, while beginning to toy with the idea of a referendum, was still far from reaching a consensus on letting Montenegro go, fearing repercussions in Kosovo and amongst its minorities. In Montenegro, Djukanovic was struggling with the referendum impasse, stuck between the Scylla of his government's independence drive and the Charybdis of the pro-Yugoslav opposition's blunt refusal. Hence, the parties' relative willingness to be cajoled by the EU High Representative.

By contrast, in 2005–6 the dangers of pursuing independence had largely subsided, while the Montenegrin government's commitment to independence was as strong as ever.[10] Subsiding danger was largely due to developments in the wider region. Regional cooperation initiatives, such as the Stability Pact and the South East European Cooperation Process (SEECP) were beginning to show their first concrete results, as the Western Balkans proceeded with bilateral free trade agreements, and cooperated on key policy issues, ranging from transport and energy to organized crime and border management. Moreover unlike 2001–2, Macedonia's potential conflict with its Albanian minority had stabilized through the Ohrid agreement, and Bosnia was beginning to endorse the responsibilities of operating its complex three-entity federation. Perhaps most important, following the March 2004 ethnic violence in Kosovo, Serbs became more resolute in resolving their national question and the international community agreed to tackle Kosovo's final status in 2006. In other words, the birth, ill-functioning and demise of the State Union, as well as the opportunity costs involved in its survival, depended critically on the domestic and wider regional developments in the Western Balkans. With these provisos in mind, let us turn to the EU's impact, in relation to the fulfilment of its declared aims and interests in Serbia and Montenegro.

The value of the EU benefit: stabilization and association awaiting accession

The first variable explaining both the ability of the High Representative and the Commission to exert a strong influence on Serbia and Montenegro as well as their failure to consolidate a stable and integrated State Union rests in the relative value of what the Union held on offer to the two parties.

Raising the value of the SAP through the prospects of accession

Between 1997 and 1999, the EU articulated its approach to the Western Balkans in regional terms. The rationale was that of fostering cooperation, post-conflict reconciliation and refugee return, the consolidation of the Dayton accords, and the prevention of further secessionist conflict. Yet particularly after the 1999

Kosovo war, the Union appreciated the need for a far more substantive engagement with the region. Hence, in addition to the Stability Pact for Southeastern Europe, the EU developed the SAP, a tailor-made initiative for the Western Balkans. Like other EU contractual approaches and most notably the accession process, the SAP was meant to prepare the Western Balkans to sign and implement bilateral contractual agreements with the EU, i.e. the SAAs. The SAP would assist the countries' adoption of the laws, rules and standards of the EU single market, and it would establish forums for political dialogue through the Stabilization and Association Councils.

Yet, unlike the accession process, initially the SAP was not supposed to usher the way to full accession. Although this was hinted at during the launch of the Stability Pact in 1999, the EU's appreciation of the need to bind the region to its structures did not translate into a concrete commitment to that effect. EU actors could not imagine that the war-torn Balkans, in which a dictator against whom it had waged war was still in power in Belgrade, could enter the EU in the foreseeable future. Hence, the SAP simply aimed to support the establishment of a Western Balkan free trade area, and more generally to induce cooperation in the region. But this prospect alone was hardly appetizing to countries which had just undergone years of violent conflict in the process of separation. The limits and disincentives inherent in the EU's regional approach were quickly understood. By the June 2000 Feira European Council, the Union for the first time labelled the Western Balkan countries as 'potential candidates'. Naturally, Milosevic's FRY was excluded from the bargain.

The EU prospects for Serbia and Montenegro, and indeed for the rest of the region, improved dramatically after the fall of Milosevic in October 2000. In November 2000 at the Zagreb Summit, the five Western Balkan countries (Albania, Bosnia-Herzegovina, Croatia, Macedonia and FRY) and the EU officially endorsed the goals of the SAP and affirmed the European perspective of the region (European Council 2000). Thereafter, being no longer viewed as an alternative to European integration, regional cooperation conditionality started bearing fruit. The Zagreb summit also agreed on trade preferences for industrial goods and a significant rise in EU financial assistance through the newly established instrument, the Balkan-tailored 'Community Assistance for Reconstruction, Development and Stabilization' (CARDS).[11] Since November 2000, CARDS to Serbia and Montenegro has amounted to more than €2bn. It was initially concentrated on budgetary support, humanitarian assistance and reconstruction, and over time it has shifted its focus to the more long-term goals of democracy, good governance, institution-building, socio-economic development and EU integration. It is in this context of deepening EU engagement that Solana brokered the Belgrade agreement (Lopandic and Bajic 2003).

Yet the region's EU prospects were still vaguely articulated at the Zagreb summit. With the assassination of Djindjic in March 2003, the EU was reminded again of the need for constant support for the fragile Western Balkans. Hence at the June 2003 meeting in Thessaloniki, the European Council unambiguously declared that '(t)he future of the Balkans is within the EU....(p)reparation for integration into the European structures and ultimate membership into the EU…is now the big challenge ahead' (European Council 2003a, paragraph 2). The conclusiveness of the SAP was thus transformed. From being a much-criticized alternative to accession, it became the antechamber to the full accession process. The gatekeeping steps towards accession were the following: the Commission would first draw up a feasibility study for the opening of negotiations on a SAA; following conclusion and implementation of the agreement, the country could apply for full membership; on the basis of a subsequent decision by the European Council, the Commission would conduct accession negotiations leading to full membership. Thus the road was long, with many stages and accompanying benchmarks. But by 2003 a roadmap was in place, unambiguously raising the value of bilateral ties between the Western Balkan countries and the Union. The message was strengthened when under the Barroso Commission, the Balkans were shifted from the competence of DG External Relations to that of DG Enlargement. The Commission's steering role during the SAP gave it high potential to influence developments in the State Union of Serbia and Montenegro.

Yet the State Union was precisely what reduced the value of EU relations, in so far as its ill-functioning prevented the parties from progressing along the SAP. The beginning of the Commission's feasibility study required a prior agreement and implementation on the internal market Action Plan. However, this was delayed by many months, and was only patchily cobbled together in July 2003. The lack of economic harmonization after June 2003 continued to hinder the Commission's study, leaving the State Union at the bottom of the pile of the Western Balkans, with Croatia and Macedonia having entered the accession process, and Bosnia and Albania being further ahead in the SAP.[12]

Perceptions and assessment of the SAP in the region

Upgrading the status of the SAP into the preparatory stage of accession was of key importance because of the value ascribed to membership in Serbia and Montenegro. Since Montenegro distanced itself from Milosevic's regime, its government has been critically dependent upon and supportive of the West in general and Europe in particular. In June 2005, the Montenegrin parliament adopted a resolution committing Montenegro to European integration, a resolution that was widely supported both by the government and by the opposition. In Serbia, official attitudes U-turned after October 2000, when EU integration became a key goal of the new regime. One year later, the Serbian parliament adopted a resolution in favour of European integration, and in 2005 the government endorsed a comprehensive strategy to pursue that goal. Official attitudes have reflected public sentiment, where in both Serbia and Montenegro, opinion polls have regularly rated support for EU accession at well over 70 per cent. Particularly instructive of the value ascribed by the parties to the EU is the fact that Article 3 of the Belgrade agreement explicitly stated that its goal was that of establishing a common market so as to facilitate its 'integration in European structures, the EU in particular…..'. Back in 2002, the two parties had thus agreed to harmonize their economies precisely because of the prospect of EU integration.

But when scratching beneath the surface of this unreservedly positive assessment, several doubts arise, doubts which partly explain the EU's failure to induce the parties to commit to, and develop, their State Union. True for the Western Balkans in general, the EU has been viewed with a good dose of scepticism and mistrust in Serbia and Montenegro (Noutcheva 2004). This is partly due to its passivity during the unfolding Balkan tragedy in the 1990s as well as to the perceived double standards frequently displayed by Europe since then (Batt 2005: 63–4). But it is also because when comparing the EU's treatment of the Balkans with that of the CEECs, the former have noted a categorically lower degree of EU commitment towards them, despite the fact that beyond economic transition, the Balkans have also borne the costs of post-conflict reconstruction. EU measures such as twinning, technical assistance and trade liberalization, forthcoming to the CEECs, have been either denied or sparingly granted to the Balkans (Pippan 2004). On issues such as visa facilitation, the EU has been slow and reluctant to move forward, despite the problems caused in the Balkans by the CEECs' adoption of the Schengen *acquis*.[13] In this context, even an important EU commitment such as that made in Thessaloniki, has had a lower positive impact than expected. Mistrust rose further as the Balkans observed the Union's growing 'enlargement fatigue' and more specifically 'Balkan fatigue', particularly in the aftermath of the crisis over the EU Constitutional Treaty. Several European actors indeed publicly took note of the dangers involved if Europe's commitment to the Balkans were to waver (Rehn 2006; International Commission on the Balkans 2005).

In addition, Solana's intense involvement in establishing the State Union was resented in Belgrade and Podgorica, reducing further the value ascribed by them to EU relations. The High Representative's insistence on reconstituting federal unity between Serbia and Montenegro was resented by the latter, particularly in view of the West's (including the EU's) unreserved support for Montenegrin de facto independence before October 2000. Solana was portrayed in Montenegro as the 'last defender of Yugoslavia' (Commission 2003b: 52). Also in Serbia, Solana's role was criticized, given that on substance, the High Representative had ultimately yielded to most of Djukanovic's demands. The unworkability of the Belgrade agreement and the Constitutional Charter were to some extent blamed on Solana's excessive pressure to force onto the parties a State Union that neither wanted. Amongst the most nationalist circles in Belgrade, the EU was vehemently accused, being defined as 'evil' by Serb nationalists (Massari 2006: 264).

The Commission was also accused, particularly in Montenegro. Montenegrin independists argued not only that the Commission forced on them integration with Serbia at the expense of their own development and institution-building. In addition, they argued that the Commission distorted the original meaning of the Belgrade agreement itself. Whereas the agreement had loosely stated that internal economic harmonization would occur through EU integration, when it came to negotiating an Action Plan, the Commission sided with Serbia, insisting that Montenegro should raise its tariffs to Serbian levels (and thus above

EU levels). According to some observers, this reduced Montenegro's commit-ment to EU accession.[14] Perhaps more accurately put, if the price to be paid for EU accession was to renounce on the goal of independence, then acces-sion may not have been worth the bargain for the Montenegrin government. An independent Montenegro could be pro-Western, but not necessarily an EU-member state. Some in Montenegro may have actually preferred to see the country develop as a European microstate outside the Union, developing as a tourism and tax haven. Proponents of this view included both elements of the business lobby and the criminal elements thriving on the smuggling econ-omy. The prospect of membership was evidently not a sufficient prize to induce the Montenegrin government to make the State Union work and renounce its independence ambitions.

According to others, the high value attributed to EU accession was precisely what reduced incentives to engage in State Union politics. Pragmatic Serbs and pro-independence Montenegrins argued that their immediate priority was to pursue domestic reform, not least because of its necessity for EU integration. To the extent that the State Union was viewed as a hindrance to reform and thus to progress in the SAP, resistance against it rose. In Serbia, the politi-cal platform of G17 Plus captured this logic at its best. As put by one party leader: 'we spent 18 months on a constitutional agreement and four months on an Action Plan. But with a poverty level of over 60 per cent we cannot afford to waste one day'.[15] To exemplify their arguments, several interlocutors in Serbia highlighted the case of the Schengen system. Until Hungary's EU acces-sion, approximately 4.5m people crossed annually the Serbian–Hungarian border, boosting Serbian trade and employment levels. With Hungary's adoption of the Schengen *acquis*, cross-border movement of Serbian citizens into Hungary has been restricted. In order to return to the status quo ante, Serbia would need to access the EU's visa-free list, requiring its compliance with stringent EU demands. Yet, pro-independence Serbs argued that the unwieldy State Union and Montenegro's problems in smuggling and organized crime hampered efforts to comply with EU demands, entailing significant costs to Serbian citizens. While the State Union partly acted as a scapegoat for Serbia's own failings, the argument linking the defi-cient State Union to the restrictions on movement resonated amongst the Serbian public.

EU institutions unanimously asserted until 2006 that progress with the SAP and ultimate accession would be faster together than apart. They argued that internal harmonization would represent a 'mini-experiment' in EU integration, and that it would have to take place in any event in the context of EU accession. Yet the EU never elaborated precisely on how progress in the implementation of the State Union was linked to the SAP.[16] Furthermore, the timeframe of the SAP invalidated the EU's logic in the eyes of many in the region. Serbs argued that although EU integration would require a reduction in tariff levels in the long term, Serbia need not bear the costs of doing so in its early years of transition (in order to harmonize with Montenegro). Montenegrins argued that unlike rich and stable federations in the EU, Montenegro did not have the luxury to experiment in *sui generis* federal experiments, but had to confront its costly and complex domestic reform challenges.

The credibility of the obligations

Beyond the value of the benefit, the EU's impact on Serbia and Montenegro also lies in the obligations that EU institutions put forth to condition progress in the SAP and to enhance the region's accession prospects.

The EU High Representative's negative conditionality

Javier Solana's success in brokering the Belgrade agreement and the ensuing accords on the Constitutional Charter and the State Union parliament largely rested in the credibility of negative conditionality. Conditionality within the SAP was not directly relevant to the survival of the State Union, and focussed instead on the Copenhagen criteria, in addition to the Balkan-specific requirements on refugee return, cooperation with the ICTY and regional cooperation. Nevertheless, the High Representative repeatedly claimed that a constitutional link between Serbia and Montenegro was an informal yet clear requirement of EU accession. This acted as a blunt form of negative conditionality, particularly vis-à-vis the secessionist Montenegrin government. In the run-up to negotiations which culminated the Belgrade agreement, Solana (2001) unambiguously threatened the Montenegrin president: 'Djukanovic has to know that separation is not a rapid train to the EU … and it would jeopardize prospects for international assistance, economic development and EU integration'.

However, the credibility of Solana's negative conditionality also generated dis-incentives, deepening the political divide in Montenegro and threatening to desta-bilize the region. These came to the fore after 2001, complicating both Montenegrin domestic politics and spilling over into the State Union. Solana's conditional-ity provided strong incentives to the pro-Yugoslav opposition in Montenegro to spoil any debate on a referendum, an eventuality that had been legitimized by the Belgrade agreement and to which Djukanovic had remained unwaveringly com-mitted to. In 2001, the obstructionism of the pro-Yugoslav bloc was legitimized by making reference to the EU and Solana's position (ICG 2002: 7).

The same trend emerged in the run-up to the referendum in 2005–6, when the pro-Yugoslav opposition hardened its position, relying on Solana's veiled threats not to recognize Montenegro's independence (ICG 2005: 10). These threats induced the Montenegrin government to alter the referendum law, accepting the EU's negative conditionality on a 55 per cent electoral hurdle. Had the Montenegrin government not accepted the EU's recommendations and gone ahead with a referendum without EU approval, both the unionists as well as many Albanians, Croats and Bosniaks may have boycotted the referendum, leading to a failure to reach the 50 per cent quorum and a deepened division in the country. Yet accepting the EU's negative conditionality was a risky gamble, which could have destabilized the region further. Before the referendum, it was generally understood that an eventual majority in favour of Montenegrin independence would have been narrow (as indeed it turned out to be). Many believed that if a majority was reached, it could have lied between 50 and 55 per cent. By insisting on a 55 per cent threshold through negative conditionality, the EU was considered as having forced a risky gamble for the sake of retaining the State Union. Had the result fallen in the 50 and 55 per cent range, the EU (and Serbia) would not have recognized Montenegro's independence, while the Montenegrin government could have boycotted the State Union (given that more than half of its electorate would have voted against it). The threat of instability in the region could have been raised to new heights (ICG 2006b: 6).

The Commission's positive conditionality

The Commission also used conditionality to shape the nature and conduct of the State Union. Unlike Solana, it rested its influence on the positive conditionality embedded in CARDS and the SAP. The numerous stages foreseen in the SAP also meant that the Commission could successfully exert its influence over time. Specified conditions had to be met for the beginning of the feasibility study, for the study to conclude that SAA negotiations could begin, for a successful opening and closing of negotiations, as well as for all the additional benchmarks of the ensuing accession process.

More precisely, the Commission relied on its power to decide when and whether to begin and how to conclude its feasibility study to exert influence on the content and implementation of the internal market Action Plan. By specifying clear and binding conditions, the Commission aimed to reshape the Belgrade agreement into a more centralized federation. Commission officials repeatedly called for more 'critical mass' behind the State Union in order to proceed with the SAP.[17] In its reports up until 2004, the Commission claimed that 'a prerequisite for contractual relations with the EU remains the implementation of an internal market and a single trade policy' (Commission 2003b: 1).

Yet the Commission's insistence generated disincentives in both republics. In Serbia, the Commission's conditionality legitimized criticisms against the looseness of the State Union. In Montenegro, Commission conditionality caused alienation and resentment, as Podgorica was constantly blamed as the principal obstacle to the State Union's progress in the SAP. The Commission judged the State Union's reforms against the standards of a tight federation. In turn, most of the failures in meeting EU benchmarks were blamed on the smaller and independist Montenegro, while Podgorica's internal reforms were hardly acknowledged (ICG 2002). Former Commissioner Patten also repeatedly told the Djukanovic government that Montenegro's economic integration with Serbia was a strict precondition for its EU accession (Patten 2003a). It is in this context that the vision of a microstate outside the EU took root in Montenegro, as many independists sought a way to escape the Commission's constant criticism and conditionality. Many in Montenegro also compared unfavourably the Commission's perceived obsession with a federation with Washington's more relaxed approach. The US has been an important partner for Djukanovic since 1997, providing $240m per year to Montenegro. Unlike the Commission, it was viewed as far more sympathetic to Montenegro's independence.

Moreover despite the credibility of its policies, the Commission failed in its intent. The beginning of the feasibility study was delayed until September 2003, after the parties agreed on their Action Plan. Yet the problems in subsequent implementation delayed the publication of the feasibility study for over one year. The study was published only after the Commission and the Council accepted the failure of their economic harmonization conditionality in October 2004, resigning themselves to conducting twin-track SAA negotiations. Following the Montenegrin referendum, the Commission also abandoned its condition to conclude a single SAA with Serbia and Montenegro, and the SAP has proceeded separately with the two republics.

The Commission's cross-cutting conditionality also created disincentives to make the State Union function. Until the EU's decision to conduct twin-track negotiations was taken, both republics claimed that they were being slowed down by Commission conditions on the other republic. Serbia criticized Montenegro's insufficient efforts to eradicate smuggling and organized crime, its weak administrative and judicial capacity and its high external imbalances – issues that have been much criticized by Brussels. Montenegro instead blamed Serbia for the slowness in the State Union army's reform, and criticized Belgrade for the weak protection of human rights in the Serbian Constitution, for the insufficient cooperation with the ICTY,[18] for the unresolved status of Kosovo, and for the pending territorial disputes with Croatia and Bosnia – again, all issues which the Commission raised in its reports and in the European Partnership document. In the economic realm, Montenegrins pointed to Serbia's inflationary pressure (in 2005 Serbian inflation was 16 per cent as opposed to Montenegro's 3.5 per cent), its slow and patchy privatization and price liberalization, and its uncompetitive market environment. Following the decision to conduct twin-track SAA negotiations, although the EU repeatedly claimed that the progress of each party would depend on its own pace reform, the EU's insistence to conclude a single SAA continued to generate mixed incentives. This became painfully clear when in May 2006 the EU decided to suspend SAA negotiations with *both* Serbia and Montenegro given Serbia's failure to compliance with its ICTY obligations. The EU's decision unwillingly bolstered the Montenegrin independist camp in the run-up to that month's referendum vote.

The limits of social learning

Beyond conditionality, EU institutions hoped and believed that Serbia and Montenegro would be persuaded of their self-interest in building a functional State Union, which would act as a prelude to their EU integration. Through the political dialogue conducted in forums established under the SAP, such as the EU–FRY Consultative Task Force in 2001 followed by the Enhanced Permanent Dialogue in 2003, EU actors expected the parties to undergo a process of learning, whereby they would voluntarily alter their perceptions on the desirability of the State Union.

They also hoped that local actors would appreciate the tangible benefits of staying together following the implementation of a harmonized internal market.[19]

It was not only the non-implementation of many EU priorities that delayed the SAP to the extent of hindering regular dialogue in 2002–4. Also and most importantly, there has not yet been a genuine process of learning in the region. This is partly because of the lack of sufficient time, particularly in Serbia, to become acquainted with and internalize European norms and standards. At the level of the wider public, it is instructive to note that a mere 3 per cent of Serbian students has visited Western Europe (Batt 2005: 68). In addition, the unsolved national questions, first and foremost that of Kosovo, have hindered further Serbia's democratic consolidation.

But more worryingly, the discourse of the EU and of Europeanization has been used by some local actors to legitimize unchanged positions (Huysseune and Noutcheva 2004). Hence, the Montenegrin pro-Yugoslav parties' self-labelling as pro-European, despite their persisting scepticism of several EU conditions (e.g. on the ICTY). The same goes for the Serbian public, where although 70 per cent favours EU membership, a far lower percentage supports EU conditions (on the ICTY, minority rights and decentralization for example). According to some observers, Serbia's EU discourse could become particularly dangerous if, and when, it is used to cover and legitimize a new strand of nationalism, which, while not bent on the former Greater Serbia agenda, it is nonetheless committed to an ethnically defined Serbian nation. It is precisely in this context that some Serbian actors were content to see Montenegro secede.

The EU's political management of State Union affairs

A State Union that no party desired was established largely because the High Representative appealed to the high value ascribed to EU ties for the retention of a constitutional link within the FRY. Yet despite the perseverance of both Javier Solana and the Commission in nurturing the State Union, and their constant and careful conditionality tying the development of the State Union to progress in the SAP, the State Union began drifting towards dissolution at the very moment of its inception. Much of the EU's failure to induce federal unity between Serbia and Montenegro lies with the widely held beliefs in the region of the political imperatives and interests underpinning the conduct of different EU actors.

Javier Solana stepped into the affairs of the region with an explicit conflict prevention mandate. The Belgrade agreement was viewed by many in Brussels, Belgrade and Podgorica as a personal accomplishment of the High Representative. In the region, the State Union was dubbed by many as 'Solania'. From the outset, local actors took note of Solana's high (or excessive, depending on political perspectives) degree of interference. Many doubted whether Solana's conflict prevention operation had been a success at all, given the possibility that there may not have been a conflict to prevent. Yet criticism of the High Representative rose exponentially when Solana persisted in his unreserved defence of the State Union, irrespective of its unsatisfactory content and performance. Many felt that Solana's

Table 3 The dispute between Serbia and Montenegro and EU relations

Population (2006)	Serbia 10.6m and Montenegro 620,000	
Key Historical Dates	1878	At the Congress of Berlin, Serbia is recognized as an independent country
	1910	Montenegro is recognized as an independent kingdom
	1918	Integration of Montenegro in the kingdom of Serbs, Croats and Slovenes, renamed Yugoslavia in 1929
	1946	The communists take control of Yugoslavia transforming it into a federation, with six republics including Montenegro
	1974	Montenegro's autonomy in Yugoslavia is increased
	1991	The socialist Yugoslav federation dissolves
	1992	The FRY is established, including Serbia and Montenegro
	1997	Montenegro distances itself from Milosevic's Serbia
	1999	The Kosovo war. Montenegro affirms its aspiration to independence
	2000	The downfall of Milosevic
	2002	The Belgrade agreement between Serbia and Montenegro
	2003	Serbia and Montenegro agree on a Constitutional Charter
	2006	Montenegro's referendum and recognition as an independent state by the international community
EU Relations	1991	EU sanctions on FRY
	1999	The Stability Pact for Southeast Europe. The EU launches the SAP
	2000	The Feira European Council labels the Western Balkan countries as 'potential candidates' for membership. With the fall of Milosevic, the EU lifts sanctions on Serbia. At the Zagreb summit, the five Western Balkan states and the EU endorse the goals of the SAP and affirm the European perspective of the region
	2002	Montenegro unilaterally adopts the euro
	2003	The Thessaloniki European Council officially endorses the EU membership perspective of the Western Balkans
	2004	The European Council agrees to conduct the SAP with Serbia and Montenegro on a 'twin-track' approach
	2005	The EU's Feasibility Report concludes that Serbia and Montenegro can open SAA negotiations
	2006	The EU suspends the SAP with Serbia and Montenegro. It recognizes Montenegro's independence and accepts to pursue two independent SAPs with Serbia and Montenegro
EU Financial Assistance	CARDS (previously OBNOVA) assistance to Serbia and Montenegro amounted to over €2.9bn in 1991–2002. Over €2bn have been disbursed since the fall of Milosevic (annual average €400m)	

attachment to the State Union had more to do with his personal prestige than with a genuine preoccupation with the region's reform, development and EU integration.

Differences between member states on the survival of the State Union, driven by different political considerations, damaged further the EU's reputation. Similarly to the High Representative, Madrid and Rome exerted constant effort to forestall a referendum in Montenegro, the former possibly fearing a precedent for the

Basque Country, while the latter concerned about the consolidation of a safe haven for organized crime in Montenegro. On the contrary, following the US's more hands-off approach, Berlin, Budapest and Vienna were readier to accept Montenegro's secession (Whyte 2005).

Equally problematic was the exclusive EU integration mandate of the Commission. Local actors frequently criticized the perceived political imperatives underlying the Commission's role, hidden behind its technocratic approach. A technocratic approach is more often than not an invaluable Commission asset. It can enhance the Commission's credibility by signalling its commitment to the mechanisms of passive enforcement, as well as its aversion to political compromise with third party actors. Yet in the case of Serbia and Montenegro, the Commission's insistence on conditions underlying the establishment of a tight federation were viewed differently. Many Montenegrins felt that the Commission's physical presence in Belgrade (rather than also in Podgorica) through its delegation induced its officials to view the political dispute exclusively through Serbian lenses.

Moreover, rather than to the benefit of the region, the Commission's stance was perceived as being driven by the self-interested objective to avoid conducting two sets of SAPs, culminating in the accession process of two (rather than one) new member state. Indeed when compared to the US's more hands-off approach towards Montenegro's independence, it is clear that the EU had an interest in retaining federal unity not least to avoid having to absorb a higher number of new member states in an already overcrowded Union. But understandable as these interests may have been in Brussels, they generated little sympathy in a region still outside the Union, which is struggling with questions of a far more critical and existential nature.

6 The glaring gap between rhetoric and reality in the Israeli–Palestinian conflict

EU interests and objectives in the Israeli–Palestinian conflict

The Middle East has always been a principal area of European foreign policy concern, and was indeed one of the two subjects dealt with at the first European Political Cooperation meeting in November 1970. The aim of a peaceful resolution of the Arab–Israeli conflict and more specifically of the Israeli–Palestinian conflict is motivated by several interests, whose salience has remained high over the decades. The overarching interest is that of stability in the Middle East; stability which is marred principally, albeit not exclusively, by the festering conflict. Stability is in turn necessary for the fulfilment other corollary interests, including energy security, the eradication of political violence and migration management. Peace and stability in Israel and Palestine are considered important also because of Europe's historical responsibility towards the conflict parties; from the Jewish holocaust to the betrayal of the Palestinians during British mandatory rule. Religion is another key variable, calling for the peaceful coexistence between the three monotheistic religions in the region. Finally, the Israeli–Palestinian conflict is an important item on the transatlantic agenda, given US's interests in the region. Given the overarching importance of transatlantic relations, EU actors have considered convergence and cooperation with the US over the Middle East to be of utmost importance.

To pursue this set of interests, the EU has defined with rising clarity and coherence its goals in the conflict. Since the October 1973 war, member state positions have increasingly converged. Common positions are based on two interconnected pillars, which crystallized over the decades into a well-defined view of the conflict and its resolution.

The first pillar is the need to respect the self-determination rights of the Israeli and Palestinian peoples. The EC/EU historically upheld Israel's right to statehood, living in peace with its neighbours within secure and internationally recognized borders. The European position towards the Palestinians was instead defined progressively over the decades. In 1973, the nine member states affirmed their support for the 'legitimate rights of the Palestinians' (European Council 1973). By 1977, the definition of these legitimate rights acquired a collective and territorial character, as the member states acknowledged the 'national identity' of the Palestinians, who deserved 'a homeland' (European Council 1977). Greater clarity came in 1980, when the Venice Declaration backed the Palestinian right to self-determination (European Council 1980).

In view of the Oslo process in the 1990s, the member states refrained from specifying further what a solution should entail, limiting themselves to supporting negotiations and the institutionalization of the Palestinian Authority. It was only with the deterioration of the peace process after the 1996 assassination of Yitzhak Rabin and the election of Benjamin Netanyahu that the EU resumed its declarations on the desirable end-point. Initially, the European Council did not venture beyond suggesting that a solution should not exclude the option of a Palestinian state. The 1999 European Council in Berlin went a qualitative step further, stating that 'the EU is convinced that the creation of a democratic, viable and peaceful sovereign Palestinian state … would be the best guarantee of Israel's security' (European Council 1999a).

With the collapse of the Oslo process, the resumption of violence and the end of negotiations in 2000–1, the Union felt emboldened to articulate further its vision for a peaceful Middle East. This entailed the creation of two states, Israel and Palestine, living in peace and security within internationally recognized borders. The state of Palestine would be viable, independent, sovereign, peaceful and democratic, and it would entail the end of Israel's occupation. It would be established along the 1967 borders, with minor adjustments agreed by the parties, and Jerusalem as a shared (or divided) capital. The means to achieve a two-state solution would be through negotiations, and only through negotiations.

The second pillar of EU goals has been the importance of respecting human rights and international humanitarian law (IHL) as well as democratic standards and good governance. Most European declarations on the Middle East conflict since the 1970s have condemned Palestinian violence and terrorism, pointing to the violations of rights and law that such acts entailed. With the outbreak of the second intifada, EU statements have also affirmed the PA's responsibility in taking all necessary measures to combat terrorism.

Vis-à-vis Israel, since 1973 member states have condemned the acquisition of territory by force, have called upon Israel to end the occupation of the territories it conquered in 1967, and have opposed Israeli settlements in the occupied territories (OTs). The 1980 Venice Declaration went further, specifying that settlements are not only a 'serious obstacle to peace', but that Israel's confiscation and/or razing of land and property for the purpose of establishing settlements to be populated by Israeli nationals violates the Fourth Geneva Convention prohibiting the deportation or transfer of one's own civilian population into occupied territory (European Council 1980, paragraph 9). The 1990 European Council in Dublin reiterated its call on Israel to adhere to the Geneva Conventions and acknowledged the member states' own legal obligations under those Conventions by calling for their 'further action' to ensure the protection of the human rights of the population under occupation (European Council 1990).

Also on the human rights and IHL front, the EU remained silent during the Oslo years, despite ongoing violations and shortcomings in the fields of rights, democracy and the rule of law. EU criticisms resurfaced following the collapse of the Oslo process. Since 2000, the Union has intensified its calls to halt and reverse settlement construction, including policies inducing settlement expansion (e.g. subsidies and tax incentives). EU actors have also condemned the whole array of human rights and IHL violations, ranging from Palestinian suicide bombings and the launching of rockets on civilian targets, to Israeli military incursions, extra-judicial killings, closures, and all other forms of collective punishment. The Union repeatedly affirmed that Israeli security and Palestinian self-determination should be pursued exclusively within the confines of international law. Since 2002, the EU also began speaking out against Israel's barrier within the OTs, declaring that – like settlements – the barrier hinders peace and is illegal under international law. Its illegality stems from its confiscation of land and property, its hindrance to movement and its deprivation of essential services to the civilian Palestinian population.

Finally, an area that has received increasing European attention since the late 1990s has been that of democracy and good governance in the region. While occasionally addressing Israel's discrimination against the Palestinian minority in Israel, the EU has paid little attention to flaws in Israel's democracy. Instead, European policy-makers became increasingly concerned with the nature of the future Palestinian state. Since the 1999 Berlin European Council, all EU statements advocating a Palestinian state added that such a state should be democratic as well as independent, sovereign, peaceful and viable. With the eruption of the intifada, the European Council stated that the reform of the PA is essential and would be supported by the Union. While not arguing that reform should be a precondition for negotiations, the Union hinted that it was necessary both to enhance Palestinian democracy and to secure an end of violence and progress in the peace process.

In focussing on Palestinian reform, EU institutions concentrated on the judiciary, the fiscal system and the security sector, as well as on the administration and the executive, on elections, the media and the education system, and on the promotion of civil society in support of the peace process. In particular, EU recommendations called for the ratification and implementation of the Basic Law and the Law on the Independence of the Judiciary. They focussed on the training of judges and the refurbishment of courts. They insisted on the transparency of public finances through the consolidation of revenues in a single IMF-monitored account controlled by the Finance Ministry, on strengthened audit capacities, as well as on a freeze on public sector hiring. And they concentrated on free and fair (EU-monitored) elections, the redistribution of competences within the executive, the accountability of non-ministerial institutions, and the restructuring of municipalities, ministries and the security sector.

Since 1973, European declaratory diplomacy on the conflict thus developed consistently and progressively. By the turn of the century, and in particular since the collapse of the Oslo process, common positions stipulated clearly both what the ultimate objective was and what the necessary means to achieve this were. The aim was that of a two-state solution based on the 1967 borders. The means were negotiations, the respect for human rights and international law, and democracy and good governance in Palestine. These positions were not only formulated as an EU vision for the Middle East. Their attainment was expressly recognized as being an integral element of the EU's own security interests (European Council 2003b). For this reason, the Union has clarified that it 'cannot commit itself to any other path' as far as the conflict and its resolution are concerned (European Council 2005a, paragraph 12).

The evolution of the Israeli–Palestinian conflict

To what extent have developments on the ground matched the EU's wishes, particularly since these have been spelled out clearly in the 1990s and 2000s? The following sections first review briefly the evolution of the conflict since its inception and then turn to the developments since the collapse of the Oslo process in 2000.

From the 1948 war to the Oslo process

In Israel and Palestine, the conflict emerged with a distinct identity-based character, as the Zionist endeavour to construct a Jewish state in the Holy Land was resisted by the Arab and Muslim worlds, including the local Palestinian population (both Muslim and Christian) living under British mandate. Following the Arab rejection of the 1947 UN partition plan (which provided for two – albeit not ethnically homogenous – states), the 1948 war, the ensuing flux of Palestinian refugees and the creation of the State of Israel (on approximately 80 per cent of mandatory Palestine) epitomized the crux of the identity-based conflict. There are two primary issues left pending from 1948. The first and most salient is the fate of the Palestinian refugees, numbering between four to six million.[1] Most refugees are scattered in and outside camps in Jordan, Lebanon, Syria, the West Bank and the Gaza Strip. But many also live in Europe, in North America and in the Gulf. The second issue is the status of the Palestinian minority in Israel (i.e. the descendants of those who were not expelled in 1948 and who now represent around 20 per cent of Israel's population). While enjoying Israeli citizenship, the Palestinian minority suffers from different forms of discrimination, caused directly or indirectly by the definition of Israel as a Jewish state (Mossawa 2001). Touching on the nature of the State of Israel, these two issues represent the most intractable aspects of the conflict. These are the issues on which the EU has been largely silent.

The conflict acquired a distinct territorial character in 1967. The June 1967 war resulted in Israel's occupation of the West Bank and East Jerusalem (administered since 1948 by Jordan) and of the Gaza Strip (administered since 1948 by Egypt) as well of the Syrian Golan Heights and the Egyptian Sinai. The post-1967 period saw Israel's accelerating construction of Jewish settlements (and infrastructure) and the seizure and destruction of Palestinian land and property in the West Bank, Gaza Strip and East Jerusalem. The Palestinians organized their resistance through the Palestinian Liberation Organization – PLO (established in 1964), turning both to political violence and terrorism and to international diplomacy. The territorial dimension of the conflict acquired greater salience both regionally and internationally with the first intifada in 1987, when the Palestinians in the West Bank and Gaza Strip mounted a largely unarmed rebellion against Israel's occupation.

The ensuing Oslo process in the 1990s, grounded on the 'land for peace' formula embedded in UNSC resolution 242, set the territorial dimension at the forefront of peace negotiations. Settlements, Jerusalem, borders and security, and water became the primary focus of the talks. When compared with the 1948 issues – and most importantly the refugees – these items (with the exception of Jerusalem) appear far more amenable to compromise in principle (Susser 2000). The PLO's 1988 acceptance of a two-state solution could meet the Zionist priority to secure a Jewish state through the withdrawal from some Palestinian-inhabited land. Israeli–Palestinian track-two initiatives such as the 2003 Geneva accords show that compromise on these items could be possible. The territorial dimension of the conflict is where the EU has pronounced itself with greatest clarity and coherence.

Yet while a settlement along these lines became increasingly feasible in the minds of local and international actors, the Oslo years saw the emergence of a growing gap between peace diplomacy and realities on the ground. Arguably, this gap lies at the core of the collapsed peace process (Bishara 2001). While negotiations proceeded, the Palestinian leadership never completely renounced the use of political violence, although the unrest of the first intifada largely came to a halt by the mid-1990s. The nascent PA also became increasingly corrupt, authoritarian and opaque in its functioning (Nabulsi 2005). Successive Israeli governments instead accelerated the construction of settlements in the West Bank, East Jerusalem and the Gaza Strip, strengthening Israel's grip of those territories that were set to be released in return for peace and security. Indeed from 1993 to 2000, the number of settlers increased from 240,000 to 373,000 (Foundation for Middle East Peace 2002). In other words, at the level of diplomacy, the peace process seemed to move towards the fulfilment of at least one of the EU's declared aims, namely that of Israeli and Palestinian self-determination through statehood. Yet the peace process, coupled with developments on the ground, ran contrary to the second pillar of the EU's strategy, namely the respect of human rights, democracy and international law. These breaches of rights and law, which were largely neglected by the peace process, not only distanced the actual prospects of a two-state solution, but also sowed the seeds for the demise of the Oslo process itself.

The second intifada

The peace process collapsed after the failure of the Camp David II summit in August 2000 and the outbreak of the second intifada in September. While negotiations continued up until the Taba talks in January 2001, the intifada led to a growing distance between EU goals and events on the ground, making the former ever more fading chimeras.

The violation of human rights and international humanitarian law

The second intifada led to Israel's full reoccupation (in all but administrative terms) of the Palestinian territories. This came with mounting human rights and humanitarian law violations, resulting in an ever-rising number of Palestinian casualties. As a result of a long list of violations, the Palestinian population suffered from a deepening humanitarian crisis, leading to over 40 per cent unemployment and a poverty rate of over 75 per cent (World Bank 2003). Israel has been held responsible by the international community and by local and international NGOs for the use of excessive force, extrajudicial killings and for sweeping restrictions on movement through closures, checkpoints and curfews.[2] Restrictions on movement have impaired the right to work, the right to education and the right to healthcare. Restrictions have also applied to goods and humanitarian aid. The nature of these restrictions has shown that their objective has not been strictly security-related, but has been politically dictated by the aim of imposing collective punishment on the Palestinians and an internal fragmentation of their territory.

In what has been dubbed a 'matrix of control', Israeli settlement construction has accelerated, including an expanding network of settlement blocs and highways connecting them particularly in the West Bank and in East Jerusalem (Halper 2000; Foundation for Middle East Peace 2005). In addition, in June 2002 the Israeli government approved the construction of a barrier in the West Bank. The barrier takes many shapes and forms, including walls, trenches, electrified and razor wire and military roads. Israel has also built walls and electrified fences around major Palestinian population centres, subdividing the West Bank into dozens of separated enclaves. Israeli authorities have described the barrier as a 'separation' or 'security' fence. As the names suggest, Israel has justified its construction as a necessary measure to separate Israelis and Palestinians in order to provide security to the former. However, as the details reveal, 'separation' and 'security' are not the wall's sole intents. This is principally because the barrier is not being built on the 1967 borders, but cuts deep into the West Bank particularly in the areas of Qalqilya and Salfit in the northern West Bank, in East Jerusalem and in Bethlehem in the southern West Bank (Bt'selem 2006).[3] While the exact figures depend on its final routing, the barrier may end up annexing approximately 10 per cent of the West Bank, separating East Jerusalem from the West Bank, and violating the human rights of over 300,000 Palestinians, by either restricting or denying their access to land, work, water and basic services (PLO 2003; UNSG 2003b). In view of its nature and effects, the International Court of Justice (ICJ) deemed the barrier illegal in July 2004.

Palestinian groups have also perpetrated grave human rights violations, which have amounted to or approached war crimes (Human Rights Watch 2002). These have taken primarily the form of suicide bombings targeting Israeli civilians in Israel. The identified responsible groups have been Hamas, Islamic Jihad, the Popular Front for the Liberation of Palestine and the al-Aqsa Martyrs Brigade. Suicide bombings and other attacks aimed at civilians are squarely prohibited by Protocol 1 of the Geneva Conventions governing the laws of national liberation.

Photo 3 Israel's Wall separating Palestinians from Palestinians in Jerusalem. May 2006.

However, the legal difficulty has arisen from the fact that the Conventions only refer to the obligations of states and state-like actors. Moreover, the criminal provisions of IHL are based on the doctrine of command responsibility, according to which, people in positions of authority who fail to undertake adequate prevention are also held accountable.

An issue has therefore been to what extent the PA, as a state-like actor, should be held responsible for attacks against Israeli civilians. International NGOs did not find evidence that the PA planned, ordered or carried out suicide bombings or other attacks on Israeli civilians (Human Rights Watch 2002). However, the PA leadership under Yasser Arafat was criticized for not taking adequate action to prosecute those responsible for the attacks. During the 2005–06 Palestinian unilateral ceasefire (or more accurately lull in violence – *tahadia*) there was a sharp decrease in suicide attacks. Hamas' adherence to the *tahadia* mitigated the effects of an increasingly powerless PA under president Mahmoud Abbas and Prime Minister Ahmed Qureia to rein in violence. However, the question of legal responsibility resurfaced in full force following Hamas' victory in the 25 January 2006 parliamentary elections and its formation of the PA government in March 2006. If political violence, and in particular acts of terrorism, were to be carried out by a Hamas government, this would entail a violation of the Geneva Conventions, as well as the constitutive laws of the PA, which renounce the use of violent resistance. If instead Hamas carried out acts of violence outside the confines of a Hamas-led PA, it would violate the constitutive laws of the PA calling for the monopoly over Palestinian force.

Pre-empting a two-state solution

Israeli policies have dramatically reduced the prospects of a two-state solution. Settlement construction has been a permanent feature of all Israeli administrations since the 1967 war. Yet in recent years, settlement expansion has accelerated dramatically, leading to a subdivision of the West Bank into over fifty enclaves, the separation of East Jerusalem from the West Bank, the separation of the northern from the southern sections of the West Bank, and the sealing of the Jordan valley from the rest of the West Bank. The result has been a reversal of facts on the ground. Initially West Bank settlements were isolated enclaves in Palestinian territory. Over time, Palestinian towns have become isolated enclaves in Israeli territory. As expressed by Israeli journalist Amira Haas (2005), this is not a matter of two states for two peoples, but rather of 11 states: the state of Israel, and alongside and within it the states of Gaza, Hebron, Bethlehem, Ramallah, Jericho, Tulkarem, Qalkilya, Slain, Nablus, and Jenin. Each of these states is separated from the others by growing Jewish territorial contiguity…. The construction of the West Bank barrier forms part of this logic, given its de facto annexation of approximately 60 per cent of the settlements, 90 per cent of the settler population as well as key swathes of land around Qalkilya, Salfit, Jerusalem and Bethlehem (PLO 2002). Another element of Israel's policy has been the weakening of the PA through the physical destruction of its infrastructure, the myriad of restrictions on movement and the withholding of its tax revenues.

This has been coupled with the fragmentation of the Palestinian national movement itself, divided between the PA and the PLO, between Palestinians in the OTs and those in the Diaspora, between West Bankers and Gazans, and perhaps most critically between the secular Fateh and the Islamic Hamas, as well as divided internally within the declining Fateh faction. The weakening of the PA and its control over the Palestinian public and territory supported the Israeli thesis that, due to the absence of a Palestinian 'partner for peace', Israel should proceed with unilateral actions.

Indeed, this is precisely what the Israeli government has done, through its strategy of unilateral disengagement. This strategy, while not putting a legal end to Israel's occupation, led to Israel's withdrawal from the Gaza Strip and from four

1967 Pre-Occupation Border
22% of Historic Palestine

The Wall (2004)
12% of Historic Palestine

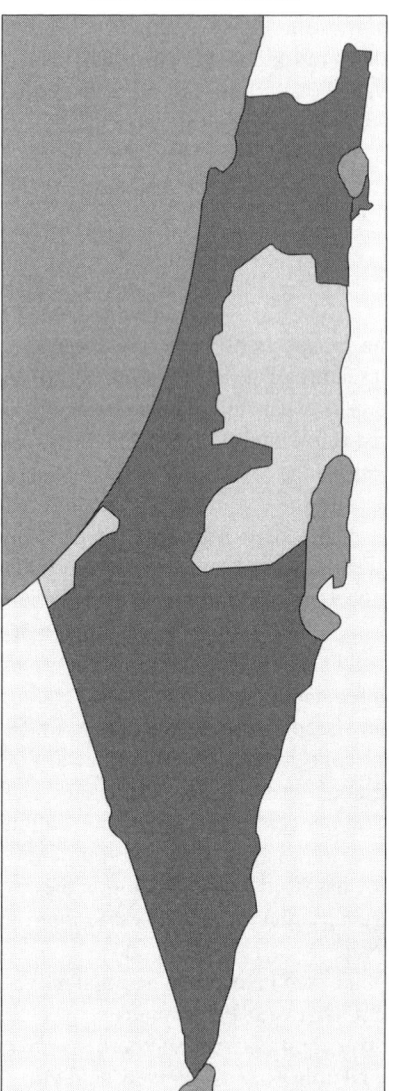
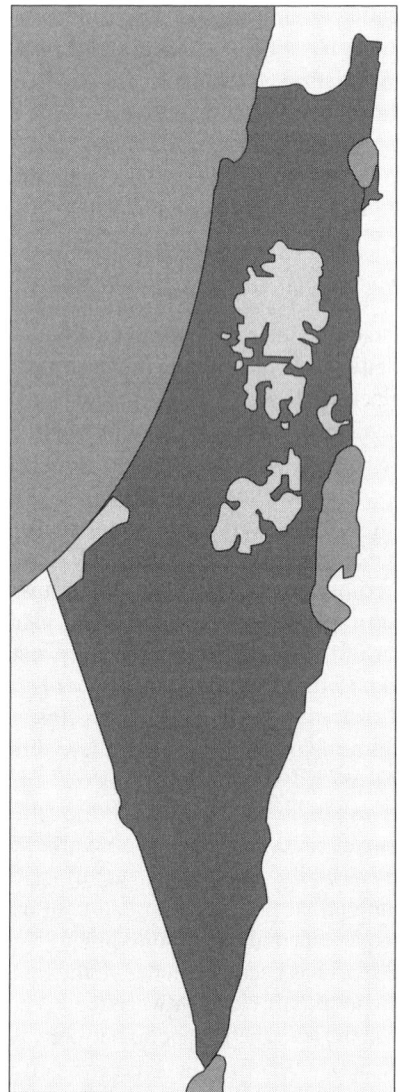

Map 4 Israel and Palestine 1967 and 2004.
   Source: PLO Negotiations Affairs Department, Negotiation Support Unit. http://
   www. nad-plo.org/maps/wall/jpeg/killing.jpg.

settlements in the northern West Bank in August 2005. The policy, first outlined by Ariel Sharon in December 2003, had a double rationale. First, it intended to deal with the 'demographic threat', to which the Israeli right became sensitive to by the turn of the century (Sheuftan 1999; Soffer 2001). This is the realization that according to demographic trends, Israeli Jews will become a decreasing minority in the area between the Jordan River and the Mediterranean Sea. Disengagement represents a formula to maximize Israeli land annexation while minimizing the number of Palestinians included in it.[4] Second, the plan emerged from Sharon's need to propose an alternative to a negotiated two-state solution, at a time when the Quartet was pressing for an implementation of its sponsored Roadmap. Disengagement – as opposed to the Roadmap – provided a more palatable alternative to the Israeli government (and public). It would be unilateral and would not require a Palestinian 'partner'. It would cede less territory, retain Israeli effective control and it would avoid compromise on the two most critical issues on the peace agenda, namely Jerusalem and refugees.

Many in the international community supported Israel's disengagement plan. The EU declared that disengagement represented the 'best chance of sustained peace in the region for many years' (Commission 2005b: 2); although it qualified that this would necessitate the implementation of the Roadmap and Gaza's access to Egypt and Israel, to third countries (through a port and airport) and to the West Bank (through a safe passage). The US-brokered Movement and Access Agreement in November 2005 regulated the management of border crossings for goods and people between Gaza and Egypt. The EU became an integral part of this agreement, monitoring the Rafah crossing. But not only did the arrangement allow Israel to retain partial control over Palestinian borders and crossing points. Its practical implementation has been hampered by the almost permanent closure of the Karni crossing for trade and by the standstill on the opening of a safe passage between Gaza and the West Bank and on the reconstruction of the Gaza sea and air ports. Moreover, Israel retains complete control over Gaza's airspace and territorial waters, it has reserved the right to reinvade the Strip, and it has reduced further the access of Gazan workers into Israel. Israel's overwhelming military assault on the Gaza Strip in the summer of 2006 following Hamas' abduction of an Israeli soldier demonstrates that the Gaza disengagement has all but ended Israel's occupation of the Strip and opened prospects for peace.

The primary logic behind international optimism surrounding the Gaza disengagement was linked to the hope that it would trigger a domino effect on settlement dismantlement in the West Bank and a resumption of negotiations. Indeed the Gaza disengagement led to a growing support in Israel for settlement dismantlement. This triggered a split within Likud and the formation of a new party in late 2005 – Kadima – established by Sharon and taken over by Ehud Olmert in January 2006. Kadima, which included also several members of the Labour party, won the March 2006 Israeli elections on a pledge to pursue 'convergence' ('realignment'/'ingathering'). Convergence extended the logic of disengagement to the West Bank. Its aim remained that of solving the 'demographic problem' and proceeding with a unilateral definition of Israel's eastern borders without negotiating with the Palestinians. More specifically, the convergence plan entailed the withdrawal of some settlements from the West Bank, alongside the consolidation of other major settlement blocs, such as Ma'ale Adumin, Ariel and Gush Etzion, as well as all the settlements in the Greater Jerusalem area (Katz 2006). As opposed to the Gaza disengagement, convergence in the West Bank would not foresee the withdrawal of military presence and would include Israel's exclusive control of the Jordan valley. As put by Olmert himself: '(T)he idea is that most of the settlements that would have to be removed …will be converged into the blocs of settlements that will remain under Israeli control' (Weymouth 2006). Since the Gaza disengagement, Israel has indeed tightened its grip on large portions of the West Bank and East Jerusalem. Developments in 2005–06, such as the routing of the barrier in Jerusalem, the construction of settlements and roads in and around the city and the planned expansion of settlements and development projects (i.e. the E1 plan) connecting Ma'ale Adumim and Jerusalem unambiguously point to a rationalized yet tightened Israeli hold over Palestinian territory (PLO 2005). In addition, plans for further settlement withdrawal have been put on ice since the Israeli war in Lebanon in the summer of 2006.

Progress, limits and relapse in Palestinian reform

Prior to, and over the course of, the intifada, criticism against the PA and its leadership had mounted from the inside. The population resented the leadership for having failed to deliver a just peace through negotiations and better standards of living. They complained about the widespread corruption, inefficiency and authoritarianism of the Authority. Divisions emerged between the 'old guard', including the revolutionary PLO leadership from Tunis, and the 'young guard', including secular and Islamic groups, indigenous to the OTs, leaders of the intifada and connected to the grassroots (Shikaki 2002; Tamari 2002).

In response to mounting domestic and external (American, European and Israeli) pressures during the intifada, some steps forward were made. In 2002, a Basic Law and a Law on the Independence of the Judiciary were adopted. Significant progress was made in the management of PA finances, as PA revenues were included in a single transparent account, the President's budget was cut and an effective audit system was developed. According to the IMF in 2005: 'the PA has a level of fiscal responsibility that rivals the most fiscally advanced countries in the region' (Commission 2005f). In 2003, the security sector was partly restructured, as the former twelve (poorly coordinated) security apparatuses were streamlined into six sectors.

The passing away of Yasser Arafat in November 2004 initially accelerated the reform momentum. Security sector reform proceeded with the consolidation of three apparatuses under the Ministry of Interior, as well as with a facelift to the personnel service through the retirement of security officials, the training of forces and the recruitment of former militants. Preparatory work was undertaken to establish a National Security Council, as well as to create effective parliamentary budget and oversight committees. In the fiscal domain, transparency in public finances was enhanced through the control of the president's funds and the shift in fiscal control from the presidency to the finance ministry. In foreign affairs, there was an overhaul in the diplomatic service with the introduction of rotation in diplomatic appointments. In the judiciary, the legislative framework was prepared to clarify the relationship between the Ministry of Justice, the Higher Judicial Council and the Public Prosecutor. There was an intensified dialogue between the secular and Islamic camps, both aimed at including Hamas in the PLO and PA institutions and at ending the violent intifada. The March 2005 inter-factional 'Cairo Declaration', which formalized Hamas' adherence to the *tahadia* and provided for Hamas' participation in the parliamentary elections, embodied the basic compromise on these issues.

There were also clear limits to the reforms. During Arafat's rule, reforms were often superficial and inconsequential. The cabinet was reshuffled in 2002, but with few exceptions, changes were largely cosmetic. The 2003 creation of the prime minister's post did not come with its empowerment, as most control remained in the president's hands. After Arafat's death, some deficiencies remained and others emerged or exacerbated. Despite the rebalancing of roles within the executive following Mahmoud Abbas' election as president, relations between the President and former Prime Minister Ahmed Qureia were often tense. Problems in the judiciary persisted, hindering the effective separation between the judiciary and the executive and the actual independence of the former. A law passed in October 2005 exacerbated this problem by entrusting ministers with the power to appoint judges (Reuters 2005). In the security sector, the President and the Minister of Interior faced acute problems in restructuring and recruiting former militants. In the fiscal sector, increased transparency in accounts was not matched by greater responsibility in the conduct of fiscal policy. Despite the World Bank's wage bill containment plan, the PA engaged in uncontrolled public sector hiring and rising salaries in the fall of 2005 in anticipation of parliamentary elections and as a means to recruit former militants in the security services. By January 2006 the PA's monthly deficit had reached $70m (Quartet's Special Envoy for Disengagement 2006).

Most worryingly, the post-Arafat period saw mounting chaos and fragmentation in the OTs, as intra and inter-factional tensions escalated triggering infighting (Sayigh 2005). Despite the inter-factional understanding reached in Cairo in March 2005, by July clashes erupted in Gaza between Hamas militants and PA security forces, in the wake of Israel's disengagement and in view of the PA's postponement of elections originally scheduled for that month (largely due to Fateh's fears of a strong showing by Hamas). Inter-factional clashes took place again in the autumn of 2005, particularly in Gaza. Tensions also mounted within Fateh itself, first triggering violent acts perpetrated by Fateh activists against PA institutions in April 2005 and then leading to a split in the movement in the run-up to the elections in January 2006. The split was between the old-guard-dominated Fateh and the young guard, which provisionally seceded into a new movement called The Future (*el-mustaqbal*). On the eve of the elections, the split was patched over for the sake of avoiding electoral defeat.

Fateh's unrelenting decline and Hamas' growing support and its effective and clean management of the municipalities under its control since 2004–5 contributed to the crushing electoral victory of Hamas in January 2006. The Change and

Reform Platform (Hamas) won 74 seats in the 132-seat Palestinian Legislative Council (PLC), compared with Fateh's 45 seats. The election results all but eased inter-factional tensions. On the contrary, the transition has been hampered both by the international response to Hamas' victory and by Fateh's permeation of PA structures and its strategies to retain power. This led to an attempted re-centralization of power in the President's hands and shift of control from the PA government to the PLO (where Hamas is not represented). For example, in February 2006, the old Fateh-dominated PLC created a constitutional court with the power to veto new legislation and with judges who would be appointed by the President without parliamentary approval. The President brought official media agencies under his control. Following elections, Abbas affirmed his overall control over the security forces. In response, the Hamas Minister of Interior formed an alternative security force. These and other developments escalated tensions between Fateh and Hamas both at elite and rank-and-file level, triggering rising lawlessness and chaos on the streets of Gaza in 2006. Escalating intra-Palestinian violence dangerously edging towards civil war in Gaza in 2006–7 led to the Mecca agreement between Fateh and Hamas in February 2007 on the formation of a national unity government.

Assessing EU impact on the Israeli–Palestinian conflict

Regardless of whether EU aims have been met or otherwise, the underlying premise in what follows is that the EU, as a secondary external actor, could not have represented a major determinant of the conflict. Developments have been dictated mainly by domestic factors, interacting with wider regional and international events. More specifically, the inherent flaws in the Oslo process which came to a head at the Camp David II summit, the unwillingness of Arafat to rein in the intifada in its early stages, the election of the Likud led by Sharon and the subsequent escalation of violence and accelerating colonization of the OTs underlie the shift away from a two-state solution and the mounting violation of human rights and IHL.

In particular since 2000, several interrelated features have constrained the EU's role. In Israel, the feeling of existential threat aroused by Palestinian suicide attacks was pivotal in explaining Sharon's freehand in crushing the Palestinian uprising in complete disregard of rights and law. The growing Israeli popular desire to 'disengage' from the Palestinians and the rising awareness of the 'demographic threat' posed by them have underpinned the 'separation barrier', the Gaza disengagement, the convergence plan and the general preference for a unilateral pursuit of Israel's perceived interests. In Palestine, the intifada meant that maximalist goals of promoting a two-state solution were downscaled to minimalist goals of crisis management, poverty alleviation and institutional survival.[5] The deepening Israeli occupation on the one hand and Palestinian political disarray on the other hindered Palestinian reform. At the international level, the US neglect of the conflict and its acceptance of the human rights and international law violations on the ground also explain the unfolding of events. In addition, the post 9/11 blunt American approach to the question of Palestinian reform focussing on 'regime change' and the demonization of Arafat up until his death hindered his succession and weakened internal voices that had long called for reform. Likewise since 2006, the international boycott of the Hamas government has exacerbated polarization within the OTs, failed to weaken popular support for Hamas and eliminated all chances of pursuing effective reform at a time when its prospects could have been highest.

Yet, irrespective of its power, status and resources, the EU has also been an important external actor in the conflict. In the light of the EU's bilateral relations with the parties, has the Union put to best use its instruments to contribute to a realization or approximation of its stated goals? The answer in what follows is largely negative.

The value of the EU benefit: association, aid and the ENP

When compared with the Union's contractual ties with other non-candidate countries, both Israel and the PA rank high on the EU's list of priorities, judging by the relationships they enjoy. In addition, particularly when it comes to the ENP and financial assistance, EU relations with Israel and the PA have not suffered from time inconsistency problems, i.e. the time lag between the demanded conditions and the delivery of the benefit, which either decreases the credibility of the former (in the case of ex post conditionality) or the value of the latter (in the case of ex ante conditionality). This would suggest that, while lower than in the case of accession countries, the EU's potential influence on the two parties and thus on the conflict could be high.

The objective value of EU relations

In the case of Israel, the first EC trade agreement dates back to 1964. Further preferential trade agreements were signed in 1970 and in 1975. In 1995, Israel and the Community signed a Euro–Mediterranean association agreement, which entered into force in 2000. Its main components are political dialogue, free trade in industrial products, freedom of establishment, free movement of capital, the harmonization of competition rules, and economic, social and cultural cooperation. Additional agreements have been signed on procurement, the liberalization of agriculture, and on Israel's inclusion in EU scientific and technical cooperation and in the European Global Navigation Satellite System (Galileo). Israel's has also been included in the pan-Euro-Mediterranean system of cumulation of origin rules.

In the case of the PA, association has been less extensive. Building on the 1986 regulation giving rise to a separate preferential import regime for Palestinian products, in 1997 the EC–PLO interim association agreement entered into force, allowing for limited trade liberalization and the establishment of political dialogue. But bilateral ties have primarily taken the form of financial and technical assistance. Since 1971, EC aid has been channelled to Palestinian refugees through UNRWA (the UN Relief Works Agency). In 1987 this was complemented by assistance to Palestinian civil society. In the context of the Oslo process, the member states stepped up their economic support to the Palestinians through a joint action, this time directed primarily to the PA. In 1994–8, the EU committed Ecu 400m in grants. It committed a further €600m in 1998–2002. Through these monies, the EU financed the establishment of PA institutions as well as key infrastructure projects, such as the Gaza airport and seaport.

Aid to the Palestinians rose further during the intifada, amounting to around €300m per year (or €500m if member state contributions are included) in 2000–5. With Israel's withholding of revenue transfers to the PA, the EU provided approximately €10m per month in direct budgetary assistance in 2003. As Israel partially resumed revenue transfers in 2003–5, the Union refocused its assistance, through a Reform Support Instrument, to private sector development, municipalities, social services, fiscal and judicial reform, election monitoring and the establishment of the Palestinian Central Elections Commission. Through the Partnership for Peace Programme, EU funds promoted people-to-people contacts and NGO activity aimed at fostering dialogue and combating incitement. In 2005, through EU COPPS (Coordinating Office for Palestinian Policing Support), upgraded through a European Security and Defence Policy (ESDP) police support mission and complemented by the ESDP Rafah monitoring mission, the Union also heavily committed itself to reform the Palestinian security sector.

In addition, in 2003 both Israel and the PA were included in the ENP. Particularly in the case of Israel, the ENP Action Plan spells out a long list of EU benefits, ranging from reinforced political dialogue, to economic and social cooperation, trade and internal market integration, cooperation in justice and home affairs and in the areas of transport, energy, environment, information society, research, and civil society. The ENP also provides important political benefits to Israel, namely the refocussing of relations from the multilateral (Euro–Mediterranean) to the bilateral (EU–Israel) level. The EU–Israel Action Plan indeed states that one of its aims is to fulfil the promise set out in the 1994 Essen European Council meeting, which foresaw special bilateral ties between Israel and the Union (Commission 2004d: 1).

However, despite the developed nature of these bilateral ties, there are clear limits to their objective value and thus to the EU's potential influence on the parties. Israel is not included in the customs union, it is not part of the European Economic Area and it does not have any prospects of entering the accession process. Israeli officials and analysts frequently cite all the measures that the EU could have and has not undertaken (Tovias 2004). The Palestinians are even further away in terms of EU integration. As Palestinians often complain, even the limited provisions for preferential trade remain largely unimplemented, due to Israel's non-recognition of the EC–PLO Interim Agreement and wider Israeli obstacles posed to Palestinian international trade.[6] During the intifada, many EU-funded projects, such as the Gaza sea and air ports, were destroyed by Israeli raids. Finally, the ENP benefits to Palestine are hardly discernible. At best, the Union, through its Action Plans with both Israel and the PA, could push for the implementation of the trade aspects in the existing EC–PLO interim agreement. However, the international community's unheeded calls to Israel to respect the terms of the Movement and

Access Agreement following the Gaza disengagement do not set a promising precedent.

The subjective value of EU relations

Turning to the subjectively perceived value of bilateral relations, both Israelis and Palestinians accord high importance to EU ties. Israel is a small country, whose openness to international trade is key to its economic survival. The EU is Israel's largest trading partner, accounting for one third of Israeli exports and around 40 per cent of Israeli imports. The political value attributed by Israel to the EU is far more controversial, but arguably more important. During the second intifada, Israelis frequently referred to the 'crisis' in EU–Israel relations. Israel's strategic relationship with the US has also overshadowed the murkier political ties with the EU. However, Israel lives at the EU's doorstep, it is surrounded by real and perceived enemies and the US remains on the other side of the Atlantic. Beyond the rhetoric, Israel's links to Europe are valued highly, and the desire of finding a place of belonging in Europe (rather than in the Middle East) is deeply embedded in the Israeli Jewish majority (of European descent). The subjective value of EU ties with the Palestinians is also high. In economic terms, the EU represents by far the largest donor to the Palestinians. Without EU aid since 2000, the PA may well have collapsed. Politically, Palestinians frequently accuse Europe of its inadequate political role. However, they would warmly welcome a stronger European involvement, given their view of the US bias in favour of Israel and their appreciation of the multifaceted weaknesses of the Arab world.

This is not to say that Israel and Palestine aspire to join the EU, and thus that their exclusion from the accession process limits their perceived value of EU ties and the EU's potential influence on them. However, it does mean that the influence the Union could exert on the parties is likely to be lower than for candidate or aspiring candidate countries. In the case of the Palestinians, the question is clear-cut. Neither have elites nor the public ever expressed the desire to join the Union. Palestinians would welcome a more active EU role in the region. But this is viewed exclusively within the realm of foreign policy and is linked to their prime objective of securing viable and independent statehood.

As far as Israel is concerned, the picture is far more nuanced. At first glance it appears that the prospect of EU accession could have a strong hold amongst Israelis. A 2004 poll revealed that 85 per cent of Israelis would support an application for EU membership (Dahaf Institute 2004: 60). Yet this desire seems to stem more from a general wish to exit the turbulent Middle East and to enter a European security community, than from a thorough realization of what membership would mean. EU accession would entail a radical transformation of the Zionist project through the adoption of the Copenhagen political criteria (Dror and Pardo 2006: 31). While the majority of the Israeli public could be willing to compromise on the territorial aspects of the conflict, there is hardly a domestic constituency ready to compromise on the Jewish nature of the state. Hence, even in the hypothetical situation in which EU membership were on offer, it seems unlikely that the Israeli Jewish majority could be mobilized to pursue this goal. Far more appetizing to most Israelis would be other forms of 'virtual membership', allowing Israel to benefit from close political and economic ties with Europe, without the intrusive conditionality that full accession entails. Although it is yet to materialize, this is what the ENP holds on offer to Israel.

The credibility of EU obligations

Despite the high value of relations with Israel and the PA as non-accession countries, EU influence on them has hardly matched its potential. The reason largely lies in the obligations side of the contractual equation. With the partial exception of EU policies targeted to Palestinian reform, the Union has failed to make full and adequate use of its instruments in view of the lack of credibility of its obligations.

The lack of credibility of ex post conditionality

Beginning with the association agreements with both Israel and the PA, the problem (true for all EMP members) has been the lack of credibility of ex post conditionality embedded in the 'human rights clause'. The clause, mentioned in all association agreements, includes two components. The 'essential elements' article establishes human rights and democratic principles as essential elements of the agreements (Article 2). The 'non-execution' article calls for 'appropriate measures' which 'least disturb the functioning' of the agreements, in the event of their material breach (Article 79). While not necessarily representing a material breach (as defined by Article 60.3 of the 1969 Vienna Convention on the Law of Treaties), if, and when, it does, a violation of human rights and democracy could justify a suspension of the agreement. In other words, the benefit (i.e. association) is delivered on an understanding that its essential elements will be respected. Otherwise, the Union reserved the right to suspend the agreement by appealing to the non-execution article. Yet, for both legal and political reasons discussed in Chapter 2, ex post conditionality is rarely applied. Hence, while the front-loading of the benefits avoids the reduction of value that often applies to ex ante conditionality, the back-loading of the obligations reduces their credibility and thus the EU's influence on third parties. Indeed, despite the grave human rights, democracy and international law violations in the Israeli–Palestinian context, no attempt has been made to use ex post conditionality. The relevance of the human rights clause has been rather that of engaging in soft forms of pressure through political dialogue, which, however, has not led to any discernible effect on either party.

The ENP offers the scope for a more graduated and possibly more effective use of ex ante conditionality. Particularly vis-à-vis the Palestinians, the ENP Action Plan with the PA states that one of its primary purposes is to promote the Authority's political and economic reform through the delivery of conditional EU benefits (Commission 2004e: 1). Yet the ENP has shied away from conditionality in practice and after the election of Hamas, the entire ENP process with the Palestinians has been frozen. The EU–Israel Action Plan instead mentions 'facilitating efforts to resolve the Middle East conflict, strengthening the fight against terrorism and arms proliferation, promoting the respect for human rights, improving the dialogue between cultures and religions, cooperating in the fight against anti-Semitism, racism and xenophobia' (Commission 2004d: 3). But these issues are only mentioned in an open-ended way and in the context of political dialogue. When it comes to the 'priorities for action' where conditionality could be used, only one in six bullet points refers to the conflict and human rights, and does so in a general manner. Furthermore, the Plan only loosely states that 'progress in meeting these priorities will be monitored…. On this basis, the EU and Israel, will review the content of the Action Plan' (Commission 2004d: 3).

Abandoning passive enforcement

When it comes to Israel, with few exceptions, the Union has never exerted any form of conditionality.[7] At times, this has led to schizophrenic EU behaviour, whereby declarations condemned Israeli policies, while EU actions concomitantly delivered valuable benefits. One such incident was in the autumn of 2004, when the Commission negotiated an ENP Action Plan with Israel while the Council vociferously criticized Israeli raids in Gaza and backed the ICJ opinion on the illegality of the West Bank barrier. On other occasions, the EU has simply failed to act in response to Israeli defiance of its conditions. For example, Israel's disregard of the EU's conditional support for the Gaza disengagement (i.e. respecting the terms of the 2005 Movement and Access Agreement and re-engagement in the Roadmap) has not been met by any EU response. The Union has at times admitted the need for greater coherence. In 2005 for example, the Commission stated that 'the EU must increase the effectiveness of its messages rejecting the recent upsurge in settlement activity (Commission 2005b: 7). But no attempt was made to suggest how this could be done and no action has followed suit.

Beyond the lack of conditionality, when it comes to Israel, the EU has displayed a categorically different problem as well. By far the most serious way in which the Union has damaged its credibility and thus its potential influence on the conflict has been its reluctance to rely on its legal mechanisms of passive enforcement. The dispute over the preferential export of Israeli goods produced in settlements is emblematic in this respect.[8] While receiving sparse attention from academia and civil society, this problem lies at the very core of the conflict. This is not simply because it is connected with settlements. It is mainly because the issue exemplifies a key structural feature of the conflict, namely, the international community's acquiescence to Israel's right to differ in its respect for international law.

Since 1975, the territorial scope of all EC–Israeli agreements has been limited to the 'territory of the State of Israel', thus excluding on the basis of international law, the territories occupied in 1967. As such, the Community does not entitle preferential treatment to products, wholly produced or substantially processed in Israeli settlements (Patten 2003b). Yet Israel has determined the origin of its exports in a manner that does not distinguish between production carried out within its borders and in the OTs. This has resulted in the preferential treatment of Israeli settlement products, putting member states in violation of their Fourth Geneva Convention obligations,[9] and causing a material breach of the Association Agreement. The Commission and the member states have acknowledged the need to rectify the situation, pursuing several avenues to this end (The Mattin Group 2005). All have been marginally effective at best (leading to *ad hoc* duty recovery) and at worst they have been legally hazardous by threatening to accommodate Community law and practice to Israel's illegal policies.

The last move in this ongoing saga has been the agreement on a 'technical arrangement' in 2004–5 to ease the administrative burden of verifications on member state customs authorities. The arrangement, which entered into force in February 2005, consists in Israel naming the localities of production on the proofs of origin of its exports to the EU. The Commission then provides member state customs services with a list of settlement localities, allowing these to deny preferences without verifications when the stated localities fall beyond Israel's territorial scope (Council 2004d, paragraphs 39–40). The arrangement has the advantage of lightening the administrative burden on member state customs to carry out onerous verifications (necessary to ensure duty recovery). Furthermore, since its entry into force, no evidence suggests that the technical arrangement has failed in its practical intent to deny preferences to detected fraudulent exports.[10]

However, the technical arrangement has seriously imperilled the EU's standing on the conflict. The political quid pro quo behind the informal agreement with Israel was the decision to include Israel in the system of pan-Euro-Mediterranean cumulation of the rules of origin covering the Barcelona group and the Eastern European candidates and neighbours. In December 2005, the Council of Ministers amended the Protocol on Origin providing for Israel's inclusion in the system of cumulation.

This has generated two sets of problems. On a practical level, it has become much harder to ensure that goods which are partly produced in settlements are denied preferential treatment. This is because of the practical difficulty of detecting goods co-produced in settlements and other EU neighbouring countries. It is also because, with the exception of the EEA states, the technical arrangement has not been underwritten by non-EU countries included in the system of cumulation. On a legal level, the technical arrangement and the ensuing amendment of the Protocol on Origin could undermine the EU's interpretation of Israel's territorial scope. There is an inbuilt contradiction in the technical arrangement. Although it seeks to prevent the preferential treatment of settlement products (through the specification of the localities of origin), it also entitles Israel to represent all localities as situated within the State of Israel and to issue proofs of origin on that basis. It follows that if Israel is legally entitled to issue proofs of origin for settlement products, then their preferential treatment could also be considered legal under the association agreement. In turn, the arrangement could lead to the Union's recognition of Israel's territorial scope as covering the OTs. This may be the case, despite the fact that the amended protocol was accompanied by a unilateral declaration reconfirming the EU's unchanged interpretation of Israel's territorial scope.

The origin rules problem exemplifies how, in the case of Israel, the Union has disregarded the mechanisms of passive enforcement, risking a distortion of its own law and practice in order to accommodate illegal Israeli policies. The lawful and politically desirable solution (according to the EU's own normative stance) would compel the Union to rely on the legal instruments at its disposal, ranging from broad verifications, to arbitration and partial suspension. In principle, the Union has clarified that these remedies would not amount to 'sanctions', but would represent the only legal mechanisms to ensure the proper implementation of the agreement (The Mattin Group 2005: 27). But in practice, it has shied away from the mechanisms of passive enforcement. By relying on a politically non-confrontational deal couched in technical terms, the EU has failed to solve the problem while risking to exacerbate it in both legal and practical terms.

Perhaps most important, the EU's conduct has signalled to Israel that EC law is up for political bargaining. No third country on the receiving end of such signals is likely to take seriously EU obligations. Moreover, the Union's behaviour has cast doubt over its own commitment to the rules and values it diffuses. This has also reduced the prospects for the assimilation of EU rules and norms through learning and persuasion; mechanisms of influence that could be effective in Israel given its developed economic, social and cultural links to Europe.

The origin rules problem has wider applicability. One key area is that of research. As in the case of trade, only legal entities within the territory of the State of Israel are entitled to benefit from funds available in EU research programmes. Yet Israel, in line with its public policy, has considered Israeli entities within the OTs as eligible. An informal search of the Fifth Framework Programme database revealed that two settlement companies benefited from EU funds (Rockwell and Shamas 2005: 22–4). As in the case of trade, the Union took no action to ensure Israel's respect of its rules. Future problems are likely to emerge in other fields as well. In the case of procurement, no EU precautions are being taken to avoid the possibility that European companies may participate in Israeli tenders for the construction of infrastructure in the OTs. In the context of the ENP, the European Neighbourhood and Partnership Instrument (ENPI), which is specifically tailored to border regions, does not include adequate safeguard mechanisms to ensure that funds will not be directed to support actors or actions that contravene public international law.

The credibility of ex ante conditionality on Palestinian reform...
and its limits

EU obligations on Palestinian reform were increasingly credible between 1999 and 2005. Beginning in 1999, the Commission began criticizing the shortcomings of the PA and advanced recommendations for change. The recommendations of the EU-sponsored Rocard–Siegman Report became a first basis on which to specify EU conditions for the delivery of financial assistance (Sayigh and Shikaki 1999). They were complemented by the recommendations of the PLC in 2001, of Palestinian NGOs and of the June 2002 100-day reform plan. A further step was made in the

EU-PA Action Plan, where clear steps were spelled out in the areas of democracy, human rights, the judiciary, fiscal transparency, the security sector and the administration.

EU conditionality was relatively effective in those years. Particularly through budgetary assistance, EU threats to withhold aid at key points in time proved pivotal in triggering specific reforms aimed at fiscal transparency and judicial independence.[11] This also helped the resumption of Israeli revenue transfers and US aid to the PA in 2003–5. Particularly since the eruption of the intifada, the Union went the extra mile to monitor the use made of EU funds, ensuring that these were not redirected to finance political violence or incitement. EU institutions commissioned an independent enquiry on the use made of EU monies, finding no evidence of their misuse.

This is not to say that EU involvement in PA reform was fully successful in those years. The reasons underlying the Union's limited success partly derived from the sui generis situation in Palestine. First was the limited capability of the PA as a non-state actor to fulfil EU obligations. In a war-torn, occupation-ridden and non-state context, credible obligations required a careful distinction between reform priorities that the PA could meet, priorities that required Israeli cooperation, and priorities that needed external support. Making such distinctions in practice was no simple feat. Second and relating to the security sphere, was the problem that the targets of conditionality were not the direct authors of violence against Israel. Beyond back-channel contacts, the EU has had no official contact with, and thus leverage on, actors such as Hamas, which was included in the EU's terrorist list in 2003. EU conditionality targeted the Fateh-controlled PA, in opposition to the Islamic camp. In 2000–5 it was thus unclear how, and to what extent, the EU could have influenced the perpetrators of violence through its relations with the PA alone.

However, the Union itself was largely responsible for its own shortcomings. In terms of negative conditionality, while threats of suspending budgetary assistance were relatively credible, the EU could not credibly threaten to withdraw the bulk of its assistance for a sustained period of time. Doing so would trigger the collapse of the Authority and it would consequently oblige Israel to undertake the financial responsibilities that derive from its legal status as occupying power. EU actors have never realistically contemplated this outcome. Both Israel and the PA were aware of this, reducing the credibility of EU threats.

The magnitude of this dilemma rose to the fore prior to and after the Palestinian elections, highlighting the inconsistency of the EU's negative conditionality. This contributed to a reversal of the marginal steps forward that the EU had promoted in the previous five years. In December 2005, Javier Solana threatened to withhold EU aid to the PA in the event of a Hamas victory, unrealistically hoping to weaken Hamas' popularity given the PA's dependence on EU funds. Following Hamas' victory, both the Council and the Commission first toned down their rhetoric, accepting that the elections had been free and fair (as reported by EU monitors), and waiting to judge the formation and conduct of the new government. In the meantime, the Union disbursed €120m to the PA and UNRWA, and criticized Israel's decision to withhold PA tax revenues. Taking the lead from the Quartet, the

EU embraced the notion of conditional engagement (Council 2006a). The General Affairs Council urged Hamas to disarm, to renounce violence and terrorism, and to recognize Israel's right to exist. It also called upon the new government to accept previous agreements between Israel and the PLO and negotiations with Israel, as well as to commit itself to the rule of law, reform and sound fiscal management.

Yet the Union gave Hamas only two months to fulfil these all-encompassing conditions. In April 2006, the Council of Ministers decided to withhold budgetary assistance, making the uneasy distinction between humanitarian and development aid on the one hand and budgetary assistance on the other. This distinction poorly reflected reality. Since the eruption of the second intifada, 60 per cent of the PA's budget has been spent on salaries, which provided for the vast majority of health and education services and supported 25 per cent of the population in the economically free-falling OTs (Quartet's Special Envoy for Disengagement 2006 and UNSG 2006).

By May 2006, blunt negative conditionality plunged the OTs into a grave economic crisis that threatened the collapse of the PA without necessarily harming Hamas, in terms of either finance provision (deriving from non-Western sources) or of public support. Israel's withholding of PA revenues ($50m per month), the severing of ties between Israeli and Palestinian banks and the US Congress' Palestinian Anti-Terrorism Act made the EU's aid freeze untenable in the medium term. Through the Quartet, the EU insisted on a marginal U-turn to blunt negative conditionality. Aid would be partly resumed through a Temporary International Mechanism (TIM) intended to bypass the Hamas government by relying on the presidency, on international organizations and on the direct provision of supplies to sectors such as health and education. In July 2006, in the wake of Israel's assault on the Gaza Strip, the Commission announced the delivery of €50m in humanitarian aid in additional to the €34m already granted, and the €105m channelled through the TIM. In other words, having exerted much effort in 2002–5 in creating and empowering the post of prime minister, and shifting the control of PA finances and security from the presidency to the Ministry of Finance and the Ministry of the Interior respectively, the EU worked assiduously in 2006 to undo these results.

The EU's shortcomings have not been confined to the inconsistent to-ing and fro-ing of its threats. Turning to positive conditionality, the EU's obligations have often been incomplete, inadequate or inconsistent. At the height of its concern with PA reform in 2002–5, the EU's reform priorities were often not followed up in order to yield effective long-term results. In the case of judicial reform, after the EU's success in inducing the Law on the Independence of the Judiciary, the Commission's attention waned, despite the persistent shortcomings in this sector. In other cases, the Union pushed for reforms which were not necessarily the most desirable or urgent. The EU-sponsored Basic Law, while being hailed by some, was criticized by many Palestinians given the absence of territorially defined statehood (Shedada 2005).

More problematic still, while some areas received disproportionate EU attention (such as the post of prime minister in 2002–3 or security sector reform in 2004–5), others received none at all. Questions which arguably lie at the forefront of Palestinian democracy were largely neglected by EU actors. The Union showed little interest in the non-inclusiveness of the Palestinian political system (i.e. the exclusion of the Islamic factions from the PA up until the 2006 elections and from the PLO). The Union also showed remarkably little interest in the duality between the PLO and the PA. Up until 2006 it actively promoted the PA over and above the PLO, despite the latter's greater representativeness (representing also the Palestinian refugee Diaspora). The Union's attention only turned to the PLO after the 2006 elections, in its attempt to bypass the PA Hamas government.

Finally, in the post-election context, EU conditionality on Hamas has suffered from a fundamental lack of clarity and from an overemphasis of words over action. The EU's (and Quartet's) conditions have been vague and have not been accompanied by a framework for implementation.[12] Hamas has been called upon to recognize previous agreements. Yet the Union has not specified whether this means accepting the *legitimacy* of previous agreements, qua international agreements on which the PA itself is founded; or whether this means recognizing the *substance* of those agreements, which any government has the right to debate, question and renegotiate, as Israel itself has done. The February 2007 Mecca agreements declared *respect* of previous agreements indeed initially left the EU at loss as to how it should react. Hamas has been called upon to accept negotiations with Israel. Yet the operational meaning of this condition is incomprehensible in a situation in which it is the PLO that negotiates with Israel, and in which it is Israel that refuses to negotiate with the Palestinians, regardless of whether they have been led by Arafat (2001–4), by Abbas (2004–5) or by Hamas (2006). Hamas has been called upon to recognize Israel's existence. Yet does this mean the recognition of Israel's 'right to exist', i.e. a demand which could be considered the outcome of a peace process rather than the precondition for it? Or does it mean the de facto recognition of Israel, a demand that Hamas could be induced to meet by pressing for its adherence with the two-state solution, embodied in the 1988 PLO Charter (of which Hamas wants to be a part), the 2002 Arab League Beirut declaration and the 2006 inter-factional 'prisoners initiative'. Lastly, Hamas has been called upon to end violence. Yet all emphasis has been placed on words (the rhetorical renunciation of violence) rather than the far more relevant sphere of action. In terms of action, Hamas has demonstrated its ability to comply, as illustrated by its ceasefire between the 2005 Cairo declaration and the 2006 escalation in the Gaza Strip. Yet little EU thought has been put into how this condition could be operationalized and strengthened by establishing effective monitoring mechanisms to ensure that Hamas abides by its commitments.

The political management of EU contractual relations with Israel and Palestine

The degree of political management of EU contractual relations explains much of the gap between EU rhetoric and policy practice towards the conflict, and most of the flaws relating to the lack of credibility of EU obligations towards the conflict parties.

During the Oslo process, this meant that the Union largely neglected the failures of the PA in the field of democracy and governance, driven by the symbiotic relationship which had developed between Fateh and the PA, and by Arafat's particular mode of governance. As put by one observer: 'the PA regime was built with international funds at the cost of democracy, transparency, accountability, the rule of law and the respect for human rights' (Le More 2005: 988). Its primary purpose was that of conducting negotiations in the framework of Oslo and concomitantly acting as the protector of Israel, irrespective of democratic, human rights and good governance standards. Violations were often viewed as the necessary evil in order to rein in the 'Palestinian street' and maintain political momentum in negotiations (Roberts 2005: 19 and 24). When it came to Israel, the Oslo process was conducted on the premise that, while Israel cooperated, the international community would accept its right to differ on the interpretation and application of international law. The Union deemed the continuation of negotiations to be more important than the parties' unilateral actions, paying little attention to how these would ultimately trigger the failure of the peace process itself.

Post-Oslo, political imperatives continued to dictate EU contractual relations. On the positive side, this meant that the EU made progress in strengthening the credibility of its obligations on Palestinian reform, particularly in 2002–5. The Commission in particular specified conditions increasingly clearly and made extra efforts to monitor compliance. This was done in a political context in which Palestinian reform was the mantra of the day in both the US and Israel. In 2002–5 the EU vigorously pursued conditionality on Palestinian reform, which had begun back in 1999, partly because of the new-found attention to this in the US and Israel. Its purpose was thus only partly genuine. Beyond pursuing reform as an end in itself, the EU pushed for reform as a means to re-engage Washington in the peace process and to remove any reason or excuse for Israel's refusal to negotiate. This also explains the undue attention on issues such as the creation of the prime minister's post during Arafat's presidency or the reform of the security sector, at the expense of other, perhaps more crucial, areas of reform. However, the EU's shortcomings in those years and the reversal of its successes since the 2006 Palestinian elections demonstrate the flaws inherent in a policy aimed primarily at unilaterally ending Palestinian violence and securing an agreement with Israel, rather than at promoting democracy and good governance as ends in themselves.

Security and conflict settlement do not necessarily compete with democracy. On the contrary, particularly if the focus is on conflict resolution over and above settlement, democracy and good governance are essential conditions for peace in the region. However, to the extent that EU actors may believe that particular manifestations of Palestinian democracy may hinder a putative agreement with Israel, its policy goals could become competing, if not mutually exclusive. In the pre-election period this manifested itself in the EU's neglect of issues such as the exclusion of the Islamic factions from the legal Palestinian political system. Far more dramatically, in the post-election period this has led to the EU's promotion

Table 4 The Israeli–Palestinian conflict and EU relations with Israel and the PA

Population (2006)	7m in Israel of whom 1.4m Palestinian citizens. 2.46m in the West Bank and East Jerusalem and 1.43m in Gaza	
Key Historical Dates	1917	The UK issues the Balfour Declaration promising a 'national home' for the Jews in Palestine
	1936	Arab Revolt, which persists until 1939
	1947	UN Partition Plan
	1948	War establishing the State of Israel and leading to the expulsion of 770,000 Palestinian refugees to the Gaza Strip, the West Bank, Syria, Lebanon and Jordan
	1956	The Suez campaign
	1964	The establishment of the PLO
	1967	In the June war, Israel occupies East Jerusalem, the West Bank, the Gaza Strip, the Golan Heights and the Sinai. UNSC resolution 242 calls for the withdrawal of Israel and the establishment of peace
	1970	'Black September', in which the Hashemite regime cracks down on the PLO in Jordan
	1973	The October war between Israel, Egypt and Syria
	1979	Peace treaty between Israel and Egypt
	1982	Israel's invasion of Lebanon to crush the PLO
	1987	Eruption of the first intifada in the OTs
	1991	Madrid peace conference sponsored by the US
	1993	Declaration of Principles between Israel and PLO
	1994	Interim Israel–PLO agreement establishing the PA
	1995	Yitzhak Rabin is assassinated
	1996	Israel–PLO Wye Rier accord on partial Israeli redeployment
	2000	Camp David II summit, eruption of the second intifada and end of the Oslo process
	2005	With Arafat's death in 2004, Mahmoud Abbas is elected PA president. Israel unilaterally withdraws from the Gaza Strip
	2006	Parliamentary election of Hamas. Israel's war in Lebanon
EU Relations	1964	First trade agreement between the EC and Israel
	1970	Second EC–Israel preferential trade agreement
	1975	Third EC–Israel preferential trade agreement
	1986	The EC provides a separate preferential import regime for Palestinian products
	1995	Under the EMP, the EC signs an association agreement with Israel and an interim agreement with the PLO
	1996	The EC–PLO interim agreement enters into force
	1999	Israel–EU scientific and technical cooperation agreement. Israel is associated to the EU Framework Programmes
	2000	The EC–Israel association agreement enters into force
	2003	Israel and the PA are included in the ENP
	2004	Israel accedes to the Galileo system. Publication of the ENP Action Plans for Israel and the PA
EU Financial Assistance	€400m in grants to the PA in 1994–8 and €600m in 1998–2002. €300m per year in 2002–5. Aid is suspended in 2006 and only partially resumed through a Temporary International Mechanism	

of a re-centralization of power in the presidency (which it had forcefully fought against in the last years of Arafat's rule) and in the (much-denied) attempted creation of parallel governing structures to bypass the Hamas government. This has led to a failure to positively induce moderation within Hamas and in an exacerbated polarization between the internationally supported Fateh and the boycotted Hamas. It has also failed to quell the popularity of Hamas amongst the Palestinian public and to wider perceptions amongst Palestinians of Europe's hypocrisy when it comes to its rhetorical support for democracy and the rule of law.

In the case of EU–Israel relations, political considerations have damaged far more seriously the credibility of the EU's role. The Union has been influenced politically by several Israeli strands of argument. First has been Israel's accusations of Europe's alleged anti-Israeli bias and its anti-Semitism.[13] EU member states and particularly countries such as Germany and Austria, for evident historical reasons, have been highly sensitive to any criticism of this kind. A second major line of Israeli reasoning has been that of separating 'politics' from 'economics', by compartmentalizing the conflict from wider EU–Israel relations and advancing EU–Israel economic integration in view of Israel's economic development compared to its neighbours (Heller 2004). This intuitively compelling argument has in practice meant the deepening of EU–Israel economic ties irrespective of Israel's conduct in the conflict, and in turn the Union's acquiescence to Israel.

A final reason explaining why the Union has largely bent to Israel's wishes has been the leverage that Israel can exert on Europe itself. In economic terms, close EU–Israel trade ties have benefited Europe as well as Israel (the Union enjoys a strong trade surplus with Israel). In geostrategic terms, Israel and the Israeli–Palestinian conflict represent a major dossier on the transatlantic agenda, of primary interest to Europe. This has meant that when it comes to the Israeli–Palestinian conflict, EU interests have not been exclusively related to the goal of promoting the solution affirmed in its Middle East declarations since the 1970s. Advancing such a solution does reflect EU interests, when these are understood as promoting a stable, peaceful and developed neighbourhood. Yet equally, if not more importantly, there are other objectives, which are related to the transatlantic rather than the Middle Eastern agenda and which are not spelled out in EU declarations on the Israeli–Palestinian conflict. The goal of seeking transatlantic understanding and cooperation on the Middle East has been, to varying degrees, a key preoccupation of all member states. This also explains why, in many instances the Union has not put its policy instruments to the service of its declared goals in the conflict, prioritizing instead the aim of playing second fiddle to US policy in the region. The ensuing political imperative not to antagonize Israel has meant that the Union has abdicated on the use of conditionality. It has also and far more seriously meant that the EU has discarded the mechanisms of passive enforcement, risking bending its own laws for the sake of accommodating illegal Israeli policies and precluding other forms of non-coercive positive influence on Israel.

7 Caught between neglect and competing mediation in Georgia's secessionist conflicts

EU interests and objectives in Georgia

EU interests in Georgia are primarily driven by the geostrategic position of the South Caucasus coupled with its proximity to the Union. The importance of the Caucasus is given by its location as transit hub for Azeri and Central Asian oil and gas. Caspian energy is viewed as essential to reducing Europe's dependence on Russian and Middle Eastern supplies (Commission 1997). The Baku–Supsa pipeline transporting oil across the Black Sea (operational in 1999), followed by the Baku–Tbilisi–Ceyhan pipeline and its sister Baku–Tbilisi–Erzerum gas pipeline (operational in 2006) have been strategic priorities for the Union.[1] Georgia lies at the centre of these interlocking energy routes. Developments in the South Caucasus are also important because of the region's proximity to the Union, particularly in view of enlargements to Romania and Bulgaria, and to Turkey in future. The Caucasus is thus set to become a direct EU neighbour. As such instability, violence and organized crime in the region risk having dangerous spillover effects into the EU.

Energy interests and proximity have generated a set of corollary stakes in peace and stability in the South Caucasus, pursued by promoting state-building, democracy, human rights, the rule of law, poverty reduction, market reform, as well as peace processes and regional cooperation (Council 2005). The EP has explicitly promoted a 'Stability Pact for the South Caucasus', i.e. an EU initiative modelled on the precedents in the CEECs (the 1993 Balladur Pact) and in the Western Balkans to encourage regional cooperation and conflict resolution (European Parliament 2003). While the Commission and the Council have shied away from such an intensive mode of EU involvement, they have emphasized the EU's aim to promote solutions to the Caucasian conflicts. This is for two main reasons. First, events since the late 1990s have demonstrated that conflicts in the region are all but 'frozen', and that their unfrozen nature imperils EU interests. Second, EU actors have appreciated the nature of the vicious circle besieging the Caucasus – trapped between conflict and stagnant development. They are increasingly aware that conflict has been a primary cause of the economic, humanitarian and political problems in the region; and that failings in domestic reform have hindered the prospects for peace (Commission 1998a). As put by former Commission President

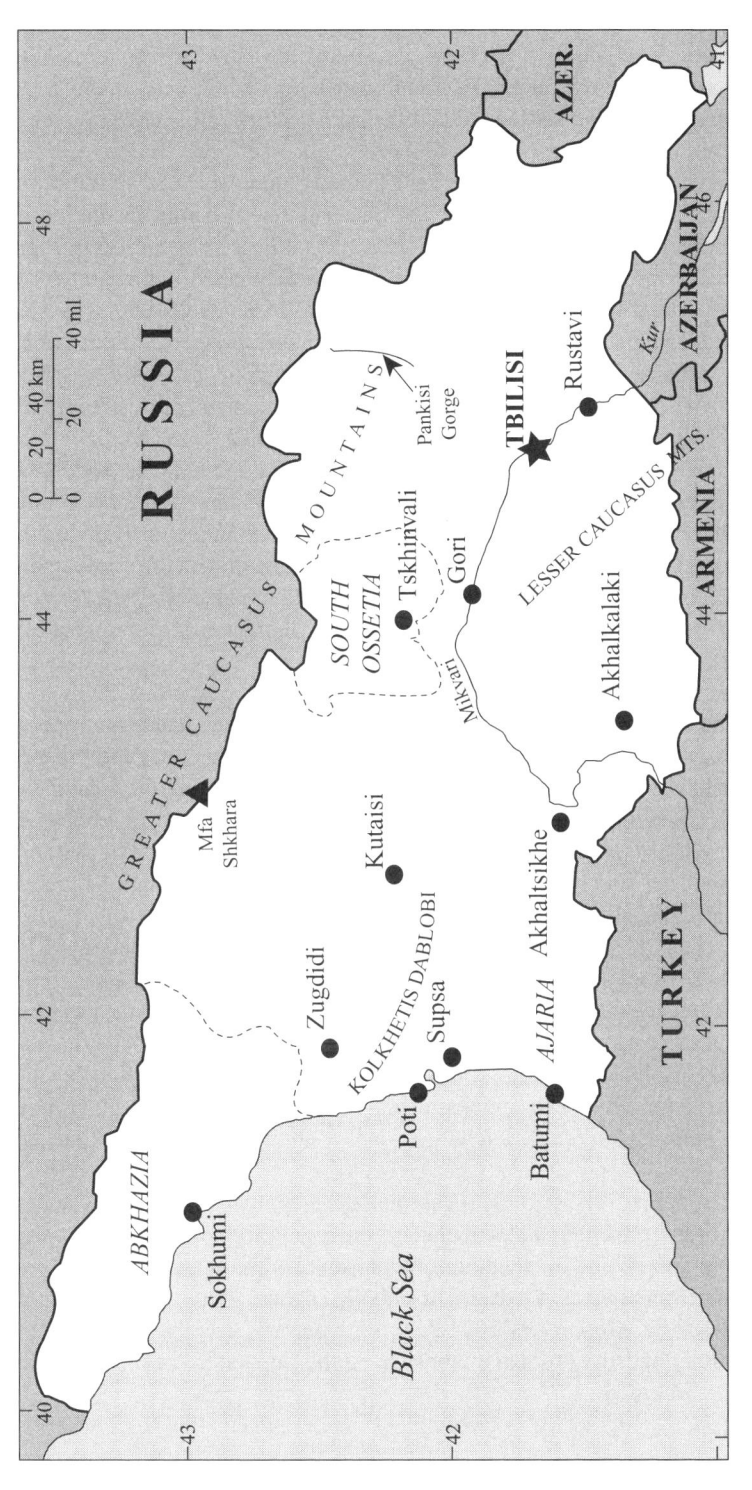

Map 5 Georgia, Abkhazia and South Ossetia.
Source: The World Fact Book. https://www.cia.gov/cia/publications/factbook/geos/mj.html.

Romano Prodi (2004) on a visit to Georgia: 'we realize that resolving the conflicts in South Ossetia and Abkhazia is essential for Georgia's long-term stability. But progress towards conflict settlement and the implementation of Georgia's reform agenda ... are interlinked. Neither is possible on its own'.

Indeed, evidence suggests that in the Caucasus there is a close link between democracy and good governance on the one hand and conflict resolution and regional cooperation on the other. The festering conflicts have opened the space for organized crime, reducing the degree of good governance and respect for the rule of law. One of the most striking examples was in South Ossetia. The South Ossetian leadership, controlling the de facto statelet following military victory in 1992 and basing its political claims on its desire to integrate with its North Ossetian kin within Russia, has refused to establish an international customs regime between North and South Ossetia. Hence, the Roki tunnel connecting North and South Ossetia has seen an uncontrolled flow of goods and persons across what is legally an international border. Goods such as flour, cigarettes, dairy products, kerosene and petrol are smuggled from Russia into South Ossetia. They are then sold in Georgia and beyond, given that the Georgian government does not establish customs control on the South Ossetia–Georgia frontier, considering the former to be part of Georgia proper. This has reputedly cost Georgia over 80 per cent of its annual customs revenues (ICG 2004).

The absence of strong, democratic, law-abiding and prosperous states in the Caucasus has also hindered conflict resolution. On the one hand, metropolitan states such as Georgia and Azerbaijan have not represented appealing prospects for the breakaway regions to reintegrate into. On the other hand, the weakness of democracy, civil society and economic development within breakaway entities like Abkhazia, South Ossetia and Nagorno Karabakh has hindered political pluralism, necessary to foster inter and intra-communal dialogue and reconciliation (although not necessarily the abandonment of the goal of independence).

Closing the circle, the persistence of conflict and the consolidation of failing states has reduced prospects for regional cooperation. The inter-state conflict between Armenia and Azerbaijan over Nagorno Karabakh has been the key obstacle in this respect. However, Georgia's internal problems, its problematic ties to Russia and its simmering ethno-political conflicts have also hindered its potential to act as the key promoter of regional cooperation in the Caucasus (given it represents the only state in the region with normal relations with its South Caucasian neighbours).

Viewed from Brussels, stability, peace and development in the South Caucasus also calls for the effective independence of the region from excessive, exclusive and competing meddling by neighbouring powers. Unlike Washington, however, the EU has not manifested the desire to actively contain the influence of regional actors like Russia (Coppieters 2004). On the contrary, member states such as Germany, Italy and the UK have emphasized the imperative not to antagonize Russia in its backyard.

Turning more specifically to Georgia, EU actors have called for a sovereign, democratic, well-governed and peaceful Georgia (Coppieters 2000b). Particularly after the rise to power of Eduard Shevardnadze in 1992, the member states threw their weight behind newly independent Georgia. This meant unreserved EU support for Georgia's territorial integrity and Georgian claims to sovereignty over the breakaway regions of South Ossetia and Abkhazia. Virtually all EU declarations on these two conflicts have emphasized the non-negotiable principle of Georgia's sovereignty and territorial integrity, as well as the return of refugees and IDPs (Council 2001c, 2002, 2004c, 2006c). At the same time, the Union has rejected the use of force as a means to re-establish Georgia's territorial integrity. Particularly in view of the fragile ceasefires in place, EU declarations have emphasized the imperative of stabilization and demilitarization, and put their weight behind negotiations mediated by the UN and the OSCE in Abkhazia and South Ossetia respectively.

On the specific solutions to Georgia's two conflicts, EU actors have remained largely silent. On Abkhazia, the EU has simply called for 'maximum autonomy', permitting Abkhazians 'to express their identity within Georgia' (Council 1999). The Union has also supported the December 2001 proposals drafted by UNSR Dieter Boden on behalf of the Friends of the UNSG on Georgia (i.e. France, Germany, Russia, the UK and the US). But this one-page document only outlined extremely general ideas on the distribution of competences between Georgia and Abkhazia (Council 2001c). On South Ossetia, the EU has been even vaguer. It has only expressed support for South Ossetian autonomy within Georgia, for the demilitarization of the conflict zone and for unspecified confidence-building measures (OSCE 2003).

The emergence and development of the conflicts

Both the Abkhaz and the Ossetians are culturally and linguistically distinct from Georgians. In addition, while Abkhazia at times has been part of Georgia proper, on other occasions it has enjoyed prolonged periods of self-rule. Abkhazia was an independent kingdom between the eighth and tenth centuries and an independent principality between the thirteenth century and 1864, when it became the last Caucasian entity to fall under Tsarist rule.

From latent tensions to violent conflict

The outburst of these two ethno-political conflicts first occurred during the period of Georgian independence in 1918–21, when Georgian Mensheviks accused the Abkhaz and the Ossetians of collaborating with the Russian Bolsheviks, while denying both meaningful autonomy in the 1921 Constitution. When in 1921 the Bolsheviks occupied Georgia, the two potential conflicts were frozen, although tensions between Georgians and Abkhazians continued to simmer. Within the emerging Soviet ethno-federal system, Georgia became a Socialist Soviet Republic (SSR); a status which was ultimately denied both to Abkhazia and to South Ossetia. Abkhazia was initially given the status of an SSR in 1921, and in 1922 it entered the Soviet Union together with Georgia through the short-lived Transcaucasus Soviet Federated Socialist Republic. In 1925 Abkhazia took part in a quasi-confederal arrangement with Georgia, but in 1931 its status as an SSR was abolished. Hence, when the Transcaucasus Federated Socialist Republic was dissolved in 1936, Abkhazia was downgraded into an autonomous republic within the Georgian SSR. South Ossetia was given a lower degree of autonomy, i.e. that of an autonomous *oblast* (region) in the Georgian SSR.

Ethnic tension rose during Soviet rule. Georgians largely considered South Ossetia as an artificial entity, while the South Ossetians resented both the separation from North Ossetia and their lower status as *oblast* compared to them (North Ossetia was an autonomous republic within the Russian SSR). In the case of Abkhazia, resentment mounted as a consequence of the rule of Joseph Stalin and Lavrenti Beria's in 1933–53. The two – ethnically Georgian – Soviet leaders pursued aggressive policies of 'georgianization' in Abkhazia, through education, culture and migration policies. This led to a sharp decline in the proportion of ethnic Abkhaz in Abkhazia. Whereas in 1897 the Abkhaz constituted 55 per cent of the population of Abkhazia, by 1989 this figure had dropped to a mere 18 per cent. Abkhaz resentment and ensuing protests in Sukhumi, the capital of Abkhazia, led to a reversal of Soviet policies in the 1970s. Constitutional revisions included Abkhaz overrepresentation in the Abkhaz Supreme Soviet and an increase in its administrative autonomy (although most decisions were taken in Tbilisi and Moscow). Georgians criticized the ethnically discriminatory nature of these arrangements. The Abkhaz rebuked that these were insufficient measures to compensate for past policies of georgianization.

By and large, the Soviet lid quashed potential conflict in Georgia until Gorbachev's *perestroika*. The period of profound change within the Soviet space in the late 1980s re-ignited ethno-political claims. Tensions escalated with the rise of Georgian nationalist Zviad Gamsakhurdia in the 1990 election of the Georgian SSR, and his ensuing election as independent Georgia's first president in May 1991. Gamsakhurdia's ethno-nationalism alienated further the Abkhaz and South Ossetians. In 1989, the Popular Front (Ademon Nykhaz) within the South Ossetian regional council demanded an upgrade of South Ossetia's status into an autonomous republic. In response, the Georgian Supreme Soviet banned the formation of regional parties, triggering the Ossetian boycott of the Georgian 1990 elections and its declaration of sovereignty within the Soviet Union. In retaliation, in December 1990 Gamsakhurdia abolished South Ossetia's *oblast* status, sparking the eruption of armed clashes in January 1991. The clashes quickly escalated into a full-blown war, with Ossetians being on occasions supported by Russian troops. The war ended in June 1992, leaving behind a legacy of death, destruction and displacement. Prior to the war, there had been much intermingling between communities, with 26,000 Georgians and 65,000 Ossetians living in South Ossetia, and 95,000 Ossetians living in the rest of Georgia. The war shrank South Ossetia's population to 35,000, with 40,000–50,000 Ossetians fleeing Georgia and 10,000 Georgians fleeing South Ossetia into Georgian-controlled territory.

The war in South Ossetia induced Gamsakhurdia to ostensibly placate ethno-political tensions in Abkhazia. Tensions had been on the rise since the 1989 clashes in Sukhumi over Abkhaz education rights, the 1990 Abkhaz call to be recognized by Moscow as an SSR, and the ensuing Abkhaz participation in the 1991 Soviet referendum on the future of the Soviet Union (which had been boycotted by Georgia). In 1991, Gamsakhuurdia adopted an electoral law guaranteeing Abkhaz overrepresentation in Abkhazia's parliament within independent Georgia. Yet this arrangement was short-lived, as Georgia plunged into civil war in the winter of 1991–2. The civil war culminated with the ousting of Gamsakhurdia by a coup and with the invitation by the putchists to Eduard Shevardnadze to return to Georgia to lead the country in March 1992. However, the rise of Shevardnadze did not put an end to civil unrest. Supporters of the ousted president (known as Zviadists) regrouped in western Georgia (i.e. Mingrelia – Gamsakhurdia's native land), backed by Georgians–Mingrelians in Abkhazia. In retaliation, the pro-Shevardnadze Georgian parliamentarians blocked the power-sharing arrangements in the Abkhaz parliament. In Tbilisi, the Georgian authorities also reinstated the 1921 Georgian Constitution, which failed to specify Abkhazia's autonomy.

As a ceasefire was being brokered in South Ossetia, a new war was thus in the offing in Abkhazia. With the collapse of the electoral arrangements and the reinstatement of the 1921 Constitution in July 1992, the Abkhaz voted to restore the 1925 Abkhaz Constitution, which provided for treaty-based (i.e. confederal) ties to Georgia. Ostensibly aimed at protecting the rail link from Zviadist insurrectionists in Abkhazia, Shevardnadze's troops entered Sukhumi in August 1992 triggering an all-out war. While Georgian forces were initially victorious, the Abkhaz ultimately acquired control of the entire territory by October 1993. Their victory was possible through the support of Russian troops and north Caucasian fighters (including the renown Chechen commander Shamil Basayev). The Abkhaz victory shrank the population of Abkhazia to approximately 150,000 from its former 545,000, with the flight of around 250,000–280,000 refugees and IDPs (mainly Georgian, but also Abkhaz, Greeks, Armenians and Russians).

Frozen peace processes and unfrozen conflicts

Since the end of the two secessionist wars, the EU's aims to secure peace and stability in Georgia have been deeply frustrated. The peace processes in South Ossetia and in Abkhazia have not produced tangible results. Moreover, trends over the years have moved away from the reintegration of the secessionist regions into Georgia, shifting relentlessly towards their integration into Russia.[2]

Some steps forward have been made within (rather than between) the conflict parties. In Abkhazia, important steps forward were made in the development of civil society and – particularly after the 2004–5 presidential elections – in the functioning of democracy and the growth of political pluralism. In Georgia, domestic change occurred through the spectacular 'rose revolution' in 2003, which ousted Shevardnadze and his regime through peaceful means. Post-revolutionary Georgia has engaged in an impressive campaign to fight organized crime and corruption and has reasserted sovereignty over the Black Sea region of Ajara.[3] However, other worrying trends have emerged instead, and the Georgian leadership has engaged in dangerous brinkmanship over South Ossetia. This has reduced

Photo 4 The former Iveria hotel in Tbilisi hosting Georgian refugees from Abkhazia. July 2000.

prospects for negotiated peace settlements, encouraged the remilitarization of the conflict zones, and exacerbated Georgian–Russian tensions.

Frozen peace processes and competing mediation

In South Ossetia, the war ended with a ceasefire agreement signed in Sochi in 1992. The agreement established a joint peacekeeping force (PKF), including Georgian, Russian, and Ossetian units (the latter being a South Ossetian force under a North Ossetian commander). In addition, the agreement mandated the OSCE to monitor the South Ossetian territory. Beyond the conflict zone, this also included an OSCE border monitoring operation on the Russian–Georgian frontier between 1999 and 2004 (largely in relation to the war in Chechnya). Georgia has been dissatisfied with the peacekeeping arrangements, given the presence, in its view, of three out of four actors favouring South Ossetia (Russia, South Ossetia and North Ossetia). It has also demanded an upgrading of the OSCE's involvement in monitoring the Roki tunnel. However, despite Georgian misgivings, the joint PKF did act as a confidence-building forum and was relatively effective in monitoring demilitarization and securing the ceasefire until 2004. Yet the inherent flaws caused by its internal make-up were revealed in full-force when in 2004, it failed to prevent the re-eruption of violence and the ensuing remilitarization of the region.

The 1992 ceasefire agreement also established the Joint Control Commission (JCC), featuring Georgia, South Ossetia, North Ossetia, Russia and the OSCE. The JCC's peace process has focussed on three interlinked issues: refugee return, economic rehabilitation and security. The peace process made marginal steps forward especially up until 2001. In 1996, the parties agreed to a memorandum to 'enhance security and confidence building measures', foreseeing the progressive demilitarization of the conflict zone, refugee return and rehabilitation. Political status talks started in 1999 and led to the 'Baden declaration' in 2000 during an OSCE experts group meeting. The declaration envisaged South Ossetian autonomy within Georgia, security guarantees and demilitarization. However, after Eduard Kokoity's election as South Ossetian president in 2001, the South Ossetian side denied the very existence of the Baden declaration.

In Abkhazia, the peace process has been even more frozen and international involvement has been even more complex. In terms of peacekeeping, the Russian-brokered May 1994 ceasefire agreement foresaw the stationing of a Commonwealth of Independent States (CIS) force. In practice the CIS PKF has consisted of Russian troops. In July 1994, the UN deployed an observers' mission (UNOMIG). Like the OSCE in South Ossetia, UNOMIG's mandate has been limited and it has been powerless to prevent the occasional re-eruption of violence.

The results of the peace process in Abkhazia have been even more meagre than in South Ossetia. As put by Coppieters (2000a: 16), there have mainly been 'negotiations about negotiations'. The first, and most promising steps forward were made immediately after the war. In April 1994 under Russian mediation, the parties signed a 'declaration of measures for a political settlement of the Georgian–Abkhaz conflict', foreseeing joint competences in the fields of foreign affairs, borders and customs, energy, transport, communication, environment, and human and minority rights. Yet the declaration was not followed by substantive negotiations, as the Georgian side pulled back from its initial commitments. Also in 1994, the parties reached a quadripartite agreement (between Georgia, Russia, Abkhazia and the UN High Commissioner on Refugees) on the voluntary repatriation of Georgian IDPs to the formerly Georgian-inhabited Gali district in Abkhazia. However refugee return has been limited and unstable primarily due to the lack of security in the region.

The international dimension of the peace process was institutionalized in 1997, through the UN Geneva Process. The Geneva Process includes the conflict parties,

Russia as facilitator and the UNSR, and it grants observer status to the OSCE and the Group of Friends of the UNSG on Georgia. Mirroring the South Ossetian peace process, the Geneva Process established a Coordinating Council with three working groups on refugees, economic rehabilitation and security. The Geneva process has been largely unsuccessful. This is not least because it has been viewed with utmost suspicion by the Abkhaz, who – not without reason – have felt that, with the exception of Russia, all other actors have unreservedly backed the Georgian stance on territorial integrity (Stewart 2003). As put by one Abkhaz analyst, 'Georgia's territorial integrity, rather than being a subject of negotiations, has been the framework and premise underlying the peace process'.[4] This has led to the paradoxical situation in which negotiations, when they took place at all, were often conducted within the Group of Friends itself, and more precisely between Russia and the rest. It took over three years (1999–2001) for the Group of Friends and the UNSR Dieter Boden to agree on what became known as the 'Boden document' in December 2001 – a modest one-page outline sketching a tentative division of competences between Tbilisi and Sukhumi. But despite Russia's approval, the document was rejected out-of-hand by the Abkhaz, on the basis of its support for Georgia's territorial integrity. Negotiations on status have been stalled since then.

Russia has also played an independent role in the peace process, which while controversial, has yielded some results. In 1997, under Primakov's mediation, Shevardnadze and former Abkhaz leader Vladislav Ardzinba almost concluded a common state agreement, a commitment which was later abandoned by the Georgian side. In March 2003, President Putin mediated and took part in the Georgian–Abkhaz agreement in Sochi. The Sochi agreement set aside the thorny question of status and tackled practical aspects concerning the status quo. It provided for the re-opening the rail link between Russia and Georgia through Abkhazia, and for the renovation of the of joint electricity infrastructure (the Inguri hydroelectric station), in exchange for the return of Georgian IDPs to Gali. The rail link between Russia (Sochi) and Abkhazia (Sukhumi) was restored in 2002, but due to disputes over border control, its extension to Georgia has been stalled. The other elements of the package deal also remain pending (Khashig and Kupatadze 2005).

The Russian dimension in both conflicts has other, less benign, facets. Russia undoubtedly played a decisive role in securing the military victory of the two breakaway regions. Since the end of the two wars, several Russian policies have weakened Georgia and consolidated the de facto independence of South Ossetia and Abkhazia from Georgia – although not as independent entities – and their progressive integration into Russia. Russian peacekeepers have not encouraged demilitarization and have often served as border troops between the two entities and Georgia proper.

In the economic domain, South Ossetia and Abkhazia are part of the Russian rouble zone and the survival of both regimes hinges on their border with and thus their economic ties to Russia. Despite the 1994 and 1996 official CIS embargoes on Abkhazia, trade restrictions have been partially lifted since 1999 and Abkhazia has benefited from growing Russian trade, tourism and private investment. In 2002

Russia reopened the rail link between Sochi and Sukhumi. Russia has also exploited its economic and energy-related influence on Georgia to exert pressure on it. In 2006 it banned Georgian wine and mineral water exports to Russia. In the winters of 2001 and 2006 it cut off energy supplies to Georgia in a clear (albeit denied) act of confrontation. In the summer of 2006, the only crossing point between Georgian controlled territory and Russia was closed.

In the domain of visa and citizenship policies, Russia has fully integrated the two breakaway regions. In December 2000, Russia imposed visas on Georgian citizens, while exempting South Ossetian and Abkhaz residents from this requirement. Since 2000 (and the abolishment of Soviet passports), it has allowed South Ossetians and Abkhazians to acquire Russian passports, and the vast majority of them have done so, having no other option for movement. Moscow has then used the presence of Russian citizens in these regions to claim a legitimate stake in their political future. For example during the Abkhaz presidential elections in 2004–5, Russia openly backed Raul Khajimba and secured his post as vice-president in January 2005, despite the fact that the majority of the population had backed his rival Sergei Bagapsh in the October 2004 elections.[5] In South Ossetia a large proportion of the elite in charge of the 'power ministries' are retired Moscow officials.

Finally, Russia has used the presence of its military bases to exert pressure on Georgia. Despite its commitment at the 1999 OSCE summit in Istanbul to dismantle its bases in Georgia, Russia retains two bases in the Armenian-populated region of Alkhalkalaki and in Batumi near the Georgian–Turkish border.[6] Its base in Gudauta (Abkhazia) has been dismantled, although its troops and equipment have reputedly shifted to the Russian PKF there.

Citing these realities, Georgian authorities (both under Shevardnadze and Saakashvili) have portrayed Russia as the principal instigator and cause of the stalemates (Eurasia Insight 2004). Its peacekeeping functions have been dubbed as a form of occupation and its role in the peace processes has been accused of deepening Russia's grip on the South Caucasus. In turn, Georgia has repeatedly expressed its wish to see the departure of the Russian peacekeepers from Abkhazia and South Ossetia. In February 2006, the Georgian parliament voted to review and replace the joint PKF in South Ossetia with an OSCE or EU force (Fuller 2006). In July 2006, the parliament voted in favour of a withdrawal of the Russian peacekeepers from both South Ossetia and Abkhazia.

Russia clearly has strong interests in the status quo. However, Georgia's characterization of Russia's role as the prime source of conflict in the region has been neither productive nor accurate. Georgia's exclusive finger-pointing at Moscow has backfired, by angering Moscow and the two secessionist regions (which have considered Georgia's attitude as yet another demonstration of disrespect for their capacity for self-determination). It has also reduced European incentives to influence the conflicts, with Europe fearing that it would antagonize Russia by doing so.

Georgian accusations also fail to capture the complexities of Russia's role. Russia certainly exerts much influence on the two breakaway regions and there has been an undeniable process of integration of the two into Russia proper. But as the 2004–5 Abkhaz election debacle demonstrates, Russian control in the two entities is also limited (given that Moscow's candidate was ultimately not elected as president) (Antonenko 2005: 258–64). Moreover, Russia's support for Abkhazia and South Ossetia has not entailed a formal support for their independence, an observation that the Abkhaz and Ossetians are quick to make.[7] Recognizing secession or annexation in the South Caucasus would set a dangerous precedent for Russia, in view of its war in Chechnya. Finally, Russia's policies towards Georgia have not derived from a premeditated and monolithic strategy. The military, the security services, regional leaders and the Duma have openly supported (both verbally and militarily) the secessionist regions. However, the Kremlin, the foreign ministry and the ministry of defence, aware of Russian interests in a stable Georgia, have been far more cautious and have stood behind political initiatives such as the 2003 Sochi agreement (Antonenko 2005). In other words, ambiguous as its role may be, Russia is both part of the problem and an indispensable part of the solution.

Unfrozen dynamics on the ground

While the peace processes have been largely frozen, the conflicts themselves have simmered incessantly. Georgian peace offers have been vague and unappealing, while the positions of the secessionist leaderships and their societies have progressively hardened. The conflict parties have also taken unilateral steps to strengthen their (non)negotiating stances. This has led to the occasional re-eruption of violence in Abkhazia and Ossetia, remilitarization, and the flourishing of organized crime especially in South Ossetia.

Under Shevardnadze, Georgia's negotiating position, while reasonable at first glance, was hardly appealing upon closer inspection. Partly to distinguish himself from his predecessor Gamsakhurdia, and partly in view of military defeat, Shevardnadze did not espouse radical ethno-nationalism. Since the 1995 Georgian Constitution entered into force, Shevardnadze advanced the proposal of an 'asymmetric federation', which would grant Abkhazia and South Ossetia different degrees of autonomy. Yet neither did Shevardnadze specify what such an offer entailed, nor did he federalize Georgia's Constitution to demonstrate the credibility of his offer. He rather waited for an external (Western) saviour to overturn the balance of power in Georgia's favour. In the meantime, Georgia increasingly acquired the features of a failing state, thus hardly representing an alluring prospect for the two breakaway entities. Over the 1990s and early 2000s, Georgia became characterized by rising poverty and unemployment, rampant corruption, macroeconomic disarray, a crumbling security apparatus and the privatization of violence through the rise of partisan groups (especially operating in western Georgia and Abkhazia). Tax collection stood at a mere 14 per cent GDP, 24 per cent of the labour force was officially unemployed, the shadow economy ranged between 40 and 70 per cent GDP, and in 2002 the economy's size was only 38 per cent of that in 1989 (in purchasing power terms) (Lynch 2006: 22).

Georgia's 'rose revolution', led by Mikhail Saakashvili, Zurab Zhvania and Nino Burjanadze following the rigging of the November 2003 presidential elections, renewed the impetus in state-building and conflict resolution. In Ghia Nodia's words, the new leadership overturned the 'Potemkin' democracy of the past, passing important reforms in a 'prolonged revolutionary syndrome' (Coppieters and Levgold 2005: 3). Following the repeat presidential elections in January 2004, President Saakashvili publicly recognized his predecessor's failings. In his address to the UN General Assembly in September 2004, he emphasized the importance of transforming Georgia into a state where the secessionist entities would want to reintegrate into. In terms of domestic reforms, the new leadership, backed by a young and western-educated elite, made impressive strides forward in eradicating systemic corruption, curtailing the powers of the Abkhaz government-in-exile, downscaling the inefficient public sector, engaging in large-scale privatization, tripling state revenues, shrinking the shadow economy, improving infrastructure, and reforming the education system, the judiciary, the civil service, and, above all, the police and the armed forces (Nodia 2005). Coupled with the reassertion of control over previously out-of-bounds areas such as Ajara or the Pankisi gorge, and the dismantlement of partisan groups, the new leadership succeeded in meeting the Weberian criterion of state control (with the exception of the secessionist entities themselves).

In terms of peace proposals, Saakashvili presented his 'peace plans' in September 2004 (at the UN General Assembly) and in January 2005 (at the Parliamentary Assembly of the Council of Europe). These foresaw constitutionally guaranteed 'broad autonomy' for Abkhazia and South Ossetia (broader than that granted by Moscow to North Ossetia). With regard to South Ossetia, Saakashvili proposed dual citizenship (i.e. Russian and Georgian), a free economic zone, as well as guaranteed Ossetian representation in federal institutions and an elected Ossetian government and parliament with wide-ranging competences. Carried out in successive stages, the South Ossetia peace plan would begin with normalization of relations and demilitarization, followed by economic rehabilitation and refugee return, international monitoring of the Roki tunnel and confidence-building measures, finally concluding with final status talks.

Yet not all is 'rosey' in post-revolutionary Georgia (Haindrava 2005). While the Georgian state is undoubtedly stronger, it is not in every respect more democratic. Opposition is feeble and ineffective.[8] The new leadership has weakened the system of checks and balances, strengthening the presidency at the expense of the legislature. Saakashvili has staffed the Central Electoral Commission with personnel close to him and has rejected direct elections for Tbilisi's city mayor. The authorities have passed new media laws hindering the freedom of expression, and Georgia's human rights record remains worrying particularly in the areas of torture and prison conditions. More relevant to the secessionist regions, following Tbilisi's reassertion of power over Ajara, Saakashvili failed to use the occasion of the June 2004 Ajaran elections to establish genuine democracy there. The new constitutional law, theoretically promising Ajara significant autonomy, in practice has established Tbilisi's control over the region. The Georgian government has pointed out that Ajara does not have the ethno-political distinctiveness of South Ossetia or Abkhazia, that the Ajarans have not demanded greater autonomy, and that the law could be revised to provide for greater decentralization in future.[9] Notwithstanding, the Ajaran precedent – both in terms of means pursued (brinkmanship) and constitutional result (lack of autonomy) – has undermined the credibility of the federal offers made by Georgia to Sukhumi and Tskhinvali.

Turning to the secessionist entities, while South Ossetia's first leader Lyudvig Chibirov became increasingly conciliatory towards the end of his tenure, these trends were reversed with the election of Eduard Kokoity in November 2001. The new Ossetian leadership hardened its position, as Kokoity refused to discuss South Ossetia's political status within Georgia and called for unification with North Ossetia in the Russian federation. In Abkhazia, after its military victory, the Abkhaz rejected a federal solution. Until 1999, Abkhaz leader Ardzinba was ready to discuss a treaty-based confederation or free associated state with Georgia. Yet, not least because of Georgian backtracking from the 1994 agreement on the division of competences and from the 1997 'common state' Russian proposal, the Abkhaz position hardened. In the 1999 referendum, the Abkhaz voted in favour of independence, and since then the leadership, both under Ardzinba and under his successor Bagapsh has rejected negotiations with Georgia aimed at a federal/confederal solution. The leadership's stance on independence has been shared by virtually the entire spectrum of Abkhaz civil society as well as by the wider public (with the exception of Georgian returnees in Gali).

On the ground, the simmering conflicts have triggered a resumption of violence on several occasions. In Abkhazia, Georgian paramilitaries (the White Legion and the Forest Brothers) became increasingly active after 1996, operating in Abkhazia and Mingrelia. In May 1998, well after the Georgian IDPs had begun returning to Gali, clashes erupted between Georgian guerrillas and Abkhaz militias. Russian peacekeepers failed to prevent and halt the violence, creating widespread destruction and a renewed exodus of 30,000 Georgian IDPs. Clashes erupted again in the Kodori gorge in 2001, causing the shooting of a UNOMIG helicopter. More generally, in Tbilisi bellicose rhetoric is often heard. This is true not only of radical factions, such as the former Abkhaz government-in-exile in Tbilisi, but at times also by the Georgian leadership itself, both under Shevardnadze and Saakashvili.

In South Ossetia, inter-communal confidence increased in the late 1990s, with a gradual process of demilitarization and refugee return underway. This was reversed in the summer of 2004. Following his election, Saakashvili, exhilarated by his quick success in Ajara, shifted his focus on South Ossetia with a twofold tactic. First, he aimed to 'win the hearts and minds' of the Ossetians by offering them a package of goodwill measures, including the provision of fertilizers, ambulance services, broadcasting in Ossetian, the payment of pensions and the resumption of rail links. Second, he aimed to replicate the successful brinkmanship used in Ajara. Saakashvili engaged in an anti-smuggling operation in South Ossetia through the closure of the Ergneti market on the outskirts of Tskhinvali (where most of the smuggled goods from Russia were sold) in June 2004. The government

Photo 5 The former Ergneti market in South Ossetia. August 2000.

also deployed troops ostensibly aimed at patrolling the anti-smuggling operation. Brinkmanship dangerously backfired. The closure of Ergneti exacerbated
Ossetia's economic problems by halving its revenues. It raised Kokoity's popularity and increased South Ossetian dependence on Russia.[10] Moreover, the closure
did not eradicate the smuggling economy as different routes were soon found
to transfer goods into Georgia. Finally, the Ossetians viewed the deployment of
Georgian troops as a clear act of provocation, triggering clashes in August 2004.
The clashes halted direct dialogue between the parties, hampered the movement
of persons between South Ossetia and Georgia, broke Ossetian trust in Tbilisi and
remilitarized the region. Nearby Abkhazia watched closely developments in South
Ossetia and its trust in the Georgian regime plummeted to an all-time low.[11]

Assessing EU impact on Georgia's secessionist conflicts

Of all the conflicts analyzed in this book, those in Georgia are the ones where
the EU's potential influence is the lowest. As in any other conflict, the outbreak
and evolution of Georgia's conflicts is determined principally by the parties themselves, and not by external actors like the EU. The upheavals unleashed by the
break-up of the Soviet Union set the scene for the eruption of ethno-political
conflicts in Georgia and beyond. Georgia's troubled transition to independence
and Russia's persistent meddling in the region shaped the outbreak and outcome of the secessionist wars. Thereafter, unappealing Georgian peace proposals,

Shevardnadze's failing state and Saakashvili's more aggressive state did little to build inter-communal trust. In the meantime, the secessionist leaderships consolidated their commitment to independence and showed little interest in negotiations with Georgia. On the contrary, they established functioning de facto states, with legislative, executive and judicial organs. In their rhetoric and action, they have demonstrated their willingness to wait for a long as it takes to obtain international recognition. Especially in South Ossetia, the sustainability of the status quo is also bolstered by organized crime, which has generated strong vested interests in the continuation of the no-peace-no-war situation.

The competing rather than complementary nature of international mediation has also contributed to the conflict stalemate. The competing roles of Russia, the UN, the OSCE and the US have added confusion without reversing facts on the ground. The status quo has helped Russia retain its grip on Georgia and its sphere of influence in the Caucasus. However, Russian predominance in the region is also due to Georgia's own weakness and the unwillingness of other international actors to undertake Russia's functions. Hence, in 1993, Shevardnadze accepted Russian peacekeepers in Abkhazia and the retention of Russian bases in Georgia only when he appreciated that the West would not fill the potential void left by Russia's exit (Coppieters 2000b). Likewise, in 2003, Shevardnadze accepted the Sochi agreement with Russia partly out of frustration with the stalled UN process in Abkhazia. Equally noteworthy is the fact that the UNSC unambiguously stated that UNOMIG would leave Abkhazia in the event of a withdrawal of the Russian peacekeepers (Antonenko 2005: 234).

The effectiveness of the UN and the OSCE, as international organizations rather than monolithic actors, is also hindered by their internal divisions. The divisions between Russia and other member states caused repeated deadlocks. The three-year negotiation within the Group of Friends of the UNSG (rather than between the conflict parties themselves) on the Boden document best illustrates this deficiency. Russia's veto, blocking the renewal of the OSCE border monitoring presence on the Georgian–Russian frontier is another case in point. International organizations are also weakened by their 'state-centric' bias. Both the UN and the OSCE – representing communities of states – are inherently biased against secession. This has made them automatically more supportive of Georgia, while losing much, if not all, credibility amongst the Abkhaz and Ossetians.

Finally, the US has become increasingly active in the region and its presence has partly added to the competing nature of international involvement. Since the early 1990s, Georgia has been one of the principal beneficiaries of per capita US aid, reaching up to $3bn over the course of 1992–2005. In 2005 Georgia was earmarked for the US 'millennium challenge account' with $295m to be disbursed over five years. The US has also strongly and consistently backed the Baku–Tbilisi–Ceyhan pipeline, in view of its political (rather than purely commercial) interest to bypass both Russia and Iran. Washington backed the pipeline project well before major Western companies and the Europeans subscribed to it. The 11 September 2001 attacks deepened US involvement in Georgia, both because Georgia lies at the centre of the newly defined 'Greater Middle East' and because of the alleged evidence of al-Qaeda camps in Georgia's Kodori and Pankisi gorges. In 2002–4 the US carried out its 'train and equip' operation to upgrade Georgian defence capability in counter-terrorism. This has been followed up by a $60m 'sustainability and stability operation programme' in 2005. Russia may have benefited from increased Georgian ability to restore order in the Pankisi gorge, where Chechen fighters allegedly took refuge. Yet, added to Georgia's participation in NATO's Partnership for Peace and its ambitions to enter NATO, US involvement in the Georgian defence sector is viewed with scepticism in Moscow and has reduced Russian incentives to dismantle its military bases in Georgia.[12] Likewise, American involvement in Georgia's defence sector and the ensuing upsurge in Georgian military spending has deepened fears and suspicions in Abkhazia and South Ossetia.

With this wider picture in mind, let us turn to the EU's involvement. In view of the international and domestic dynamics fuelling conflict, what policies have been pursued by EU actors and what has been their impact on the complex web of domestic, regional and international factors underlying Georgia's conflicts?

The value of the EU benefit: PCA, assistance and the ENP

Of the EU's contractual relations with its neighbours, Georgia, like the rest of the South Caucasus and Central Asia, has enjoyed the weakest relations with the EU.

The weakness of trade and aid ties with Georgia, Abkhazia and South Ossetia

In 1996 Georgia signed an EU Partnership and Cooperation Agreement, which included an institutionalized forum for political dialogue, as well as provisions on trade, economic cooperation, culture and technology. Beyond the agreement, which entered into force in 1999, the EU has provided financial assistance to Georgia. It has been Georgia's second largest donor (after the US), disbursing €420m between 1992 and 2004 (Commission 2005a). This has included mainly Technical Assistance for the Commonwealth of Independent States (TACIS), focussed on the rule of law, good governance, human rights, democracy, poverty reduction, infrastructure, and conflict prevention and rehabilitation. In addition, Georgia has been included in EU regional programmes such as Traceca (Transport Corridor Europe–Caucasus–Asia) and Inogate (Oil and Gas Transport to Europe), designed to provide road and rail transport, prior to the completion of pipeline projects.

Aid has also been targeted to the conflict zones (covering Georgia and the secessionist entities). Since 1997, the Commission has disbursed €9.5m to rehabilitate the Inguri hydroelectric power plant in Abkhazia (providing electricity to both Georgia and Abkhazia). Rehabilitation projects have been carried out in southern Abkhazia and western Georgia (particularly in Gali, Ochamchira, Tkvarcheli and Zugdidi) to the value of €4m, focussing on education, health, infrastructure, electricity and income-generation. Since 2006 under its 'decentralized cooperation', the Commission has financed projects in northern Abkhazia through local NGOs, often in partnership with international counterparts. These have focussed on the development of civil society, income generation, and strengthening human rights and the rule of law.

In South Ossetia, the Commission provided a first €3.5m TACIS grant in 1997, aimed at rehabilitation projects with a clear bi-communal focus. It followed with a second €1.5m tranche to reactivate the Gori-Tskhinvali rail link and the Tskhinvali rail station. A third €2.5m package in 2003 was directed to rehabilitation and the construction/restoration of shelter for returnees. In addition, the Union, through three Common Foreign and Security Policy (CFSP) Joint Actions, has provided €500,000 to the JCC (Council 2001d: 4). In 2001 it co-financed the establishment of the JCC's Special Coordination Centre aimed at coordinating law enforcement in South Ossetia.

In the words of a European diplomat, aid to South Ossetia has 'bought the EU a role in the peace process'.[13] Indeed in view of its assistance to the conflict zone, the Commission has been invited to participate as an observer in the JCC and because of its direct assistance to the OSCE, the coordination with it on the peace process has improved over time.[14] In Abkhazia, this has not been the case, although three EU member states (France, Germany and the UK) are present in the Friends of the UNSG.

But, given the unsuccessful record of these peace processes, a seat in mediation forums has not entailed a positive let alone significant EU impact on conflict resolution. This raises the wider question of whether the EU's economic rather than political focus has, and can have, objective value and impact on conflict resolution efforts. Some argue not. In Georgia, the EU's economic role devoid of a political component has been criticized for adding to the sustainability of the no-peace-no-war status quo, for benefiting elites rather that the affected population, and for granting an implicit form of recognition to the secessionist entities.[15] The Abkhaz and Ossetians have complained that the EU's effectiveness has been hampered precisely by its excessive caution in avoiding official contact with the authorities. In Abkhaz eyes, this has reduced the magnitude of projects (given that the largest and most salient projects require coordination with the authorities). It has distorted the geographic nature of projects (most EU projects are focussed on the 1998 conflict zone in the Gali district, predominantly inhabited by Georgians rather than Abkhazians). It has also altered their thematic focus (predominantly on issues that can be tackled by NGOs and international organizations rather than by government authorities).

However, on closer inspection, the EU's economic focus appears to be well placed. First this is because there is no scarcity of international actors involved in Georgia's peace processes, and this – far from facilitating conflict resolution – may have complicated peace efforts further. An additional EU voice within ineffective and overcrowded mediation forums is unlikely to improve peace prospects. On the contrary, the Commission's presence in the JCC has arguably reduced the relative effectiveness of the EU in South Ossetia compared to Abkhazia, precisely because EU initiatives require the consent of this cumbersome mediation forum.[16]

Second, by focussing on the domestic conditions within the conflict parties, rather than only on relations between them, the EU may play a more useful role in sowing the seeds for conflict resolution.

In this respect, the EU's marginal impact on Georgia's conflicts is more likely to be caused by insufficient 'quantity' rather than 'quality' of input. In other words, focussing on the political and economic conditions within the conflict parties is welcome. But the magnitude of EU involvement has been extremely limited, particularly when compared with other countries in the EU neighbourhood. As far as contractual relations are concerned, the PCAs do not compare with the benefits foreseen by EuroMed association agreements or Western Balkan SAAs, not to mention the accession process itself. In the sphere of trade, the PCA limits itself to the elimination of quotas, most favour nation treatment and the inclusion of Georgia in the generalized system of preferences. These agreements do not foresee preferential treatment and trade liberalization as other contractual relations do. When it comes to Abkhazia and South Ossetia, even these meagre benefits are largely precluded, owing to the problems of non-recognition. As far as aid is concerned, an annual average of €32m to Georgia, including Abkhazia and South Ossetia, pales into insignificance when compared with the over €300m disbursed to Palestine or Serbia and Montenegro.

Aware of its relative neglect of the region, the Council of Ministers has occasionally voiced the need for a more active EU involvement in the Caucasus (Council 2001a). EU declaratory expressions of interest rose especially in 2001–2, in the light of the security incidents involving EU citizens.[17] The EU Security Strategy pinpointed the South Caucasus as an area where the EU should take active interest (European Council 2003b). But little action followed suit, other than the appointment of an EU Special Representative (EUSR) for the South Caucasus, with a far too limited mandate to meaningfully contribute to conflict resolution. Moreover, when the EU first conceptualized its neighbourhood policy in 2003, the South Caucasus was excluded from it, despite the fact that the region would have sea borders with the Union after enlargements to Romania and Bulgaria and land borders after Turkey's accession.

European involvement has marginally increased since Georgia's 'rose revolution'. Immediately following Saakashvili's election, the Council asserted that '(T)he EU now looks forward to helping Georgia and the other countries of the South Caucasus come closer to the European family' (Council 2004a). In July 2004, under the Rapid Reaction Mechanism, the EU deployed a seven-month rule of law mission (EUJUST-THEMIS) recommending reforms in Georgia's judiciary. It also disbursed a complementary €5m aimed at promoting legal, electoral and administrative reform. When the OSCE border monitoring mission was not renewed in 2005, the EUSR's mission was extended to include a locally based support team to follow up the work of EUJUST-THEMIS and to provide assistance to Georgian border guards. This was well below Georgian expectations, which hoped to see the EU replace the OSCE monitoring mission. Fearing to be seen in Moscow as 'defending Georgia against Russia', the EU refused this invitation.[18] It did, however, offer technical assistance to Georgian border guards.

Most important, in June 2004 the South Caucasus was upgraded to participate in the ENP. In response to Georgian calls for greater EU involvement in conflict resolution in the Caucasus, the Union made some timid steps forward (Lobjakas 2006). It included conflict resolution in Georgia's ENP Action Plan and it renewed and reviewed the mandate of the EUSR for the South Caucasus. It was decided that EUSR Heiki Talvitie's successor, Peter Semneby should 'contribute' to conflict resolution, in cooperation with the UN and the OSCE, rather than simply 'assist' the efforts of those organizations (ICG 2006a: 23). However much to Georgia's dismay, EU institutions emphasized only the EU's role in rehabilitation rather than an active contribution to the process yielding a settlement (Commission 2005a).

Finally, despite the much-acclaimed EU promises to offer its neighbours a 'stake in the single market', EU actors have been extremely reticent towards Georgia. More specifically, the Commission has turned down Georgian requests for a free trade agreement and visa facilitation, and it has been cautious in embracing cooperation on issues such as border control, the fight against organized crime, and the inclusion of Georgia in EU transport and energy networks and programmes. Moreover, the limited benefits foreseen by Georgia's Action Plan in practice do not cover Abkhazia and South Ossetia, which are de facto excluded from the remit of EU contractual relations.

The publication of Georgia's Action Plan was initially scheduled for 2005. It was delayed by a dispute between Cyprus and Azerbaijan over direct Azeri flights to northern Cyprus. The political reasoning behind the delay was that it would send the wrong signals if the EU proceeded with Christian Georgia and Armenia, holding back its Action Plan with Muslim Azerbaijan. Yet to most observers, the delay was paradoxical given that the ENP, unlike EU multilateral policies, is intended to proceed bilaterally between the EU and its neighbours.

Timing and subjective value of EU relations

When looking at the question of value from the perspective of the third party itself, a more nuanced picture emerges. The EU has clearly asserted that Georgia is not expected to enter the accession process (O'Rourke 2005). While the ENP aims at preventing new dividing lines in Europe, it has not been designed as an antechamber to enlargement. Georgian authorities appreciate this fact. This has had two contrasting effects on the value ascribed by them to EU relations.

In the short term, the ENP has reduced the perceived value of EU relations. Georgians, Abkhazians and Ossetians view the conflicts through balance-of-power lenses. Altering conflict dynamics in their favour requires a change in the balance of power in their favour. In this context, the parties do not value highly the EU's role, which is perceived as long-term and structural rather than short-term and geopolitical. The 'great game' in the South Caucasus is dictated by 'real' actors, namely Russia and the US (as well as NATO), by energy politics, and by the role of other regional players such as Turkey and Iran. 'Soft' multilateral actors like the UN, the OSCE, the Council of Europe, or indeed the EU, are viewed as playing secondary roles. Notwithstanding Georgian appeals to the EU to take on a more pronounced role in the peace processes (in support for Georgia's territorial integrity), the Georgian government is under no illusion that its expectation will be met.[19] The Abkhaz and the Ossetians, which in balance-of-power terms view the EU alongside the US as being 'on Georgia's side', reject the EU's involvement in mediation.

A radically different picture emerges when turning to the parties' perceptions of the EU's long-term value. Particularly since the revolution, Georgia has placed utmost importance on its 'Europeanness'. Georgian leaders have often proclaimed their attachment to Europe in terms of history, geography and culture. The Georgian security strategy unambiguously points to EU integration as a strategic priority (Civil Georgia 2005). In July 2004, the government established a 'commission for Georgia's integration in the EU' chaired by the prime minister. The commission's mandate has been to work on the implementation of the PCA and to elaborate Georgian positions on the ENP. EU departments have been set up in several ministries, aiming to harmonize Georgian legislation with that of the EU. More directly related to the conflicts, the Union is viewed as having a critical value in reconstruction, reconciliation and in providing security guarantees. A 2005 survey revealed that over 80 per cent of Georgians aspire to EU membership (The Gallup Organization 2005).

The EU's short-term inadequacy and long-term potential have had a positive spin-off in Georgia. The ENP has been criticized by EU-aspirants such as the Ukraine and Moldova because it excludes the prospects of accession. This has not been the case in Georgia, despite the country's long-term aspirations to join the Union. Georgian civil society has viewed the ENP as a means to consolidate democracy, hedge against the revival of authoritarianism, embark on sustainable development, and therefore empower Georgia to assert its independence and resolve its conflicts. The Georgian government considers the ENP as a welcome break from the EU's neglect of the past and a step towards greater European integration. Despite EU declarations to the contrary, the government does not consider the ENP as a long-term substitute for accession.[20]

Viewed from Sukhumi and Tskhinvali, the EU's long-term value is not linked to membership aspirations and indeed up until 2002–3, the EU was hardly valued at all. This was both because of its extremely limited presence in the breakaway regions, and because their primary focus was on Russia. And to the extent that Russia itself has no prospects or desire of entering the EU, and indeed has been moving way from it, the appeal of EU integration did not strike a chord in Abkhazia and South Ossetia. This perception of the Union, particularly in Abkhazia, has changed since 2003–4. The rising EU assistance and the unwelcome Russian meddling in the 2004 elections in Abkhazia has made the Abkhaz readier to embrace a European involvement in their domestic politics and development.[21] This perceived value should not be overstated, largely because of the limited knowledge within the secessionist entities of the EU, which is in turn explained by their limited contact with EU actors. For example, having been entirely excluded from discussions and negotiations over the ENP, the secessionist entities have no awareness of the policy and its potential benefits.

The credibility of the obligations

Turning to EU obligations, Georgia's PCA, like other agreements of its kind, includes an essential elements clause mentioning democracy, international law, human rights and market economy, as well as a non-execution clause in the event of a breach of the essential elements. Article 3 of the agreement also calls for regional cooperation and good neighbourly relations. However, like the human rights clause in other agreements, these have not been used to exert ex post conditionality on either Georgia, or Abkhazia and South Ossetia.

EU credibility has been higher in the case of ex ante aid conditionality. In 2003, the Commission revised in advance of schedule Georgia's Country Strategy Paper because of the deteriorating security situation and the slow pace of Georgia's reforms. It bluntly stated that 'the Georgian government has not yet shown the level of commitment to reaching the policy objectives linked to assistance which the EU may legitimately expect' (Commission 2003e: 10 and 21). The Commission committed itself to strengthening TACIS conditionality in the areas of governance, poverty reduction, the rule of law, human rights and progress in the peace processes. It promised to target primarily those areas where the Georgian authorities demonstrated effective commitment to reform. It also enforced ex ante conditionality. In view of stagnant reform, annual assistance dropped from €47m in 1999 to €15–20m in 2000–3 (Commission 2003e: 21). Conditionality was also raised as an argument for the initial exclusion of the South Caucasus from the ENP.

Yet despite its credibility, EU conditionality has not noticeably influenced Georgia's reform momentum. Less still has it affected the peace processes. Conditionality has followed rather than led domestic change in Georgia. After the reduction in aid in 2000–3, the EU stepped up its assistance to post-revolutionary Georgia because of the new regime's greater commitment to reform. While between 1991 and 2003 annual aid average was €28m, it rose to €46m in 2004–5 (Prodi 2004). Aid conditionality on Georgia has thus been consistent, responding to trends in domestic reform – but it has not induced domestic change, let alone a revolution.

The reason for this insufficiency is mainly the low level of EU engagement with the Caucasus. Another problem, as far as the conflicts are concerned, is the EU's insufficient specification of conflict-related obligations, and the perceived illegitimacy of several of its objectives. The Commission has loosely stated that EU policies in the conflict zones would be conditional on progress in the peace processes (Commission 2003e), but little has been done to clarify exactly how progress would be measured. Furthermore, the EU's conflict-related objectives have been viewed as illegitimate by the secessionist entities, given the EU's unwavering commitment to Georgia's territorial integrity. This has reduced their incentives to engage with the Union.

Another reason for the ineffectiveness of EU obligations is the relative disadvantage of the EU's ex ante conditionality as opposed to the ex post approach adopted by other international actors. Ex ante conditionality is based on the concept of exclusion, i.e. a third state is excluded from an EU benefit as long as its accompanying conditions have not been met. While ex ante conditionality may be more credible (given the difficulty of withdrawing a benefit once it has been delivered), the case of Georgia highlights how exclusion can reduce the legitimacy, and thus the effectiveness, of ex ante conditions.

A comparison between the EU's ex ante conditionality and the Council of Europe's ex post conditionality exemplifies this point. Georgia entered the Council of Europe in 1999. The Council of Europe opted for inclusion, despite Georgia's violations of democracy and human rights. This empowered the Council of Europe to make clear and detailed criticisms of and recommendations to Georgia. In February 2004, the Venice Commission disapproved of Saakashvili's constitutional amendments which enhanced the role of the presidency (Parsons 2006). In May 2004, it condemned the excessive powers granted to the president in the constitutional law on Ajara (Council of Europe 2004a,b). In 2005, the Parliamentary Assembly of the Council of Europe harshly criticized the performance of post-revolution Georgia (Council of Europe 2005). In other words, by opting for inclusion, the Council of Europe, as opposed to the EU, has been better placed to openly criticize and to advance proposals to Georgia. The EU, particularly in its ENP Action Plan, relies on some of the recommendations of the Council of Europe on issues like the electoral law and local government. Yet the Action Plan's obligations, while clearer than those in the PCA, are nonetheless much less detailed and stringent than those advanced by the Council of Europe.

Exclusion rather than inclusion also reduces the scope for compliance through learning, given the less institutionalized and frequent contacts between the conflict parties and the EU. The potential for Georgia's EU compliance through learning is extremely circumscribed. Political dialogue at expert level started in 1997 and it was upgraded through the Cooperation Council, the Cooperation Committee and the Joint Parliamentary Committee when the PCA entered into force in 1999. However, the Cooperation Committee and the Joint Parliamentary Committee only meet once a year. When it comes to the secessionist entities, EU actors have had even more limited contact with the Abkhaz or Ossetian authorities, and the scope to influence them through dialogue and persuasion has been virtually nil.

The scope for influence on Georgia through learning has increased since 2004. On the one hand, the fact that a large number of post-revolution Georgian elites have studied and worked in Europe has facilitated the scope for learning. On the other hand, the EU's more pronounced involvement in particular sectors, such as the judiciary (through EUJUST-THEMIS) has raised the potential for domestic change through learning. It has also allowed the EU to rely on the recommendations developed by EUJUST-THEMIS to specify more detailed obligations in the Georgia Action Plan on issues pertaining to the judiciary and the rule of law. More generally, Georgia's inclusion in the ENP has provided greater exposure of Georgian officials to EU institutions, their values and modes of operation. Alas, this has not applied to the Abkhaz and South Ossetians.

The political management of EU policy towards Georgia and its conflicts

Political imperatives and political neglect are two key reasons explaining the EU's marginal involvement in Georgia and its conflicts and thus underlying most of the deficiencies analyzed above.

The political imperative not to antagonize Russia has prevented the EU from deep involvement in Georgia's conflicts. Against the letter and spirit of the EU–Russia strategic relationship, it has also prevented the Union from raising the South Caucasus dossier in political dialogue with Russia (Lynch 2006: 70). Given the centrality of Russia's role in the continuation and/or resolution of these conflicts, this has created a self-imposed limit on the EU's potential to play a constructive role in the region. In view of the balance of power perceptions in the Caucasus, this weakness towards Russia has also reduced the EU's appeal and credibility in Georgia, Abkhazia and South Ossetia.

The Union justifies its absence from the peace processes on the grounds of a division of labour with other international actors. Indeed it would be futile for the EU to replicate the roles of UN, the OSCE or Russia. This is because of both the overcrowded international scene in Georgia's conflicts, and the likely opposition of Russia and the secessionist parties. Moreover, replication or attempted substitution would simply serve to reproduce the balance of power dynamics hindering conflict resolution in the region. As discussed above, the EU's value added is of a different nature. It is that of fostering long-term change within the conflict parties, rather than coercing change in relations between them. Yet by shying away from a more substantial engagement with the conflict parties and by failing to raise the issue of domestic change in the Caucasus in dialogue with Russia, the effectiveness of the EU's role has remained well below its potential. In addition, by not engaging sufficiently with the secessionist parties, the EU has done little to prevent mistrust and siege mentalities there, and in turn it has pushed Sukhumi and Tskhinvali into Moscow's open arms.

The political imperative not to antagonize Russia explains EU ineffectiveness in the South Caucasus only when considered alongside a second political factor, namely that of neglect. Particularly when compared with the EU's involvement in other neighbouring countries, the EU's role in Georgia in general and in Georgia's conflicts in particular, has been marginal. The EU's alleged strategic interest in the South Caucasus has not translated into a substantial policy involvement in the region. This is partly because Georgia's conflicts – unlike those in the Balkans or in the Middle East – have not struck a moral chord amongst European publics. It is also because the seemingly 'frozen' nature of these conflicts has reduced European incentives to actively promote their resolution. Even when conflicts have manifested their 'unfrozen' nature, violence has been relatively contained and it has not threatened major European interests. Beyond the rhetoric, it remains to be seen whether the East European enlargement and the 2006 energy crisis will alter the EU's traditional neglect of the South Caucasus.[22]

Table 5 Georgia's secessionist conflicts and EU relations with Georgia

Population (2006)	4.47m in Georgia; 150,000 in Abkhazia; 35,000 in South Ossetia	
Key Historical Dates	1783	Russian expansion into the Caucasus until the 1870s
	1864	Abkhazia is the last Caucasus entity to fall under Tsarist rule
	1918	Establishment of an independent state of Georgia
	1921	Soviet annexation of Georgia. Abkhazia enters the Soviet Union as a separate SSR
	1931	Abkhazia's status as an SSR is abolished
	1936	Abkhazia is downgraded into an autonomous republic of the Georgian SSR. South Ossetia is given the status of autonomous region in Georgia
	1989	Mass mobilizations and armed clashes in Abkhazia. Unrest in South Ossetia
	1990	Gamsakhurdia abolishes South Ossetia's region status
	1991	Georgia declares independence and Gamsakhurdia is elected president. War in South Ossetia. Civil war in Georgia
	1992	South Ossetian ceasefire agreement. Gamsakhurdia's ousting through a military coup and return of Shevardnadze to Georgia. Eruption of war in Abkhazia
	1993	End of war in Abkhazia
	1994	Abkhazia ceasefire agreement. Abkhaz declaration of sovereignty
	1998	Armed clashes in Abkhazia and renewed IDP flows
	1999	Abkhazia declares independence
	2003	'Rose revolution' in Georgia ousting Shevardnadze
	2004	Armed clashes in South Ossetia. Presidential elections in Abkhazia with heavy Russian meddling
EU Relations	1999	The EC–Georgia PCA enters into force
	2005	The South Caucasus is included in the ENP
	2006	EU publishes its ENP Action Plan for Georgia
EU Financial Assistance	€420m in assistance to Georgia in 1992–2004 (approximately €32m per year). Approximately €14m to Abkhazia in 1997–2006 (including the rehabilitation of the Inguri dam). Approximately €8m to South Ossetia in 1997–2006	

Political neglect has prevented the formulation and implementation of a coherent EU strategy towards Georgia's conflicts, which has reduced the potential impact of EU instruments in the region. This has remained the case despite the presence of the EUSR and the inclusion of the South Caucasus in the ENP. As put by one scholar, the 'EU's common foreign and security policy in the South Caucasus is neither sufficiently common nor sufficiently clear to be perceived in the region as being a "policy" ' (Coppieters 2004: 4).

8 Comparing the EU's role in neighbourhood conflicts

This book has analyzed the EU's role in five neighbourhood conflicts through the conduct of different types of contractual relations. This chapter draws together these empirical findings, examining comparatively the EU's role. It first compares the EU's impact on several dimensions of conflict. It then assesses comparatively the effectiveness of EU contractual relations in the field of conflict resolution.

Conflict dimensions and EU impact

When analyzing EU impact on conflict resolution, the first observation to make is that the evolution of the conflicts under examination has neither matched the EU's declared objectives (with the partial exception of Turkey's Kurdish question), nor any other form of peaceful resolution (with the exception of Serbia–Montenegro). Despite the inherent limits of the EU's potential contribution, what has been the actual impact of EU contractual relations on the different dimensions fuelling these conflicts or promoting their resolution?

Separatism

Not all five conflicts can be defined as separatist. The Israeli–Palestinian conflict is certainly *sui generis* in this respect. Rather than the Palestinian minority, it is metropolitan state Israel that wishes to 'secede' from the Palestinians, albeit not from most of their inhabited territory. The desire for this form of secession is due to the metropolitan state's appreciation that the minority will become a demographic majority before long, and that this would ultimately impede its continued political control of the state. In conflicts such as Cyprus or the Kurdish question, the minority does not define itself as secessionist. Segments within the minority may claim that secession is the only viable solution because of the majority's reluctance to share power with it (in the case of Cyprus) or accord it specific rights (in the case of the Kurds). Yet in both cases, when secession is espoused, it is explicitly articulated as a means to attain the goal of self-determination. This contrasts sharply with Montenegro and Abkhazia, where secession and independence are seen as an integral element of the national cause.

Turning to the EU's role, it is important to note that the EU has generally resisted secession. With the exception of the Israeli–Palestinian conflict, where the Union has vociferously promoted a two-state solution, the EU has been notoriously conservative on secession. This has reflected partly the disinclination of the international community to recognize new states, and partly the need for EU consensus, which has raised the Union's caution in breaking with broad international norms like that of territorial integrity. In addition, when it comes to neighbours with a prospect of accession, EU actors have often opposed separatism, given their preference for absorbing a smaller rather than larger number of new states. Yet despite this inbuilt opposition to secession, EU contractual relations have not always acted against it.

The secessionist drive in Montenegro was the most successful, despite the EU's reluctance to accept it. Montenegro's drift towards secession began under Milosevic's rule, when the international community – including the EU – aided Podgorica in detaching itself from Belgrade. Montenegro's separatism then embarked on the path of legalization through the Belgrade Agreement and the Constitutional Charter, mediated by the EU High Representative himself. While retaining a constitutional link between the two republics, these agreements legalized Montenegro's independence in most policy areas. Full legal separation then culminated after the expiry of the three-year 'trial' period of the State Union, with Montenegro's independence in 2006. EU contractual relations unwittingly strengthened the Montenegrin government's unwavering commitment to independence during the lifespan of the State Union. The conduct of a single SAP with Serbia and Montenegro generated strong Montenegrin feelings of being slowed down in terms of European integration by Serbia's deeper reform problems. The Commission's insistence on greater centralization at the federal level also raised Montenegrin resentment against the State Union.

In Abkhazia and South Ossetia separatism has also been strong, but unlike Montenegro, rather than drifting towards legalization, it has moved towards assimilation into Russia. As in Montenegro, the Caucasian de facto entities have been committed to independence and have established governing institutions to serve that end. Yet, as opposed to Montenegro, the EU's impact on Abkhaz and South Ossetian separatism has been virtually nil. Although the Commission's financial assistance has contributed to the domestic development of the secessionist entities, its involvement has been too limited to have a visible impact on their commitment and pursuit of independence.

Unlike Montenegro and the Caucasus, the Turkish Cypriot commitment to separatism has oscillated over the years. Rauf Denktaş believed that because of the ossified Greek Cypriot commitment to domination, Turkish Cypriot self-determination could only be achieved through a confederation, independence, or integration with Turkey. In the latter half of the 1990s, trends moved towards the de facto integration of northern Cyprus into Turkey, and were unwittingly fuelled by EU policies. By proceeding with Cyprus' accession process without an accompanying accession strategy towards Turkey, EU policies strengthened the Turkish–Turkish Cypriot commitment to secession. The tide reversed in 2003–5.

With the advent of the AKP government in Turkey, Ankara slowly disowned its long-held claim that a solution based on partition was reached back in 1974. This was matched by a quasi-regime change in northern Cyprus, and an ensuing commitment to a federal solution along the lines of the Annan Plan. Cyprus' imminent EU entry coupled with Turkey's accession process and mounting EU pressure on Turkey played a key role in triggering this shift. Yet since the failed referenda in 2004, there has been a marginal retrenchment in northern Cyprus. This has been fuelled first and foremost by disillusionment with the Greek Cypriot rejection of the Annan Plan, but also by the EU's unfulfilled promises to lift the isolation of the Turkish Cypriots.

Also the Kurdish commitment to secession has oscillated, although it never had a chance of realization in view of the overwhelming strength of the Turkish state fighting against it. In the mid-1980s, the PKK launched its violent attack against the state, in pursuit of an independent Kurdistan. As in the Caucasus, the EU had virtually no impact on Kurdish separatism during this period. After 1999, the PKK embraced the goal of a democratic Turkey in which Kurdish citizens could enjoy individual and minority rights. These calls were echoed by non-militant Kurdish civil society groups and political parties. In addition to the capture of PKK leader Öcalan, the switch in Kurdish goals was influenced by the launch of Turkey's accession process. The debilitating effect of Öcalan's capture on the PKK's capability dovetailed with the perceived opportunities embedded in Turkey's accession course. This created a discursive context for Kurdish actors to redefine their aims, shifting away from separatism and violence and towards a democratic and rights-based solution within EU candidate Turkey (Gunter 2000). However, the EU accession process was not enough to alter the PKK's stance and conduct. With the end of its unilateral ceasefire in 2004, the PKK has shifted back to more hardline positions, pursuing through violence an amorphous stateless pan-Kurdish confederation.

As in the Kurdish case, the would-be secessionist force in the Middle East (i.e. the Palestinians) has been unambiguously the weaker side in the conflict. However, unlike the Kurds, this weakness has not ruled out separatism. On the contrary, the growing consensus amongst the Zionist establishment, supported by the vast majority of Israeli Jewish public opinion, is the desire to disengage from the Palestinians and from the conflict. This desire has been fed by a security logic and by demographic calculations (Sussman 2004). Hence, the 1993–2000 Oslo process, the post-2002 construction of the West Bank barrier and the 2005 Gaza disengagement. On the Palestinian side, the existence of the PA has facilitated Israel's separatism, while the suicide bombing campaign fed the appeal of separation amongst the Israeli public. Yet, in a context of Israeli dominance and Palestinian weakness, separatism has not brought with it a viable Palestinian state, but has rather reduced the prospects for it. Despite its support for a two-state solution, the EU's policies have reinforced this trend. Over the Oslo years, the EU supported the PA and the peace process, without paying much attention to the PA's performance or to Israel's expanding grip on the OTs. Since then, EU efforts have mitigated the humanitarian effects of the intifada by pouring aid into Palestine.

Yet aid, coupled with acquiescence, has supported in practice Israel's peculiar brand of separatism.

The metropolitan state

A second dimension of conflict is that of the metropolitan state, its internal dynamics and the manner in which these have influenced relations with the minority community. In the Balkans, Serbia and the federal state have been the relatively weaker side of the conflict. Serbia undoubtedly has key advantages compared with Montenegro in terms of size and political status. In particular, the EU's recognition of Serbia as the successor state of Yugoslavia in all its reincarnations and its aversion to secession explain the EU's mediation of the Belgrade agreement and its commitment to the State Union until 2006. Nonetheless, Serbia has been debilitated by the legacy of Milosevic's rule. EU and US–NATO sanctions and military action contributed to the downfall of Milosevic, while leaving post-Milosevic Serbia on its knees. This diminished Serbia's potential to act as a pole of attraction for the smaller Montenegrin economy, and encumbered Serbia with onerous national questions, which raised Montenegro's separatist instincts. Since 2000, the EU has supported Serbia in meeting its challenges by engaging it in the SAP but this has fallen short of providing incentives for the State Union to survive, even amongst some actors in Serbia.

In Georgia also, the metropolitan state is weak. This weakness hinders conflict resolution by invalidating Georgia as a credible negotiating partner and blackening its image as a country worth reintegrating into. Georgia's weakness has been the product of civil war, military defeat and ill-governance; developments on which the EU's impact has been negligible. The 'rose revolution' reversed this failing trend, transforming Georgia into a far more confident country, which has made impressive steps towards modernization. However much remains to be done, and post-revolution Georgia displays greater propensity for military confrontation towards its adversaries. The extension of the ENP to Georgia and Saakashvili's declared commitment to Europeanization has raised the EU's scope to influence Georgia's reforms. Yet EU influence remains marginal, and it has not been used to placate Georgia's increased propensity for brinkmanship as a means to settle its conflicts.

In Cyprus instead, while unable to reverse the post-partition status quo, the metropolitan RoC has benefited from key advantages, making the Greek Cypriot community reluctant to rescind its status through a federal compromise. Since 1964, the international community has recognized the Greek Cypriot side as the only legitimate state on the island. Recognition has given Greek Cypriots exclusive direct access to international forums, which they have used to garner external support and legitimacy, particularly after 1974. Superior political standing has been matched by economic performance. After the trauma of 1974, the Greek Cypriot economy boomed through tourism, trade and offshore financial services. The EU accession process bolstered these advantages. By applying for and pursuing membership, the Greek Cypriot side strengthened its bargaining position, its leverage on Turkey and its sense of security. While these gains moderated the views of the former Greek Cypriot leadership, they contributed to the Greek Cypriot rejection of the Annan Plan and to the RoC's hardening stance since accession.

By contrast, in Turkey and the Middle East, the metropolitan state has been the stronger party in the conflict. This strength has been manifested principally through military might and political coercion. As such, while temporarily quelling the most acute manifestations of minority violence, metropolitan strength has often fuelled conflict rather than sown the seeds for resolution. This was clearly the case of Turkey in the 1980s and 1990s. On the one hand, the strength of the Turkish state manifested itself through a coercive security logic, countering the Kurdish insurrection with all means at its disposal. On the other hand, PKK violence empowered the Turkish security establishment by legitimizing a security-first logic. Yet while weakening the PKK's capability, an exclusive focus on security precluded the emergence of non-violent Kurdish voices and fomented the flames of Kurdish discontent. In those years, EU calls to tackle the Kurdish challenge through non-military means largely fell on deaf ears. With the initiation of the accession process, the EU instead helped desecuritize the Kurdish question and empower Turkish actors who were willing to tackle issue through alternative instruments. However, the post-2004 resurgence of PKK violence, coupled with a new wave of Turkish nationalism have slowed down the process of reform. These domestic trends have been strengthened by the doubts expressed in Europe on the desirability of Turkey's membership.

In Israel also, a security-first approach coupled with a unifying Zionist ideology set the tone of Israel's conduct in the conflict. The 1967 Israeli victory imbued the largely secular Zionist movement with a revisionist zeal to accomplish the messianic dream of controlling the entire land of Greater Israel. Key institutions have promoted this goal, planning and implementing Israel's expanding grip on territory. In addition, a security-first approach is firmly rooted in society. Israel's self-image as a small fledging state in the midst of a hostile and violent Middle East explains the prioritization of security and of security-based institutions such as the Israel Defence Forces. The EU has exacerbated these dynamics through acquiescence. More so than in the case of Turkey, the EU's rhetoric has condemned Israel's security measures and violations of international law. Yet, unlike in the Kurdish case, the Union has accepted Israeli calls to 'compartmentalize' the conflict in the conduct of their contractual relations. This has resulted in EU acquiescence and in the Union's contribution to an international environment that has allowed Israel to operate above international law.

The regional dimension

A third dimension of conflict broadens out the level of analysis to encompass the wider region, including kin-states or neighbouring countries. EU contractual relations have influenced the regional dimension either through contractual relations with the neighbouring/kin states themselves, or through an indirect impact of contractual ties with the conflict parties.

In Cyprus, an analysis of conflict requires an assessment of developments within and between kin-states Greece and Turkey. Over the 1990s, regional dynamics in the eastern Mediterranean exacerbated the Cyprus conflict. The mid-1990s saw the resurgence of Greek–Greek Cypriot nationalism, expressed especially in joint defence initiatives. Turkey and the Turkish Cypriots instead proceeded with closer political and economic integration. Greek–Turkish relations also worsened, reaching the brink of war in 1996 over the disputed sovereignty of the Aegean islets of Imia/Kardak. EU contractual ties with Cyprus and Turkey fuelled these trends. Turkey's annexationist policies towards northern Cyprus were announced in response to the RoC's accession negotiations coupled with Turkey's exclusion from the accession process. These negative dynamics reversed in 1999 through a change in the regional and the EU context. Greek–Turkish relations embarked on an unprecedented rapprochement. This moderated the PASOK government's stance on the conflict and raised its incentives to accept Turkey's EU's membership aims. Turkey's also altered its position on a Cyprus settlement after 2002. This occurred when the momentum of its EU accession process accelerated with the approaching prospect of opening accession negotiations.

In the Palestinian case, the pan-Arab dimension of the conflict has different aspects. Some Arab neighbours are at peace with Israel (Jordan and Egypt). This set the context for the Oslo process and it has influenced Israel's policies towards the West Bank and the Gaza Strip since then. Other Arab neighbours have their own territorial conflicts with Israel (Syria and Lebanon). These impinged on the Israeli–Palestinian peace process (e.g. Ehud Barak's initial preference for the 'Syrian track' at the expense of the Palestinian one in 1999–2000) and have generated unsavoury parallels fuelling escalation (e.g. between Hamas and Hizbollah's strategies and Israel's response to them). Finally, some Arab countries are enmeshed in the Israeli–Palestinian conflict itself, in view of their hosting of large Palestinian refugee communities (Jordan, Syria and Lebanon). Despite its importance, the EU has tended to neglect this regional dimension. In addition, EU relations with the Palestinians has increasingly focussed on the PA rather than on the PLO across the Diaspora. While this was done with the explicit aim of supporting a Palestinian state, in practice it has fed intra-Palestinian divisions besieging conflict resolution efforts.

In the Kurdish case also, the regional dimension involves countries hosting kin-communities.[1] The scattering of the Kurds across Iraq, Iran and Syria facilitated the operation of the PKK from Syria and Lebanon in the 1980s and from northern Iraq in the 1990s and 2000s. It has threatened war on some occasions (e.g. between Turkey and Syria in 1998), and it has acted as a coalescing factor in the region on other occasions (e.g. in the wake of the 2003 US war in Iraq). The regional dimension has also inspired Kurdish nationalist objectives. The PKK's original goal was that of establishing a pan-Kurdish state precisely in view of the pan-Kurdish dimension. More recently, the slide towards independence of Iraqi Kurdistan has re-ignited nationalist sentiment amongst Turkey's Kurds. As in the case of the Palestinians however, the EU has by-and-large neglected this regional dimension.

While EU actors have acknowledged their contribution to Turkey's Kurdish question, they have resisted involvement in its regional ramifications.[2] This is not to say that EU–Turkey relations have not impinged on this regional dimension. Put bluntly, if the concrete option before Turkey's Kurds is EU membership within a democratic Turkey or quasi-independence within a war-torn Iraq, the majority would opt for the former.[3] As such, EU–Turkey relations have indirectly impinged on the appeal of pan-Kurdish objectives amongst Turkey's Kurds and thus on the evolution of the Kurdish question.

In Serbia–Montenegro, the regional dimension is not 'kin-related', but rather linked to the interconnected history of unity and violent fragmentation in former Yugoslavia. Serbia's legacy of war in the Balkans and its policies towards Kosovo sparked Montenegro's desire to secede. However in 2001–2, the regional implications of Montenegro's secession were amongst the most important driving forces of the Belgrade agreement and the EU's muscular mediation of it. The escalation of tensions in Macedonia, the fear of irredentism in Republika Srupska and the uncertainty over Kosovo's status exacerbated European and Serbian unease about Montenegrin independence. Finally and more positively, reform and reconciliation in the region generated a more conducive environment for the 2006 Montenegrin referendum. The EU contributed significantly to this transformed regional context. EU-induced regional cooperation schemes, the SAP's support for domestic reform and European integration in the Western Balkans, Solana's prevention of the Macedonian conflict, and the international consensus in favour of tackling Kosovo's status all provided a more tension-free environment for Montenegro's secession.

The regional dimension of Georgia's conflicts is also related primarily to history, despite the presence of many Russians in Abkhazia and in South Ossetia, and the ethnic bonds between North and South Ossetia. The regional-Russian dimension of Georgia's conflicts resembles most that of Turkey in Cyprus. As in Cyprus, the Abkhaz and South Ossetians would not have been able to assert and sustain their de facto separation without Russian support. But notwithstanding Russia's key importance in these conflicts and their prospects for resolution, the EU has once again shied away from this regional dimension. This has avoided an antagonizing EU role in the Caucasus, exacerbating the balance of power logic prevalent in the region. However, the EU's neglect of the Russian dimension has handicapped its potential impact on the conflicts.

The international dimension

A final dimension of conflicts is the international one. This includes both the form and substance of international mediation and peacekeeping, as well as the main sources of influence of the major international players.

The formal involvement of the international community in Turkey's Kurdish question is absent, largely because of the Turkish state's refusal to accept international mediation or peacekeeping. The absence of a formal international role has allowed the principal parties to act in a largely unrestrained manner in their struggle.

Despite this, the EU has not mobilized EU–Turkey relations to 'internationalize' peacemaking efforts. Yet the absence of a formal international dimension has not made the Kurdish question immune to international repercussions. Following the US invasion of Iraq in 2003, there has been a growing rift between Turkey and the US administration over the former's accusation of the latter's insufficient effort to combat the PKK in northern Iraq. The EU has deliberately kept clear of Turkish–US relations. However, the accession process may have imbued the Turkish state with greater confidence to criticize American involvement in Iraq.

By contrast, the involvement of the international community in the Caucasus and in the Middle East is formalized; yet it is skewed and overcrowded, contributing to the frozen nature of the peace processes. In the Caucasus, Russia's overpowering role was institutionalized in mediation and peacekeeping. Alongside Russia, there has been a weak UN and OSCE presence, within which Western actors have conducted their relations with sporadic attention and uneven effort. Russian predominance, Western neglect and weak international organizations have fed each other. Russia's overpowering role is partly the result of Western unwillingness to assume greater responsibilities in peacemaking. This has added to the ineffectiveness of international organizations in the region. International overcrowding has also resulted in deadlock within international organizations and forums. Rather than mediating between the parties, external actors have tended to reproduce confrontation at the international level. In South Ossetia, the EU has 'paid its way' into the peace process. But precisely in view of its frozen and overcrowded nature, the Commission's observer status in the JCC has had little concrete effect. In fact, the EU's non-participation in the Abkhaz peace process may have been wiser. Not only is this peace process even more deadlocked, but the Commission's participation in it could hinder its direct involvement in developing the Abkhaz economy and polity.

In the Israeli–Palestinian case, international mediation is also skewed, this time with a preponderant US role. Over the Oslo process, the US was the only mediator in the conflict, with the EU playing second fiddle to it. Yet the US's specific interests in the region and its strong ties to Israel have hindered Washington's ability to act as a powerful yet impartial mediator. The flaws inherent in this skewed role were evident in the structure and conduct of the Oslo process itself, which came to the fore at the Camp David II summit and the ensuing explosion of the second intifada. Since then, the international dimension has changed in form but not in substance. With the creation of the Quartet in 2001, the mediating role of the EU, as well as of the UN and Russia, were formally added to that of the US. Yet neither did the Quartet alter the underlying dynamics of external involvement, nor did the EU effectively use the Quartet to establish its own direct role in peacemaking. The institutionalization of the EU's role was unsuccessfully used to induce Washington to re-engage in muscular mediation. More generally and detrimentally, it has added to the misperception that an international peace process was still ongoing.

In Cyprus, the UN has acted as the main international forum within which to conduct the peace process (Mirbagheri 1998; Richmond 1998). Since 1964, there has been a UN peacekeeping force in Cyprus. UNFICYP has provided stability in Cyprus, while being unable to prevent the eruption of violence in the 1960s and in 1974, and contributing to the 'frozen' status quo since them precisely in view of its stabilizing role. The UNSG has instead been the key mediator of a federal solution. Particularly in 1986–7, 1990–2 and 2002–4, the UNSG invested significant resources in the peace process, going beyond his formal mandate to provide 'good offices'. This effort stands out starkly when compared with the UN's involvement in Abkhazia. This is not least because in Cyprus, as opposed to Georgia, the UNSC has generally agreed on the contours of an acceptable settlement. Yet this international consensus has neither translated into a real and constant attention to the conflict, nor into the necessary resources deployed to promote a solution. Hence, the UN could not generate the necessary incentives to seal a deal. This is where the EU accession process stepped in. On the positive side, it added momentum and incentives in the UN peace process, as recognized by the UNSG himself (UNSG 2003a, paragraph 6). It also provided an appealing framework to embed a federal Cyprus (Tocci 2004b: 144–69). Yet on the negative side, the absence of direct EU involvement in the peace process created widespread misperceptions on the meaning of a solution in the EU. This paradoxically bolstered nationalist views and positions on both sides of the conflict.

Finally, in Serbia and Montenegro, an important international dimension is given by the role of the US and the international financial institutions (IFIs). Compared to the EU, both took a relatively hands-off approach to the State Union. IFIs took the decentralized division of competences as a given, interacting with the federal minister for international economic coordination to sign contracts, but negotiating their substance with the two republics.[4] This neither induced centralization, nor did it legitimize the chorus of cries against the State Union. The US instead, while paying lip-service to the State Union, did not view negatively its dissolution. Some American diplomats reportedly encouraged the development of Montenegro as a tourism and tax haven micro-state.[5] By contrast, the EU was far more adamant to see the State Union survive. This generated the perception in the region of an international division, which was conveniently used by domestic supporters and critics of the State Union alike. While supporters latched on to the EU's stance, critics bolstered their pro-Western credentials by focussing on Washington's more flexible views.

Comparing the effectiveness of EU contractual relations in conflict resolution

An analysis of the EU's impact on the different dimensions of conflict paints a mixed, albeit far from satisfactory, picture. Not only has the evolution of these conflicts rarely matched the desired outcomes advocated by the EU, but also the EU has often not contributed significantly or positively to an approximation of its desired goals. Let us move to a comparative analysis of why this has been the case.

The value of EU contractual relations

The five cases analyzed in this book enjoy a wide range of contractual ties with the EU, which allow for different degrees of European integration and assistance. These grant the Union different degrees of potential influence on the conflicts.

The objective value of contractual relations

The accession process and the prospect of membership in principle represent the most valuable offer the EU can make. Cyprus is thus the case with the strongest contractual relations with the Union, having embarked on an accession course in 1990, which was successfully concluded in 2004. This gave the Union higher potential to influence the Cyprus conflict than any other conflict in the neighbourhood. Cyprus' accession process provided strong objective gains to the Greek Cypriot community. The security gains embedded in the accession process raised the willingness of the Clerides government to compromise and seek an agreement prior to membership. However, the denial of those gains to the Turkish Cypriots, and the security risks they saw in the RoC's unilateral accession process, reduced Denktaş' incentives to negotiate a federal agreement.

Cyprus' accession process stands in sharp contrast to that of Turkey, which started a decade later and has been far more turbulent, uncertain and protracted. The ensuing lower value of Turkey's accession process reduced Ankara's efforts to alter its Cyprus policy in the 1990s, as well as to engage in a non-military solution to its Kurdish question. The EU's rejection of Turkey's candidacy between the 1987 Turkish application and the 1999 Helsinki European Council hardened the Turkish and Turkish Cypriot positions on the Cyprus conflict and made the EU's appeals on the Kurdish question go unheard in Ankara.

Turkey became more willing to reconsider its Cyprus and Kurdish policies after the EU upgraded its status from that of associate to that of candidate in 1999. So long as the EU excluded Turkey, it signalled to Ankara its unwillingness to share the burden of Turkey's security. This reduced Ankara's incentives to alter its domestic (e.g. Kurdish) and foreign (e.g. Cyprus) policies, both of which were considered as potentially risky for the country's security. Likewise, Turkey's Kurds became far more interested in the EU only after the beginning of the accession process, that promised the extension of political and socio-economic rights in Turkey. The same was true for the Western Balkans. So long as EU-induced regional cooperation initiatives were perceived as an alternative to membership, EU actors failed to exert significant leverage on the Western Balkans and on its arduous tasks of reconciliation and reform. As and when the SAP became a stepping stone to the accession process between the 2000 Feira European Council and the 2003 Thessaloniki European Council, EU actors gained greater influence and Solana succeeded in brokering a constitutional agreement with which neither Serbia nor Montenegro were fully content.

This is not to say that accession is a necessary requirement for an effective EU involvement in conflict resolution. Israel and the PA highlight how the EU can offer valuable benefits which are far removed from the goal of membership. Furthermore, the case of Israel shows how these gains can be increased, theoretically reaching the point of 'sharing everything but institutions', without opening the prospects of membership. In the Middle East and South Ossetia instead, aid has 'bought' the EU a place in the peace process. Although the advantages of playing a direct role in formal mediation are doubtful, they show how EU benefits need not be membership-related to be influential. Indeed in Abkhazia and the PA, both firmly excluded from the remit of enlargement, Commission assistance has contributed to shaping the domestic environment in a manner that could foster reform and conflict resolution. Yet the effectiveness of aid in conflict resolution depends critically on magnitude. The over €300m per year which went to the PA inevitably had far more weight in Palestine than the ten times lower amount given to Georgia.

Timing and the objective value of the benefit

The cases of Cyprus, Turkey and the Western Balkans also highlight the importance of timing in the delivery of EU benefits. On the one hand, a long-term gain can reduce the short-term incentives to engage in conflict resolution. Turkey's long-term accession process reduced the domestic incentives to alter Turkish policy on Cyprus or the Kurds. Domestic and foreign policy change in Turkey occurred only after 2002, with the approaching prospect of opening accession negotiations. Until then, the Turkish authorities felt that EU membership promises were projected in a far too distant future to be worth engaging in an immediate policy shift. In the Western Balkans also, the long-term nature of the SAP followed by the accession process reduced the incentives of Serbs and Montenegrins to engage in complex State Union politics. The gains of European integration were projected in a distant future, whereas the conflict parties were confronted in the present with painful and arduous reform challenges. This made Serbs and Montenegrins feel that they could not afford to indulge in complex federal constructs, unlike EU member states such as Belgium.[6]

On the other hand, the imminent or actual delivery of a benefit may have perverse effects on peacemaking efforts. In the case of the Greek Cypriots, this occurred under the Papadopolous government, when imminent EU entry and the gains associated with it, induced the Greek Cypriot government to reject the Annan Plan. Mutatis mutandis, the same may have occurred in Turkey vis-à-vis the Kurdish question. The decision to open accession negotiations with Turkey in 2005 has not prevented, and may have contributed to, the lull in Turkey's reform process. The opening of negotiations is not the aim of the accession process. Yet it is an important target in that process, which has projected Turkey into a new phase whose goal is membership itself. This is scheduled to happen, if at all, after 2014. Setting the next target in the accession process in a distant future, coupled with Turkey's fatigue effect of having met the benchmarks for opening negotiations, may have contributed to the stalled momentum in the country's reforms.

EU gains may thus be more effective in inducing conflict resolution when they can be graduated over time, even if their objective value is lower than that of membership. The SAP, the ENP and financial assistance highlight the gains of 'divisible' benefits, which can be delivered over time. In the Western Balkans, there is a sufficient number of targets in the SAP followed by the accession process to allow the Union to deliver its benefits gradually over time. If effectively used, this set of benchmarks can induce a sustained pace of reform and peacemaking efforts. The ENP also has this potential. While it is too early to tell, the benefits foreseen in the ENP Action Plans could be delivered over time in response to the reforms spelled out in the Action Plans. However while in the case of Israel, the EU is willing to offer a valuable set of new benefits, the same cannot be said of Georgia's Action Plan, which only modestly upgrades the weak ties in the existing PCA. Finally, aid is the instrument that best lends itself to graduated delivery. In the PA for example, EU assistance delivered over time and targeted to specific reforms played an important role in triggering key policy or institutional changes. The monthly delivery of EU budgetary aid in 2002–5 contributed to important institutional, constitutional and policy reforms in those years.

The subjective value of contractual relations

The importance of the objective value of EU contractual relations must be assessed in conjunction and interaction with the unfolding developments within and between the conflict parties. This determines the subjective value of EU contractual ties.

Subjectively perceived value depends on the views and objectives of domestic elites in power within conflict parties. Different views of EU benefits by different domestic actors can lead to policy reversals within a conflict party. In southern Cyprus, the Greek Cypriot establishment as a whole valued EU accession highly. But whereas the Clerides government was more inclined to accept compromise in view of the security guarantees embedded in membership, the ensuing Papadopolous leadership latched on to the stronger Greek Cypriot bargaining position derived from accession to extract concessions from Turkey and the Turkish Cypriots. This situation exacerbated after EU entry, as Papadopolous – much like Greece in the first decades of its membership – has exploited the benefits of membership to exert leverage on his rivals.

In northern Cyprus, Turkey and Georgia, policy changes following changes in government reflected different attitudes towards the EU itself. Whereas Denktaş viewed Cyprus' EU membership as a threat, his successor Talat rallied support for the Annan Plan precisely because a solution would bring with it EU accession. In Turkey, Ecevit's government turned down a federal settlement in Cyprus and failed to pursue energetically domestic reforms partly because EU accession was not genuinely supported by all the relevant forces within his coalition and in the wider establishment. For those in Turkey who were sceptical of membership, stalemate in Cyprus and a stalled political reform process was covertly viewed as a means to block the accession process. By contrast, the rise of the AKP government coupled with changing dynamics within state institutions and civil society, heightened Turkey's accorded value to its accession course. As such, Ankara became more willing to genuinely reassess its domestic and foreign policies. Also in Georgia, the 'rose revolution' and the regime change that came with it marked a decisive shift in attitudes towards the EU. While Shevardnadze paid lip-service to his European orientation, Saakashvili is far more genuine in his commitment to modernize Georgia through close ties with the EU. This also explains why – despite Georgia's declared ambition to enter the accession process rather than remain on the fringes of the EU – the Georgian government is well disposed towards the ENP, viewing it as a step towards deeper European integration.

This relates to the wider question of how a conflict party views its future orientation. In post-Milosevic Serbia and Montenegro, elites and publics alike view their future as being inextricably tied to that of the EU. This is not the case in the Middle East, where the Palestinians – like the rest of the Arab world (with the exception of Morocco) – have never expressed the desire to pursue EU integration. By contrast, in Turkey, beyond the general Kemalist tenet of Westernization, there are different degrees of genuine commitment to the specific goal of EU integration. According to some, Westernization could be secured more effectively and less expensively through NATO and close ties to European countries and the US. According to others, Turkey should forge additional alliances with Middle East and Eurasian countries.

In the secessionist entities instead, future orientations and views of the EU depend on the attitudes of the 'patron' states. After the Russian meddling in the 2004 Abkhaz presidential elections, Abkhazia has been visibly more interested in interacting with the EU. This is reminiscent of the rise in Turkish Cypriot incentives to enter the Union in 2001–2, partly caused by the growing public appreciation of Turkey's overbearing control over northern Cyprus. However, so long as the EU does not have a strong hold on the protector state itself, the secessionist entity's interest in the EU will necessarily remain circumscribed. Beyond kin-ties, this is because its non-recognized status makes the secessionist entity inherently dependent on the protector state. In other words, irrespective of the Abkhaz or Turkish Cypriot mixed feelings towards Russia or Turkey respectively, strong ties to Moscow and Ankara necessarily remain a cornerstone of their policies. Hence, the key difference between Cyprus and the Caucasus, which has entrusted the EU far more influence on the former than the latter. The fact that Turkey, despite its internal divisions, values EU integration highly and has embarked on an accession process, contrasts with Russia, which has no prospects of, or interest in, entering the EU.

Trust or mistrust of the EU is a another key variable affecting the perceived value of EU contractual relations. In Turkey, northern Cyprus, South Ossetia and Abkhazia, EU intentions are often viewed with mistrust. In Turkey, historical recollection, such as the legacy of the Treaty of Sèvres, has raised Turkish suspicions of European aims and intentions. Suspicion has increased, particularly at times of European reticence to accept Turkey into its fold. The breakaway entities in Cyprus and the Caucasus have instead been suspicious of the EU because of the

Union's unshakeable commitment to the territorial integrity of the metropolitan state and its reluctance to engage directly with the de facto authorities in these regions.

In the Western Balkans, the Middle East and the Caucasus, mistrust is also linked to perceptions of EU (in)capability. In the Western Balkans, this view is largely held because of the EU's legacy of passivity during the unfolding Balkan tragedy in the 1990s and its 'Balkan fatigue' particularly since the 2004 enlargement. In the Caucasus and the Middle East, scepticism of the EU's capability is linked to the balance of power logic prevalent in these regions. Viewed through these lenses, the EU is considered as inherently weak when compared with Russia in the Caucasus or the US in the Middle East. Hence, while Georgians and Palestinians would appreciate a muscular EU involvement in their conflicts, diluting the pre-dominance of the Russians and Americans respectively, they also doubt the EU's ability to contrast these powers.

Beyond elite views and public opinion, contextual factors also shape the per-ceived value of EU contractual relations. In Cyprus, the Turkish Cypriots became more receptive to the economic appeal of EU accession after their grave economic crisis in the late 1990s, exacerbated by Turkey's recession in 2001. This generated a strong sense amongst the Turkish Cypriots of the unsustainability and undesir-ability of the status quo. Likewise, while during the years of mounting violence in Turkey's southeast, a desecuritizing logic was unlikely to win the upper hand in the state's handling of the Kurdish question, Öcalan's capture provided a more propitious environment in which to pursue alternative solutions in the context of the accession process.

Subjective value however must be mapped against the perceived cost of the EU's demanded obligations embedded in contractual relations. While some coun-tries may value highly their contractual ties with the EU, they may not value them enough to engage in a serious reconsideration of their policies and conduct in conflict. Turkish nationalists genuinely believe that Turkey cannot afford to alter its Cyprus or Kurdish policies. This belief is key to understanding Turkish Euroscepticism and the lack of EU impact on some actors in Turkey. In Montenegro, although the Djukanovic government valued EU integration highly, it valued Montenegrin independence more. Even more starkly, in Israel, no matter how valuable relations with Europe may be, these are far from sufficient to induce the Jewish majority to revaluate the Zionist goal of securing a Jewish state. Israel is more inclined to seek its place in Europe through alternative forms of 'virtual membership'. As such it has received warmly the ENP.

Finally, the opposite problem arises when EU integration is valued more than conflict resolution. This was the case of the Greek Cypriots. Precisely because EU accession was pursued as a means to strengthen the Greek Cypriot position in the conflict, membership became the overriding goal of Greek Cypriot governments, over and above a rapid settlement of the conflict. The high living standards of the Greek Cypriots also meant that the RoC could afford to reject the Annan Plan, reap the benefits of membership, and then begin to seek a more favourable agreement. In Serbia also, the high value attributed to EU relations was precisely what reduced the incentives of some domestic actors to engage in State Union politics, given that the State Union's dysfunctionality hampered Serbia's pursuit of the SAP.

The credibility of the obligations

The credibility of the obligations is a second key variable conditioning the effectiveness of EU contractual relations and their impact on conflict resolution. A comparative analysis of the five conflicts reveals the determinants of credibility.

Ex post versus ex ante conditionality

What is the relative credibility of ex ante versus ex post conditionality? The 1963 EC association agreement with Turkey did not include ex post 'political conditionality' in the form of a 'human rights' clause. Hence, when EU actors tried to mobilize the association agreement as a source of leverage on the Kurdish question or Cyprus, their threats were dismissed by Ankara as illegitimate forms of pressure. This was particularly true in the run-up to the 1996 customs union agreement. Unlike the eastern Mediterranean association agreements signed in the 1960s and 1970s, the ensuing Euro-Mediterranean agreements with Israel and the PLO signed in the second half of the 1990s, included human rights clauses, which explicitly mentioned democracy and human rights. The same is true for Georgia's PCA. Yet the ex post conditionality in these agreements has never been used in practice. As such, it has lacked credibility and thus effectiveness.

This is not to say that ex post conditionality is inherently ineffective. The case of Georgia highlights the relative value of ex post conditionality, which is linked to the advantages of inclusion versus exclusion. Georgia's membership of the Council of Europe has entrusted that organization with greater legitimacy to criticize and advance recommendations to Georgia. By contrast, the EU, in view of its exclusionary approach towards the Caucasus, has been far more cautious in making specific requests. On the rare occasions in which it has, these have been criticized by domestic opponents, on the grounds of the EU's lack of legitimate standing in Georgia.

The EU, however, has been generally more effective in inducing conflict resolution through ex ante conditionality. EU impact on the Kurdish question became positive and visible after the launch of Turkey's accession process and the ex ante conditionality entailed in the Copenhagen political criteria. Turkey's accession process also raised the credibility of the ex post conditionality embedded in the membership obligations of pan-European organizations such as the Council of Europe. The shift in Turkey's approach to the ECtHR's judgements, on the stream of Cyprus property cases for example, is an interesting case in point. Whereas in the 1990s Ankara systematically ignored these judgements, in the 2000s it both paid the fine to Ms Loizidou (Loizidou v. Turkey) and has actively sought means to avoid future rulings against Turkey.

Effective ex ante conditionality is not limited to the accession process. Ex ante conditionality attached to financial assistance can also induce change within a conflict party. While this was not the case in Georgia, where conditionality followed rather than led domestic change; it was the case in Palestine. The EU's ex ante budgetary conditionality on the PA and the threat of suspending assistance to it promoted judicial and fiscal reforms in 2002–5. This is not to say that ex ante conditionality was fully effective in Palestine. Its limited credibility was largely self-imposed and linked to the EU's reluctance to see the PA collapse. The concomitant wish to exert negative conditionality on Hamas in 2006 while keeping the PA afloat has generated contradictory EU policies, which have undone the partial reform successes achieved in previous years. The ENP also offers the scope for ex ante conditionality, although its prospects appear poor in the cases analyzed in this book. With regard to the PA, the post-election crisis has frozen the ENP in the OTs. With regard to Israel, there has been no attempt to insert in the ENP Action Plan any form of political conditionality tied to the numerous EU benefits on offer.

The timing and targets of conditionality

Timing is important not only in affecting value, but also in determining the credibility of the obligations. The Middle East, Cyprus and the Caucasus highlight how EU conditionality in peacemaking is effective only when it is exerted on all conflict parties at the same time. If the EU exerts conditionality on PA reform but remains silent about Israel's expanding grip on the OTs, it cannot contribute meaningfully to a two-state solution. No matter how democratic or well-governed Palestinian institutions may be, they do not amount to the existence of a state. Similarly, the abandonment of EU conditionality on the Greek Cypriot side over the 1990s, followed by mounting EU pressure on the Turkish side in the 2000s, contributed to the successive retrenchments into nationalism first by one side and then by the other. This occurred because of the time gap in the accession processes of Cyprus and Turkey. This highlights how EU effectiveness in conflict resolution necessitates a similar degree of influence on all conflict parties, and thus the existence of similar contractual relations with them. This also explains why – in contrast to EU–Turkey relations – the EU's lack of influence and conditionality on Russia has castrated the Union's impact on peacemaking in the Caucasus.

Yet paradoxically, the EU's cross-cutting conditionality on Serbia and Montenegro also had a disincentivizing effect. The Commission's demands on both Serbia and Montenegro to pursue concomitantly domestic reforms, lest the SAP be suspended for both republics, generated resentment against the State Union amongst Serbs and Montenegrins. Key actors in Belgrade and Podgorica complained that their EU integration was being slowed down by the sluggish reform in the other republic. The pinnacle of this EU policy of linked conditionality was in March 2006, when Serbia's non-cooperation with the ICTY blocked SAA negotiations with both republics. This generated much resentment in Montenegro, which added weight to the government's independist platform in the referendum campaign.

The clarity of conditions

A third factor determining the credibility of conditionality, as well as the prospects for social learning and passive enforcement is the clarity of EU conditions. The importance of clarity stands out when conditionality on Turkey's individual human rights is contrasted with that on collective rights or specific 'Kurdish' issues. In the fields of individual human rights, democratic reform and the rule of law, the Commission made clear recommendations to Turkey. These acted as useful benchmarks for Turkey's reform process. Yet the same cannot be said of conditionality on minority rights or Kurdish-specific issues such as IDPs. These are the areas in the EU-induced reform process where progress has been the least. A lack of clarity in these fields reduced the potential for effective conditionality and passive enforcement. It also reduced the prospects for learning, given the unclear norms which candidate Turkey is expected to assimilate.

EU 'shyness' in specifying conflict-related obligations is not confined to the Kurdish question. In the Abkhaz, South Ossetian and Cyprus conflicts also, the Union has been reluctant to advance clear conflict-related recommendations. This is often because of the EU's absence from mediation forums. Hence, when the proposals spelled out by official mediators have been vague, as in the case of the UN in Abkhazia, the EU has limited itself to support open-ended ideas. In Cyprus, greater clarity in UN proposals came with the Annan Plan. Yet this occurred at a very late date in the accession process. Hence during the 1990s, EU calls for a bi-zonal and bi-communal federation were sufficiently vague for all parties to claim compliance.

In the EU's reform conditionality on the PA also, effectiveness has been hampered by conditions that were often incomplete, inadequate or inconsistent. In the area of judicial reform, EU conditionality was not followed up sufficiently to yield long-term results. In the area of executive reform, the EU focussed more on personalities (e.g. the empowerment of Abbas at the expense of Arafat in 2002–3) than on institutional structures. This led to time-contingent change, which was quickly reversed following a change in circumstances. Last but not least, EU conditionality neglected key questions lying at the core of Palestinian democracy and state-building, such as the non-inclusiveness of the political system or the duality between the PLO and the PA.

Twists in the mechanisms of passive enforcement

Passive enforcement can be more effective than conditionality as an instrument to induce change within and between conflict parties. This is because of its greater legitimacy and impermeability to the political influences of powerful third parties. The cases of Serbia–Montenegro and Turkey illustrate this point. In Serbia, Solana's strong pressure for the establishment of the State Union was articulated outside the confines of the SAP. In other words, EU pressure was exerted beyond the framework of contractual rule enforcement. Solana's leverage induced both parties to accept the Belgrade agreement. But it also generated resentment in the region and was viewed as illegitimate precisely because of its political rather than legal nature. The same is true in Turkey. So long as reforms related to the Kurdish question were pressed by EU actors outside the contours of the contractual relationship (i.e. association, which did not include human rights conditionality), pressure was viewed as illegitimate in Turkey. However, in contrast to the Balkans, Turkey's relative strength allowed Ankara to comfortably ignore the EU's calls in those years.

When Turkey entered the accession process, EU recommendations embedded in the rule enforcement context of the Copenhagen criteria had an entirely different effect. In this new context, Turkey understood that clear conditions such as the abolishment of the death penalty were not matters for political bargaining or sheer neglect. They were the essential preconditions for opening accession negotiations. While this passive enforcement approach to sensitive political matters was initially resisted by the Turkish establishment, it was ultimately accepted as a given. As such, once the Turkish establishment mustered sufficient will to proceed with the accession process, some of these reforms took place. Interestingly however, while the launch of accession negotiations has raised the passive enforcement characteristics of *acquis*-related matters, it has reduced those of political reforms. This is because when a candidate country begins accession talks, it should already comply with the Copenhagen political criteria. Hence, EU pressure on Turkey's political reforms since October 2005 has generated renewed resistance and resentment in Turkey.

In the case of Cyprus, this problem acquired far graver proportions. Especially after the 1995 decision to open accession negotiations with the RoC, EU actors rarely raised the wider political questions surrounding the legitimacy of an accession process with a divided Cyprus. Member states and EU institutions ignored the fact that Cyprus' compliance with basic political criteria such as democracy and good neighbourly relations was at best doubtful. This led to an unexpected twist in the mechanisms of passive enforcement. Until 1995, the Cyprus conflict and its implications on the applicability of the *acquis* in northern Cyprus was a major EU argument to raise conflict settlement as a precondition of the accession process. With the opening of accession negotiations and especially after the RoC's EU entry, *acquis* compliance paradoxically became a Greek Cypriot argument to reject the Annan Plan.

A similar problem occurred in the Western Balkans. The Commission, conducting the SAP, induced greater centralization in the State Union than that foreseen in the Belgrade agreement and the Constitutional Charter. It did so by focussing on the nuts and bolts of the *acquis* to be adopted in the region. This generated disincentives in both republics. It bolstered the views of Serbs who – like Greek Cypriots – preferred a centralized federation. It also generated resentment in Montenegro – as in northern Cyprus – which considered the Commission to be undermining the looseness embedded in the constitutional agreements brokered by Solana.

Beyond these twists and turns, by far the most counterproductive manner in which the EU has used passive enforcement is through outright neglect. This is the case of Israel and the origin rules problem, in which the EU has seriously damaged its credibility and that of the norms and rules it professes. It has done so by opting to set aside its legal mechanisms of passive enforcement, while seeking alternative channels to mitigate the costs of the ensuing legal violations. By doing so, the EU has not only accommodated illegal Israeli policies, but also risked bending its own rules and laws. It has also signalled to Israel and other third states that Community law is up for political bargaining.

Social learning and its limits

While far deeper and necessary to induce conflict resolution beyond conflict management and settlement, social learning is a long-term process. It requires deep and prolonged contact with EU actors and frameworks. Of the conflict parties studied in this book, Greece is the only one where genuine learning in the field of foreign policy and conflict resolution took place. Yet not only has Greece, an EU member state since 1981, used its membership to 'score points' against Turkey until the late 1990s; but also Greece's learning has manifested itself primarily at the level of elites rather than of the public at large. Even within elite circles, the merit for the shift in foreign policy owes much to the PASOK government of the late 1990s and early 2000s and to former Foreign Minister George Papandreou.

The record of all other conflict parties on the social learning front is far poorer. In the context of the accession process, the Greek Cypriots did undergo a process of learning in the latter half of the 1990s. Yet, this was confined to former leaders, who had governed the country (i.e. Clerides) or led accession negotiations (e.g. Vassiliou) over the decade of Cyprus' accession process. Genuine learning does not appear to have permeated the Papadopolous leadership, the majority of the establishment, or the public at large. Much like Greece in the 1980s and 1990s, the RoC is more inclined to exploit the advantages of membership to settle its scores with Turkey, than to genuinely re-evaluate its policies towards it. In the case of Turkey, a slow process of learning may be underway, particularly as its accession course gathers steam. While far from being complete, there seems to be a genuine reconsideration of Turkish aims and interests on key issues such as Cyprus and the Kurds. Yet change has occurred more through the empowerment of different domestic actors, than through the transformation of the same actors within the establishment.

The social learning potential of parties lying beyond the accession process is even weaker, highlighting another disadvantage in the EU's exclusionary approach. In Serbia and Montenegro, EU actors argued that a constitutional link between the two republics would act as a mini-experiment in European integration. This logic fell on deaf ears amongst Montenegrin independists. On the contrary, the dysfunctionality of the State Union delayed the SAP to the extent of hindering regular dialogue between the conflict parties and EU institutions. In the Balkans, and more so in the Caucasus and the Middle East, there has not been enough time and exposure to EU actors, arguments and norms for these to be genuinely assimilated by the conflict parties.

When it comes to unrecognized entities such as northern Cyprus, Abkhazia and South Ossetia, as well as to the marginalized Kurdish citizens in southeast Turkey or the boycotted Hamas in Palestine, the problem of access to the EU is even graver. In the case of Turkey's Kurds, while theoretically exposed to the accession process, in practice Brussels has not extended its influence to the underdeveloped southeast. Apart from a vague awareness of the desirability of 'more Europe' amongst Turkey's Kurdish citizens, the people of the southeast are hardly exposed to the EU. In the case of Hamas, the decision to place the entire organization on the EU's terrorist list – rather than individuals within it – has circumscribed EU contact with, and thus influence on, Hamas. In the case of unrecognized states, the problem of exposure and contact with the EU is both legal and practical. Because of the EU's reluctance to engage and interact with these conflict parties, their exposure to, and knowledge of, Europe is necessarily slim. As in the case of Hamas, this fuels siege mentalities and resentment, and pushes these entities into the arms of their protector states. The lack of contact with the external world also eliminates the scope for domestic change through learning, dialogue and persuasion.

The limits of learning are not only caused by the quantity and quality of contact. It can occur through accommodation or assimilation. When learning occurs through accommodation and it is limited to the discursive sphere, it can strengthen conflict dynamics rather than contribute to transcend them. In Cyprus, the discourse of the *acquis* and of a 'European solution' amongst the Greek Cypriots became a new and more acceptable way to legitimize long-held nationalist positions. In other words, Europeanization through learning occurred through the accommodation of a new EU discourse rather than through a genuine reconsideration of Greek Cypriot means and ends. Likewise in Montenegro, the Commission's preference for a more centralized State Union, relegitimized the Montenegrin opposition, which had been undermined by its pro-Milosevic legacy. But accommodation is not always negative. In Turkey's Kurdish question, a new EU discourse may not have altered substantive beliefs and objectives yet. Yet it has provided an alternative platform to discuss hitherto taboo subjects. As such, it is contributing to a new political space in which Turkish and Kurdish interlocutors can establish a future dialogue.

The political management of EU contractual relations

A last determinant of EU effectiveness in conflict resolution is the political management of contractual relations. Political management – beyond the blueprint of a contract – rarely bolsters the value of the contractual benefit and the credibility of the accompanying obligations. It rather tends to reduce the EU's scope to induce conflict resolution, and may instead entrench or escalate conflict dynamics.

EU neglect

In Cyprus, the Caucasus and Turkey, the lack of sufficient EU political interest in the conflicts has reduced the prospects for contractual relations to promote their resolution. Sheer neglect and reluctance to become enmeshed in complex peace-making efforts partly explain the EU's failure to promote peace in Cyprus, despite the appetizing offer of full membership and the conditionality that comes with it. With the exception of Greece and the UK, no other member state had strong or sustained interest in the conflict and its resolution. The seemingly frozen nature of the conflict reduced the perceived costs of its persistence in West European eyes. Its complex nature instead induced successive EU presidencies to pass the Cyprus 'hot potato' to their successor. The UN-mediated peace process also provided the EU with an alibi or argument to keep out of peacemaking efforts. The Union's intu-itively correct argument was that there was a division of labour between itself and the UN. This argument however, discarded the close and inevitable interactions between the two sets of actors and processes. As such initially reluctant member states, who were sceptical of Cyprus' membership, progressively accepted Greek demands to pursue the accession process without devising an accompanying strat-egy to settle the conflict. Beyond the rhetoric of the EU's 'catalytic effect' on conflict resolution in Cyprus, EU actors never developed a strategy to use the framework and incentives embedded in the accession process to truly catalyze a solution on the island. This remains the case post-accession, where the disinter-ested member states have accepted the RoC's stance on the conflict, reducing its incentives to alter its (non-)negotiating stance.

More so than in Cyprus, in the South Caucasus, EU interest has been even weaker and more sporadic. Georgia's conflicts have not struck a moral chord amongst European publics. As in Cyprus, their seemingly frozen nature has reduced European incentives to get involved. More so than in Cyprus, the con-solidated and often overcrowded international peace processes have provided a strong argument for the EU to keep out of mediation efforts. Hence, despite the EU's oft-repeated strategic interest in the Caucasus, its insufficient concern with the region goes far in explaining the absence of a concerted EU strategy to promote the resolution of its conflicts.

Neglect has also played a role in the EU's stance towards the Kurdish question. Unlike Cyprus and the Caucasus however, this is not due to the frozen nature of the conflict. EU actors have been interested and have made repeated statements against the most acute manifestations of the conflict, such as Turkey's repressive and military policies or the PKK's engagement in terrorist actions. Beyond this, EU actors have kept out of the Kurdish question. The EU has influenced positively the conflict. But it has done so through its wider articulation of EU–Turkey relations and the political transformation this has triggered in Turkey. EU actors have not specifically conditioned EU–Turkey contractual relations on the Kurdish question. Neglect of the Kurdish question contrasts with the EU's focus on other minority problems in Europe, and especially in the CEECs during the eastern enlargement. Unlike in Eastern Europe, minority problems in Turkey are not viewed as a security issue for Western Europe itself, explaining the EU's relative disinterest in the Kurdish question.

EU interests and objectives beyond conflict settlement

The specific interests of EU actors lying beyond peacemaking objectives, have also hindered the positive impact of contractual relations on conflict resolution. The Cyprus conflict was the clearest case in which the strong national interest of one member state played a pivotal role in determining the conduct of contractual relations with Cyprus and Turkey. Greek interests in Cyprus first induced Athens to persuade the RoC to apply for membership, and then to promote the Cyprus accession dossier in EU decision-making forums. In doing so, Greece success-fully lobbied for Cyprus by linking Cyprus' accession process to its consent to other EU decisions. At times, Greece linked Cyprus to its acceptance of deepened EU–Turkey relations. At other times, Athens threatened to veto enlargement both to the north and to the east if Cyprus was excluded from the process of integration. This generated strong tangential interests in other member states to accept Cyprus' EU membership.

In the case of Turkey instead, doubts in member states such as Germany, France and Austria to accept Turkey's EU membership have reduced the positive influence of EU–Turkey relations on the Kurdish question. These doubts, lying beyond the blueprint of the accession process, have had two contrasting effects. On the positive side, they have raised the attention paid by EU institutions on Turkey's compliance with the Copenhagen criteria. On the negative side, EU doubts lying beyond the confines of the Copenhagen criteria have reduced the legitimacy of conditionality on Turkey. They have also bolstered the arguments of Turkish Eurosceptics, who have incessantly claimed that whatever Turkey says or does, Christian Europe will never accept it into its club. In addition, the EU's credibility in Turkey has been damaged by the Union's stance on the Cyprus conflict, particularly after the RoC's accession. Demands such as Turkey's recognition of the RoC are considered in Turkey as a convenient shield behind which other member states have hid their discriminatory attitudes towards it.

The case of Serbia and Montenegro highlights the contradictions that emerge when different EU institutions, driven by different mandates, engage with the conflict parties. EU High Representative Solana stepped in the region with an explicit conflict prevention mandate. Having succeeded in brokering the Belgrade agreement, many felt that Solana's attachment to the State Union had more to do with his personal prestige than with a genuine preoccupation with the two republics and their future. The Commission's mandate in the Balkans was instead exclusively related to the goal of European integration, conducted through the SAP. Given the greater effectiveness of *acquis* compliance and reform within a centralized rather than a loose federation, the Commission pressed for a tighter federation in the region, generating suspicion and resentment especially in Montenegro.

Yet the most evident cases in which EU contractual relations have been driven by other interests and objectives are the conflicts in the Caucasus and the Middle East. This is not to say that the Union does not genuinely wish to promote conflict resolution along the lines of its declarations. What it does suggest is that when other aims and interests determine the conduct of EU contractual relations, these do not always coincide with the Union's conflict resolution agenda. In the Caucasus, a prime EU objective is that of fostering close ties to Russia. Hence, the EU's hands-off approach to the Abkhaz and South Ossetian conflicts and its detached approach to the Caucasus in general.

In the Middle East instead, several member states view the protection of Israel and close relations with it as the utmost priority, over and above the interests of promoting a stable, peaceful and just resolution of the Israeli–Palestinian conflict. Europe's history of anti-Semitism has generated a deep-felt EU preference – particularly within some member states – to maintain close relations with Israel irrespective of its conduct. In addition, EU economic interests in Israel make EU actors receptive to Israeli arguments to compartmentalize the conflict in the conduct of bilateral relations. Compartmentalization in practice has meant accepting deepened EU–Israel economic ties irrespective of the evolution of the conflict. Another EU priority in the Middle East is to seek close, cooperative and complementary relations with the US. This has generated strong EU incentives to accommodate American interests, strategies and policies in the conflict. During the Oslo process, this meant that irrespective of the parties' conduct on the ground, the Union deemed more important the continuation of the US-sponsored peace process, and thus refrained from criticizing the parties so as to avoid disrupting the diplomatic process. Post-Oslo, it has meant greater EU effectiveness in promoting Palestinian reform when this was the main tune played in Washington. Far more gravely, through acquiescence to Israel, it has meant that the EU has either contributed to, or done nothing to alter, the international context within which the conflict emerged, developed and exacerbated over the years.

9 Conclusions

This book analyzes the impact of EU contractual relations on conflict resolution in five regions of the trouble-ridden neighbourhood, seeking to understand the determinants of EU effectiveness in this field of foreign policy. Despite its potential, the EU's record in practice has been relatively disappointing.

In Cyprus, the EU had all cards in place to play an effective, if not decisive, role in conflict resolution. Cyprus' accession process imbued the Greek Cypriot community with a greater sense of security, which could have raised the willingness of its authorities to compromise with the Turkish Cypriots and Turkey. This seemed to be the case of the former Greek Cypriot leadership towards the end of its rule. The prospects of Cyprus' membership coupled with Turkey's accession process and the increasingly pressing conditionality on Ankara could also have induced greater moderation on the Turkish Cypriot and Turkish sides, as occurred in 2002–4. EU involvement in the context of enlargement also created a more conducive environment for reconciliation in the eastern Mediterranean triangle. Finally, Cyprus' accession process offered the UNSG an alternative framework within which to formulate a loose federal proposal, as indeed happened through the Annan Plan. Yet all these positive changes either materialized sequentially and belatedly, or were hindered by mistrust, miscommunication and domestic manipulation. As the Greek Cypriot community turned towards moderation in the late 1990s, the Turkish Cypriots and Turkey – feeling excluded from and suspicious of the EU – hardened their stance. Their shift towards compromise occurred with the change in the EU's approach towards Turkey after 1999, coupled with domestic changes in northern Cyprus and Ankara. Yet by this stage, a new leadership in the RoC – at the doorstep of EU membership – used the gains of EU entry to legitimize rejectionism and manipulate the mechanisms of *acquis* enforcement to justify its stance. The Union, which had kept out of mediation efforts, kept silent about how its name was invoked to smear the UN plan. The EU became enmeshed in an accession process with Cyprus without an accompanying strategy to settle its conflict. This was largely the result of EU neglect and the Union's ensuing slip into accepting the demands and positions of one party to the conflict.

EU contractual relations have had a far more positive impact on Turkey's Kurdish question, particularly after 1999. As opposed to Turkey's association and customs union agreements, the accession process both raised the value of EU–Turkey ties and provided a new framework in which the conflict parties could reformulate their strategies and objectives. The accession process raised Kurdish incentives to abandon secessionist and irredentist goals and to pursue a rights-based solution within Turkey. Moreover, it contributed to a desecuritization of the Kurdish question amongst the Turkish establishment. This helped to empower Turkish actors who were willing to pursue legal, political and socio-economic remedies to the problem. In addition, EU political conditionality and passive enforcement, especially prior to launch of accession negotiations, induced a fundamental political reform process in Turkey. Yet also in the case of the Kurdish question, the EU's positive influence has not matched its potential. The lack of clear obligations on collective rights or Kurdish specific issues partly explains the slower pace of reform on these fronts. EU actors have also shied away from using their influence to formally internationalize peacemaking efforts, to bring about effective Kurdish political participation in Turkey or to diffuse the pan-Kurdish dimension of the problem. This is partly the result of the relatively low level of EU interest in Turkey's Kurdish question. Most of all, it is due to the uncertain and protracted nature of Turkey's accession process and the reluctance of several member states to accept the prospect of Turkey's membership. This has fed Turkish mistrust, it has empowered Eurosceptic and nationalist forces, and it has reduced the legitimacy of EU norms and obligations in Turkey.

In the Western Balkans, notwithstanding the EU's strong commitment to the State Union, Montenegro seceded in 2006. The EU unwittingly contributed to Montenegro's independence. The international community's support for Montenegro's de facto self-rule during Milosevic's rule became difficult to reverse after Serbia's regime change. Hence, Solana's mediation of an exceedingly weak State Union. The ensuing linking of SAP conditionality on reforms in both republics gave Montenegro in particular the feeling that its European integration was being slowed down by the State Union and Serbia's deeper reform problems. In addition, the Commission's insistence on greater centralization at State Union level did not alter the Montenegrin government's commitment to independence, while it helped to relegitimize the pro-Yugoslav opposition in Montenegro. The largely dysfunctional State Union also generated disincentives in Serbia. Paradoxically, the most reform-minded actors in Serbia were amongst the harshest critics of the State Union. In view of its poor performance, reformist Serbs were more inclined to let Montenegro secede in order to concentrate on Serbia's arduous domestic transformation. Finally, Solana's insistence on the survival of the State Union until 2006 generated resentment amongst actors in both republics. This set of domestic disincentives added to the predominant trend in favour of Montenegro's secession.

Despite Montenegro's independence, the EU's contribution to conflict prevention and resolution between Serbia and Montenegro has been positive. This is because of its commitment to integrate the war-torn Balkans through the SAP and the prospect of accession. Commitment to integration is particularly important in a region whose orientation is fixed on the EU. The high value accorded by the Western Balkans to EU integration goes far in explaining the slow yet ongoing process of domestic reform and regional reconciliation. This has provided a conducive and relatively tension-free environment for Montenegro's referendum and ensuing secession. Yet precisely because of the high stakes involved in the European integration of the Western Balkans, a faltering EU commitment to the region could reverse the key steps forward achieved since the turn of the century.

As opposed to the eastern Mediterranean and the Balkans, the EU has not offered the prospect of membership to the southern Mediterranean. However, its highly developed relations with Israel and the Palestinians accords the EU a potentially important role in promoting a democratic and viable two-state solution. In the case of Palestine, financial assistance delivered gradually and conditionally particularly during the second intifada triggered important reforms in the constitutional, fiscal and judicial domains. Yet more could have been achieved in the sphere of Palestinian reform, particularly on the core questions lying at the heart of Palestinian democracy.

The EU's deliberate neglect of these issues, largely explained by its priority to support the US-mediated peace process, has handicapped its direct involvement in conflict resolution. The contradictions this gave rise to emerged in full force after the election of Hamas in 2006. In the case of Israel, the EU's involvement has been far less productive. Again this is because of the interplay between different EU interests and objectives beyond the goal of supporting a viable and rights-based two-state solution. By discarding conditionality and passive enforcement, the EU has failed to influence Israeli domestic politics and policies. By compartmentalizing the conflict in the conduct of EU–Israel contractual ties, it has reinforced the perception of European weakness in the region. The EU has also fed into the skewed nature of international involvement and it has signalled to the conflict parties that Israel may operate unsanctioned in open disregard of international law.

Finally, the EU's impact on Georgia's secessionist conflicts has been marginal, albeit not negative. Unlike the previous four conflicts, EU involvement in the Caucasus has been weak. Its contractual ties with Georgia have been conducted through the bland PCA. EU assistance to Georgia, Abkhazia and South Ossetia pales into insignificance when compared with EU assistance to the eastern Mediterranean, the Balkans and the Middle East. Although the South Caucasus was ultimately included in the ENP, the benefits foreseen in it for Georgia are well below those envisaged for Israel or for the eastern neighbours. This has limited the EU's potential influence both on separatist trends in the conflict zones and on Georgia's troubled transition process. But even if weak contractual ties have limited the EU's potential impact, the Union has had a marginally positive influence on these two conflicts. Post-revolution Georgia's declared commitment to European integration has raised the EU's leverage on the country. The Commission's targeted assistance to the conflict zones has also won it a role in the South Ossetian peace process and it has influenced domestic developments especially in Abkhazia. Yet, as in other cases, the EU's potential in the Caucasus has not been fully realized. The Union's weak specification of conflict-related obligations, its cautious approach to the secessionist entities and its excessive concern not to tread on Russia's toes has hindered EU effectiveness in conflict resolution. Much as in the cases of Cyprus, Turkey and the Middle East, these self-imposed limits are due to EU neglect, coupled with its pursuit of other realpolitik-related objectives in the region.

Taken collectively, the five conflicts studied in this book suggest that the EU's very nature offers a marked potential to contribute to conflict resolution, yet also impairs the actual conduct of the EU in this field.

The case studies suggest that EU contractual relations hold real potential to positively influence conflict resolution in two distinct yet interlinked ways. Both are inextricably linked to the EU's own nature as a non-state actor offering predominantly integration-related benefits. First, in countries with a prospect of European integration, the EU can provide an alternative framework within which to seek solutions to ethno-political conflicts. This has clearly been the case of Cyprus, Turkey and the Western Balkans. In Cyprus, the EU's potential was both local and regional. At the local level, the EU institutional set-up, the *acquis* and the possible exemptions to it, as well as the benefits in terms of domestic development, offered a conducive context to seek a loose federal agreement. At the regional level, Greece's membership, coupled with the accession processes of Cyprus and Turkey, contributed to a more favourable environment for an eastern Mediterranean-wide reconciliation. In the Kurdish question, the accession process created an appealing framework for Turks and Kurds to bridge their differences through a rights-based platform within a democratic Turkey. Turkey's accession process both raised the scope for a Turkish desecuritization of the Kurdish question and provided an alternative platform for Kurds to articulate and pursue their cause. In the Western Balkans, the framework of European integration could not prevent secession. However, the EU framework both raised the likelihood of regional reintegration and helped to prevent the outbreak of new ethno-political conflicts.

Second, the political, security and economic instruments envisaged in EU contractual relations can be mobilized to raise incentives for conflict resolution. The value of the accession process or the SAP is clear and appreciated by the recipient parties. The long-term and indivisible nature of the benefits foreseen in the accession process may reduce its potential to induce sustained progress in conflict resolution. However, the cases of Cyprus, Turkey and the Balkans highlight the clear leverage the prospect of accession can bestow upon the EU. This is particularly true when strong constituencies within conflict parties genuinely aspire to EU membership. Yet the conflicts in the Caucasus and the Middle East demonstrate that valuable EU instruments need not be limited to the accession process. Financial assistance or the benefits foreseen in the ENP may also raise the EU's influence in conflict resolution. Not only do non-accession benefits suffer less from the problems of timing and delivery, which afflict the accession process but also, these benefits are cherished by European EU-aspirants and non-European countries without membership aspirations. EU involvement in a non-accession context may be valued even if a conflict party wishes to enter the EU, such as post-'rose revolution' Georgia. It may also be appreciated by conflict parties with little interest in membership, who value close relations with the Union. In different ways, this is the case of Israel and the PA.

Beyond the direct effect on conflict parties, the EU's framework and policy instruments can complement the peacemaking efforts of other external players. Most vividly in Cyprus, the UNSG strengthened his mediation efforts in 2002–4 precisely in order to capitalize on the conflict parties' heightened incentives in view of the approaching EU entry. The UN mediators also used the EU framework to present a more appealing and comprehensive peace proposal to the conflict parties.

Given the absence of a strong EU framework in the South Caucasus or the Middle East, the same could not be done by the UN in Abkhazia, the OSCE in South Ossetia or the US in Israel–Palestine. Yet even in these cases, the policy benefits envisaged in EU contractual relations can bolster the mediation efforts of third parties. In the Caucasus and the Middle East, EU policy instruments cannot easily duplicate or counter the involvement of other 'powerful' external players. External players such as Russia or the US have tended to influence conflict dynamics in these regions through principal mediation and by lending support to one conflict party (Touval and Zartman 1989; Zartman and Aurik 1991). By contrast, the EU's 'comparative advantage' in conflict resolution has rested precisely in its relative inability to play into the balance of power logics prevalent in these regions. By operating at a deeper structural level, EU policy instruments can potentially complement other external actions by influencing the domestic root causes of conflict. In other words, EU contractual relations are potentially more effective in inducing long-run conflict transformation and resolution over and above conflict management and settlement, which are instead typical of the activities of principal mediators.

By the same token, EU contractual relations are also well placed to promote other EU foreign policy objectives. These include the promotion of human rights, democracy, the rule of law, civil society and regional cooperation; combating international crime, contributing to international security, and supporting sound socio-economic management (European Council 2003b). Beyond their relevance to conflict resolution, these goals have been pinpointed by the EU as guiding the conduct of its foreign policy. In view of their structural and long-term nature, these objectives are also well suited to being tackled directly or indirectly by the EU's framework and policy instruments embedded in its contractual relations.

Yet despite the EU's foreign policy potential, this book argues that an effective EU role in practice requires credible obligations accompanying valuable benefits. Credibility and reputation is particularly important for a non-state actor like the EU, which bases its influence in the foreign policy realm predominantly on its 'soft power' instruments and procedures. This is where the EU's record falters most. The credibility of the EU's conditions and obligations, or its scope to induce compliance through learning has been hindered by several key factors.

At times, EU actors have not specified at all, or with sufficient clarity, their desired conditions. This has been the case of collective rights in Turkey, of sensitive political questions relating to Palestinian democracy, or of federal solutions in Cyprus and the Caucasus. Particularly in the latter two cases, the EU's non-involvement in official peace processes has hindered its ability to spell out clear conflict-related obligations. At other times, the credibility of EU obligations has been thwarted by the Union's inability to target all conflict parties at the same time. In Cyprus, the sequential use of conditionality, with pressure being exerted on Turkey precisely at the time when it was being lifted on the RoC, enhanced feelings of discrimination in the former country and legitimized hardline positions in the latter. By contrast, the linking of reform conditionality in Serbia and Montenegro enhanced incentives for their separation. On other occasions still, both the manipulation of passive enforcement as well as its disrespect has seriously damaged the Union's credibility. On the one hand, the use and abuse of the *acquis* discourse in Cyprus generated Greek and Turkish Cypriot disincentives to seal a federal solution. On the other hand, the disregard of international and Community law by Israel and the EU's passivity towards it has damaged the standing of the EU and of its advocated norms in the Middle East.

Finally, in all of the conflicts in the EU's backyard, the scope for compliance through learning is extremely limited. In the case of conflict parties in the framework of accession, the potential for learning may exist, but it tends to be limited to governing authorities in close contact with the EU. For conflict parties lying beyond the accession process, the prospect for change through learning is even slimmer. Political dialogue on sensitive identity and security questions is notoriously ineffective at inducing change in conflict contexts. Furthermore, in the case of unrecognized secessionist entities, the EU's excessive caution in dealing with the relevant authorities has severely circumscribed the EU's potential in these regions and may have fuelled their retrenchment into closure and nationalism.

In all the conflict cases, political determinants lying beyond the blueprint of the contract often dictate or influence the conduct of EU contractual relations. These political determinants are sometimes explained by the EU's neglect of a particular conflict. This has been the case of Cyprus and the South Caucasus, and is even truer for conflicts further afield. In other cases, political determinants are related to other national or EU-wide interests beyond conflict resolution. In some cases, additional interests are not necessarily incompatible with the goals of conflict resolution. This is the case of genuine democracy and human rights promotion. Yet, to the extent that EU actors may believe that particular manifestations of democracy and human rights are incompatible with conflict resolution, the pursuit of their foreign policy objectives can become inconsistent. In other cases, the quest for other goals and interests through the conduct of contractual relations may inherently hinder the EU's ambition to contribute to conflict resolution. In theory, the EU's pursuit of normative milieu goals shapes the external environment in a manner conducive to the accomplishment of its strategic possession goals (Wolfers 1962: 73–6). Yet in practice, the pursuit of narrow and short-term interests has often obstructed the EU's potential to advance those long-term goals, reflecting the very values on which the Union is founded.

Notes

1 Introduction

1 The international legitimization of federal or consociational solutions (as opposed to the granting of minority rights for example) in conflicts where power was seized illegally and through the use of force is 'paradoxical' because it generates minority incentives to engage in violence in order to assert self-determination, despite the international community's denunciation of this approach (Kymlicka 2006).
2 Discussions during the conference: 'Prospects for Georgia and Abkhazia in the Context of Black Sea Integration', Heinrich Böll Foundation, University of California Irvine, Istanbul 26 June 2006.

2 The EU's role in conflict resolution: a framework of analysis

1 For example, under Article 228a of the Maastricht Treaty, the approval of an embargo or sanction requires first a unanimous common position under CFSP, and then an implementing decision under the common commercial policy voted by qualified majority voting.
2 The 2003 Wider Europe Communication stated that: 'in *return* for concrete progress demonstrating shared values and effective implementation of political, economic and institutional reforms, including in aligning legislation with the *acquis*, the EU's neighbourhood should benefit from the prospect of closer integration with the EU' (Commission 2003a) (my italics). Use of the term 'in return' signals the possible use of ex ante conditionality in the ENP.

3 The missed opportunity to promote reunification in Cyprus

1 Interview with Commission official, London, May 2002.
2 Article 4 of the Treaty of Guarantee gave the three powers unilateral 'right to take action with the sole aim of re-establishing the state of affairs established by the Treaty'.
3 UN General Assembly resolution 5412 (1983), UN Security Council resolutions 541 (1983) and 550 (1984) and Council of Europe resolution 1056 (1987).
4 Proximity talks are a process in which, rather than negotiating with each other, the parties present and discuss their positions with a third-party mediator, e.g. the UNSR.
5 These results were presented by Kudret Akay at a Wilton Park Conference held on 10–11 February 2005 in Larnaca.
6 Macedonia for example, is recognized as 'The Republic of Macedonia' by more than half of the EU's member states for the purposes of bilateral relations, even though for EU declarations it remains FYROM (the Former Yugoslav Republic of Macedonia).

7 Interviews in north Nicosia and Ankara, July 2003.
8 Interview with Greek Cypriot journalist, Nicosia, April 2005.
9 This fear was frequently raised during interviews in northern Cyprus in April 2005.
10 Interview with Turkish Cypriot political analyst, Nicosia, February 2005.
11 Interview with Greek Cypriot journalist, Nicosia, March 2002. The same argument was raised by other interlocutors, including politicians, academics and civil servants in southern Cyprus, April 2002.
12 Interview in February 2002, Nicosia.
13 For example, as late as January 2002, Clerides stated that 'the behaviour of the Greek Cypriot side will have to be such as to actually prove that we fervently desire the finding of a solution'. Quoted in Christou (2002).
14 European Council (2002) paragraph 24 states that the Union 'would accommodate the terms of … a comprehensive settlement in the Treaty of Accession in line with the principles on which the EU is founded'.
15 Foreign Minister George Papandreou at a speech in Vouliagmeni, Athens on 8 September 2002. The same argument was made in interviews with Greek Foreign Ministry officials, Athens, March 2002.
16 Interviews with the author 2002–4, Nicosia.

4 Ebbs and flows in the Europeanization of Turkey's Kurdish question

1 The village guards (korucular) are Kurdish civilians, armed and paid by the state to fight the PKK. There are approximately 60,000 village guards in the region.
2 Approximately 500,000 Turkish Kurds live in Western Europe, of whom 400,000 are in Germany.
3 The most notable incident was in 1991, when two HEP parliamentarians took their oaths in Kurdish wearing Kurdish colours. Another incident was in 1994 when DEP leader Hatip Dicle stated that 'nobody could separate the PKK from us or other friendly forces'. Quoted in Pope and Pope (2000: 275).
4 Espoused by the fourth PKK Congress on 25–31 December 1990. See also the interview with Öcalan conducted by Birand (1992).
5 As Dilek Kurban notes, the Kurdish call for 'legal protection' amounts to a call for minority rights, even if the term itself is adamantly rejected by most Kurdish actors (Kurban 2005: 29).
6 Interviews conducted with Kurdish politicians, civil servants, lawyers and NGOs in Diyarbakır, May 2004.
7 The term 'establishment' here and in what follows is used loosely. By establishment, I refer to all those actors within the executive, the administration, the judiciary, the military, the security services, the intelligence community, political parties, the media and academia, which ascribe to the Kemalist republican values. There are wide variations within the establishment, with some actors supporting greater political liberalism and others pressing for nationalist policies.
8 Interview with a specialist on the Kurdish question, Istanbul, April 2006.
9 Deep state (*derindevlet*) is a term frequently used in Turkey to mean the undemocratic underground security establishment encompassing elements of the military, the intelligence, the police, the judiciary and the administration.
10 Interview with a human rights lawyer, Diyarbakır, May 2004.
11 See for example the speech delivered by Prime Minister Erdoğan in Diyarbakır on 12 August 2005, which DEHAP Diyarbakır mayor Özman Baydemir acclaimed as a 'foundation for turning a new page in relations between Kurds and the government' (Balta-Paker 2005).
12 Views expressed in a seminar on 'The Kurdish Question' organized by the EU Institute for Security Studies, Paris, 27 October 2005.

13 This was a view supported by all Kurdish interlocutors during interviews in Diyarbakır, May 2004.
14 Presentation at 'The First Bosphorous Conference' organized by the Centre for European Reform, Istanbul, 15 October 2004.
15 This problem was frequently raised in interviews with NGOs in the region, Diyarbakır, May 2004.
16 Advisor to the mayor, Diyarbakır, May 2005.
17 Key note speech by Minister of the Economy Ali Babacan at an 'EU–Turkey Brainstorming Meeting' at European University Institute, Florence. 6–7 May 2004.
18 Interviews with Turkish diplomats and political analysts, Ankara, June 2006.
19 I would like to thank Ulrich Sedelmeier for raising this point.
20 See Joost Lagendijk, MEP, reported in Turkish Daily News (2005).
21 For example in November 2002 former French President and EU Convention President Valéry Giscard d'Estaing stated that Turkey has a 'different culture, a different approach, a different way of life ... its capital is not in Europe, 95 per cent of its population lives outside Europe, it is not a European country ... in my opinion it would be the end of the EU' (TDN 2002).

5 Mixed signals to Serbia and Montenegro

1 This point was raised by several Serbian and Montenegrin interlocutors, including those who supported separation, Belgrade and Podgorica, July 2003.
2 Declaring oneself as Serbian rather than Montenegrin became tantamount to expressing scepticism towards Montenegro's independence. By contrast, the majority of self-declared Albanians and Bosniaks in Montenegro have backed independence.
3 An argument frequently raised in interviews in Podgorica was that all the former Yugoslav republics which were recognized by the Badinter Commission as having a right to self-determination had achieved independence through war. If Montenegro was denied this right, the international community would have signalled the exclusive legitimacy of independence through violence. See also Kymlika (2006).
4 Modifications included the requirement of an absolute majority of registered voters to support independence, and the extension of the right to vote to Montenegrins residing in Serbia.
5 Interview with aide of former prime minister Djindjic, Belgrade, and with the Montenegrin Minister of Foreign Economic Relations, Podgorica, July 2003.
6 Interviews with State Union officials and political analysts in Belgrade, July 2003.
7 Interview in Podgorica, July 2003. After considerable delays caused also by trade disputes between the two republics, the State Union concluded FTAs with all the Balkan countries by 2005.
8 Interviews with political analysts and State Union officials in Belgrade and Podgorica, July 2003.
9 Including Governor of the Serbian Central Bank Mladjan Dinkic and former Deputy Prime Minister Miroljub Labus.
10 This was widely recognized by Council and Commission officials in early 2006 when the EU's official position was still committed to the State Union. Interviews in Brussels, March 2006.
11 Trade preferences were extended to textiles and certain agricultural products in 2005.
12 Interview with EU official, Belgrade, July 2003.
13 Interview with Commission official, Brussels, March 2006.
14 Interviews in Belgrade and Podgorica, July 2003.
15 Interview in Belgrade, July 2003.
16 Interview with Commission official, Brussels, March 2006.
17 Interview with Commission official, Belgrade, July 2003.

18 Particularly vis-à-vis the prosecution ICTY indictees Ratko Mladic and Radovan Karadzic.
19 Interview with Commission official in Belgrade, July 2003.

6 The glaring gap between rhetoric and reality in the Israeli–Palestinian conflict

1 The number of refugees (original refugees from Israel and their descendants) being registered by UNRWA and living either in or outside camps in Jordan, Lebanon, Syria, and the West Bank and Gaza Strip is approximately 4m. Yet figures could reach up to 5.9m if all the families of refugees residing anywhere in the world are included.
2 See reports by Palestinian NGOs such as LAW (www.lawsociety.org) and the Palestinian Centre for Human Rights (www.pchrgaza.org), Israeli NGO B'tselem (www.btselem.org) and international NGOs Human Rights Watch (http://hrw.org/reports/world/is-ot-pa-pubs.php) and Amnesty International (http://web.amnesty.org).
3 See also the regularly updated maps published by the UN Office for the Coordination of Humanitarian Affairs (OCHA) www.ochaopt.org.
4 Disengagement from Gaza raised the proportion of Jews between the Jordan and the Sea from 49 per cent to 57 per cent. See Della Pergola (2005).
5 However, already in the mid-1990s the international community had shifted its focus on relief assistance in Palestine (Le More 2005: 994).
6 Interview in the PA Ministry of Trade, March 2005, Ramallah.
7 Exceptions include the EP's delayed ratification of EC–Israel trade agreements in 1987–8 and in 1995–2000.
8 The following discussion was informed by conversations with Charles Shamas, The Mattin Group, Ramallah in 2002–2005.
9 Article 1 of the Fourth Geneva Convention prevents any state or its nationals from participating in, or facilitating, the Convention's violation.
10 Interview with Commission official, June 2005, Brussels.
11 Interviews with PA civil servant and Commission officials, Ramallah and Brussels, March 2005 and June 2005.
12 Interview with Commission official, Jerusalem, May 2006.
13 These accusations, which may be largely tactical as far as the Israeli leadership is concerned, are genuinely held amongst the public. In a 2004 poll, 64 per cent of Israeli respondents felt that EU accusations against Israel are motivated by anti-Semitism (Dahaf Institute 2004: 41).

7 Caught between neglect and competing mediation in Georgia's secessionist conflicts

1 While initially favouring an increased capacity of the Baku–Supsa oil pipeline, by 2001 the EU started backing the Baku–Tbilisi–Ceyhan pipeline not least in view of European (the Italian ENI, the French TotalFina and the British BP) stakes in it. 'BTC' is expected to transport 1bn barrels a day by 2010.
2 Although integration into Russia is supported by the South Ossetian elite and public, given the north Ossetian dimension of the conflict, Abkhaz views on integration into Russia are far more divided.
3 In Ajara, Aslan Abashidze, a de facto pseudo-monarch, retained absolute control after the collapse of the Soviet Union. While at times Abashidze supported Shevardnadze, he also refused to transfer tax revenues raised from the Batumi port to the central government. During the 'rose revolution', when Abashidze refused to recognize the

regime change in Tbilisi and closed Ajara's borders with Georgia, Saakashvili imposed sanctions on Ajara and conducted military exercises on its borders, ultimately forcing Abashidze's exile to Russia.

4 Interview with the author, Sukhumi, April 2006.

5 During the presidential elections in October 2004, Bagapsh narrowly defeated Khadjimba. The latter refused to accept the election results triggering a prolonged crisis, resolved with a Russian mediated agreement, which led to renewed elections where Bagapsh ran and won as president and Khadjimba as his deputy (Fuller 2005).

6 In May 2005, Russia agreed to dismantle these two bases by December 2007.

7 Interviews with Abkhaz officials and civil society representatives, Sukhumi, April 2006.

8 The March 2004 parliamentary elections only saw the Rightist Opposition Coalition surpassing the electoral threshold, in addition to Saakashvili's National Democratic Movement.

9 Interview with Georgian advisor to the president, Tbilisi, April 2006.

10 Interview with OSCE official, Tbilisi, April 2006.

11 Interviews with Abkhaz officials and civil society representatives, Sukhumi, April 2006.

12 Georgia received its NATO Individual Partnership Action Plan in 2004. If fulfilled, this is likely to lead to a Membership Action Plan with the aim of joining NATO by 2008.

13 Interview with the author, Tbilisi, April 2006.

14 Interview with OSCE official, Tbilisi, April 2006.

15 Interview with Georgian officials, Tbilisi, April 2006.

16 Interview with the author, Sukhumi, April 2006.

17 In December 2001 a member of staff of the EC delegation in Georgia was murdered and in June 2002 a TACIS contractor was kidnapped for five months.

18 Interview with European diplomat, Tbilisi, April 2006.

19 Interview with Georgian official, Tbilisi, April 2006.

20 Statement made by Georgian Minister for European Integration Giorgi Baramidze at a workshop organized by the Dutch liberal party (VVD) in The Hague on 17 November 2005.

21 Interviews with Abkhaz officials and civil society representatives, Sukhumi, April 2006.

22 Romania, Bulgaria and the three Baltic states have proclaimed themselves the 'New Friends' of Georgia.

8 Comparing the EU's role in neighbourhood conflicts

1 However, it should be noted that these communities are extremely heterogeneous in terms of language (e.g. Kurmancı and Zaza in the north and northwest, and Sorani in the south) and religion (mainly Sunni and Alevi Muslims). The Kurds have also been profoundly affected by the national development of their respective states.

2 This view was raised frequently by EU officials at a Seminar on 'The Kurdish Issue and the EU', organized by the EU Institute for Security Studies, Paris, 27 October 2005.

3 Interviews with Turkish and Kurdish politicians, civil society activists and academics, Ankara and Diyarbakır, May 2004.

4 Interview with World Bank official, Belgrade, July 2003.

5 Interviews with Montenegrin civil society representatives, Podgorica, July 2003.

6 This point was frequently raised by interlocutors in both Belgrade and Podgorica, July 2003.

Bibliography

Antonenko, O. (2005) 'Frozen Uncertainty: Russia and the Conflict over Abkhazia', in B. Coppieters and R. Legvold (eds) *Statehood and Security–Georgia After the Rose Revolution*, Cambridge MA, MIT Press, pp. 205–69.

Bahceli, T. (2001) 'The Lure of Economic Prosperity Versus Ethno-nationalism: Turkish Cypriots, the EU Option, and the Resolution of Ethnic Conflict in Cyprus', in M. Keating and J. McGarry (eds) *Minority Nationalism and the Changing International Order*, Oxford, Oxford University Press, pp. 203–22.

Balta-Paker, E. (2005) 'The Ceasefire this Time', *Middle East Report*, 31 August. Online. Available HTTP: http://www.merip.org (accessed August 2005).

Barkey, H. (1998) 'The People's Democracy Party (HADEP): The Travails of a Legal Kurdish Party in Turkey', *Journal of Muslim Minority Affairs*, 18:1, pp. 129–38.

Batt, J. (2004) 'The Western Balkans: Moving on', *Europa South-East Monitor*, 60, Brussels, Centre for European Policy Studies, November, pp. 1–4.

– (2005) 'The Question of Serbia', *Chaillot Paper*, 81, August, Paris, EU Institute for Security Studies.

Beleli, Ö. (2005) 'Regional Policy and EU Accession: Learning from the GAP Experience', European Stability Initiative. Online. Available HTTP: http://www.esiweb.org (accessed December 2005).

Betul Çelik, A. (2005) 'Transnationalization of Human Rights Norms and Its Impact on Internally Displaced Kurds', *Human Rights Quarterly*, 27:3, pp. 969–97.

BIA News Center (2004) 'Kurdish Demands Ahead of EU Summit', 14 December. Online. Available HTTP: http://freekurdistan.blogspot.com (accessed December 2004).

Birand, M.A. (1992) *Apo ve PKK*, Istanbul, Milliyet Yayınları.

Bishara, M. (2001) *Palestine/Israel: Peace or Apartheid*, London, Zed Books.

Bıçak, H. (1997) 'Recent Developments in Cyprus–EU Relations', in E. Doğramaci *et al.* (eds) *Proceedings of the First International Conference on Cypriot Studies*, Famagusta, Eastern Mediterranean University.

Börzel, T. and Risse, T. (2000) 'When Europe Hits Home: Europeanization and Domestic Change', *European Integration Online Papers*, 4:15. Online. Available HTTP: http://eiop.or.at/eiop/texte/2000-015.htm (accessed November 2003).

– (2003) 'Conceptualizing the Domestic Impact of Europe', in K. Featherstone and C. Radaelli (eds) *The Politics of Europeanization*, Oxford, Oxford University Press, pp. 57–82.

Brandter, B. and Rosas, A. (1999) 'Trade Preferences and Human Rights', in P. Alston (ed.) *The EU and Human Rights*, Oxford, Oxford University Press, pp. 699–722.

Brewin, C. (2000) *The European Union and Cyprus*, Huntingdon, Eothen.

Bt'selem (2006) *Under the Guise of Security: Routing the Separation Barrier to Enable Israeli Settlement Expansion in the West Bank.* Online. Available HTTP: http://www.btselem.org (accessed June 2006).

Checkel, J. (1999) 'Norms, Institutions and National Identity in Contemporary Europe', *International Studies Quarterly*, 43:1, pp. 83–114.

Christou, J. (2002) 'New Year Will Be Crucial for Cyprus', *Cyprus Mail*, 2 January.

Civil Georgia (2005) *Report: National Security Concept Finalized*, 15 May. Online. Available HTTP: http:// www.civil.ge (accessed May 2005).

Commission of the EC (1993) *Opinion on the Application for Membership from Cyprus*, COM(93) 313, EC Bulletin 6–1993.

– (1997) *Regional Cooperation in the Black Sea Area*, 14 November. Online. Available HTTP: http://www.ec.europa.eu (accessed March 2006).

– (1998a) *Bilateral Relations – South Caucasus*, Bulletin EU 6-1999, 1 March. Online. Available HTTP: http://www.ec.europa.eu (accessed March 2006).

– (1998b) *Regular Report on Turkey's Progress Towards Accession.* Online. Available HTTP: http://www.ec.europa.eu (accessed November 1999).

– (2001a) *Communication from the Commission on Conflict Prevention*, COM(2001) 211. Online. Available HTTP: http://www.ec.europa.eu (accessed January 2002).

– (2001b) *The EU's Role in Promoting Human Rights and Democratization in Third Countries*, COM(2001) 252. Online. Available HTTP: http://www.ec.europa.eu (accessed January 2002).

– (2002) *Staff Working Paper on the Federal Republic of Yugoslavia*, COM(2002) 163. Online. Available HTTP: http://www.ec.europa.eu (accessed December 2002).

– (2003a) *Wider Europe – Neighbourhood: A New Framework for Relations with Our Eastern and Southern Neighbours*, COM(2003) 104. Online. Available HTTP: http://www.ec.europa.eu (accessed December 2003).

– (2003b) *Staff Working Paper Serbia and Montenegro*, COM(2003) 139. Online. Available HTTP: http://www.ec.europa.eu (accessed December 2003).

– (2003c) *Reinvigorating EU Actions on Human Rights and Democratization with Mediterranean Partners*, Brussels, COM(2003) 294. Online. Available HTTP: http://www.ec.europa.eu (accessed December 2003).

– (2003d) *Continuing Enlargement: Strategy Paper and Report of the European Commission on the Progress Towards Accession of Bulgaria, Romania and Turkey.* Online. Available HTTP: http://www.ec.europa.eu (accessed November 2003).

– (2003e) *Country Strategy Paper in 2003–2006, TACIS National Indicative Programme 2004–2006, Georgia.* Online. Available HTTP: http://www.ec.europa.eu (accessed February 2006).

– (2004a) *European Neighbourhood Policy Strategy Paper*, Brussels, COM(2004) 373. Online. Available HTTP: http://www.ec.europa.eu (accessed September 2004).

– (2004b) *Regular Report on Turkey's Progress Towards Accession.* Online. Available HTTP: http://www.ec.europa.eu (accessed November 2004).

– (2004c) *Staff Working Paper Serbia and Montenegro*, COM(2004) 376. Online. Available HTTP: http://www.ec.europa.eu (accessed November 2004).

– (2004d) *EU–Israel Action Plan*, 9 December. Online. Available HTTP: http://www.ec. europa.eu (accessed December 2004).

– (2004e) *EU–PA Action Plan*, 9 December. Online. Available HTTP: http://www.ec. europa.eu (accessed December 2004).

– (2005a) *European Neighbourhood Policy: Recommendations for Armenia, Azerbaijan, Georgia, and for Egypt and Lebanon*, COM(2005) 72. Online. Available HTTP: http://www.ec.europa.eu (accessed December 2005).

– (2005b) *EU-Palestinian Cooperation Beyond Disengagement – Towards a Two State Solution*, COM(2005) 458. Online. Available HTTP: http://www.ec.europa.eu (accessed December 2005).

– (2005c) *Turkey 2005 Progress Report*. Online. Available HTTP: http://www.ec.europa.eu (accessed November 2005).

– (2005d) *Communication from the Commission on the Preparedness of Serbia and Montenegro to Negotiate a SAA with the EU*, COM(2005) 476. Online. Available HTTP: http://www.ec.europa.eu (accessed November 2005).

– (2005e) *Serbia and Montenegro, Progress Report*, COM(2005) 561. Online. Available HTTP: http://www.ec.europa.eu (accessed December 2005).

– (2005f) Directorate General for External Relations Website. Online. Available HTTP: http://www.delwbg.cec.eu.int/en/eu_and_palestine/overview.htm (accessed December 2005).

Coppieters, B. (2000a) 'Introduction' in B. Coppieters, D. Darchiashvili and N. Akaba (eds) *Federal Practice*, Brussels, VUB Press, pp. 7–18.

Coppieters, B. (2000b) 'Western Security Policies and the Georgian–Abkhaz Conflict', in B. Coppieters, D. Darchiashvili and N. Akaba (eds) *Federal Practice*, Brussels, VUB Press, pp. 21–58.

Coppieters, B. (2004) 'EU Policy Towards the Southern Caucasus', paper presented at the European Parliament, Committee of Foreign Affairs, Brussels, January.

Coppieters, B. and Legvold, R. (eds) (2005) *Statehood and Security – Georgia After the Rose Revolution*, Cambridge MA, MIT Press.

Cortright, D. (1997) 'Incentives and Cooperation in International Affairs', in D. Cortright (ed.) *The Price of Peace: Incentives and International Conflict Prevention*, New York, Carnegie Corporation of New York, Rowman and Littlefield, pp. 3–20.

Council of Europe (2004a) *Draft Opinion on the Draft Constitutional Law of Georgia on the Status of the Autonomous Republic of Ajara*, Venice Commission, Opinion No. 291/04, Strasbourg.

Council of Europe (2004b) *Report on the Honouring of Obligations and Commitments by Georgia*, Doc.10383, 21 December, Strasbourg.

Council of Europe (2005) *Honouring of Obligations and Commitments by Georgia*, Parliamentary Assembly of the Council of Europe, Resolution No. 1415, Strasbourg.

Council of Ministers of the EU (1999) *Declaration of the Presidency on Behalf of the EU on the Presidential Election and Referendum in Abkhazia*, 5 October 1999. Online. Available HTTP: http://www.consilium.europa.eu (accessed February 2006).

– (2001a) *General Affairs Council Meeting*, 26 February 2001. Online. Available HTTP: http://www.consilium.europa.eu (accessed February 2006).

– (2001b) *Decision on the Principles, Priorities, Intermediate Objectives and Conditions in the Accession Partnership with the Republic of Turkey*, 24 March 2001, 2001/235/EC, *Official Journal*, L85. Online. Available HTTP: http://www.consilium.europa.eu (accessed December 2001).

– (2001c) *Declaration of the Presidency on Behalf of the EU Concerning the Situation in Abkhazia, Georgia*, 12 October 2001, Presse 360. Online. Available HTTP: http://www.consilium.europa.eu (accessed February 2006).

– (2001d) *South Ossetia, Georgia – Conflict Settlement Process*, CFSP Action Profile, 2001/759/CFSP. Online. Available HTTP: http://www.consilium.europa.eu (accessed February 2006).

– (2002) *Declaration of the Presidency on Behalf of the EU Concerning the Recent "Parliamentary Elections" in Abkhazia, Georgia*, 12 March 2002, Presse 70. Online. Available HTTP: http://www.consilium.europa.eu (accessed February 2006).

– (2004a) *Declaration of the Presidency on Behalf of the EU on the Presidential Elections in Georgia*, 9 January 2004, Presse 5. Online. Available HTTP: http://www.consilium.europa.eu (accessed February 2006).

– (2004b) *Council Conclusions on Cyprus*, 26 April 2004. Online. Available HTTP: http://www.consilium.europa.eu (accessed May 2004).

– (2004c) *Declaration of the Presidency on Behalf of the EU on the Situation in South Ossetia*, 20 August 2004, Presse 246. Online. Available HTTP: http://www.consilium.europa.eu (accessed February 2006).

– (2004d) *Declaration of the EU for the Fifth Meeting of the Association Council EU–Israel*, 13 December. Online. Available HTTP: http://www.consilium.europa.eu (accessed January 2005).

– (2005) *Declaration of the Presidency on Behalf of the EU Concerning the European Neighbourhood Policy*, 25 April 2005, Presse 86. Online. Available HTTP: http://www.consilium.europa.eu (accessed February 2006).

– (2006a) *General Affairs Council Meeting*, 2706, Brussels, 30–31 January 2006, Press Release 22. Online. Available HTTP: http://www.consilium.europa.eu (accessed May 2006).

– (2006b) *General Affairs Council Meeting*, 2737, Brussels, 12 June, Press Release 162. Online. Available HTTP: http://www.consilium.europa.eu (accessed August 2006).

– (2006c) *Declaration of the Presidency on Behalf of the EU on the Situation in South Ossetia*, Brussels, 20 July 2006, Presse 256. Online. Available HTTP: http://www.consilium.europa.eu (accessed February 2006).

Cyprus News (2001) 'Turkey Threatens to Annex Northern Cyprus', *Cyprus News* 7 November. Online. Available HTTP: http://www.cyprusnews.com (accessed November 2001).

Dahaf Institute (2004) *Appendix: Tables of Distribution of Responses – Israeli's Attitudes Towards the EU*, Tel Aviv, Dahaf Institute. Online. Available HTTP: http://www.eu-del.org.il/english/dahaf_second_poll_tables_of_results.doc (accessed March 2005).

De Witte, B. (2002) 'Politics Versus Law in the EU's Approach to Ethnic Minorities', in J. Zielonka (ed.) *Europe Unbound*, London, Routledge, pp. 137–60.

Della Pergola, S. (2005) 'For First Time, Jews Are No Longer a Majority Between the Jordan and the Sea', *Ha'aretz*, 11 August. Online. Available HTTP: http://www.haaretz.com (accessed August 2005).

Diez, T. (2002) 'Why the EU Can Nonetheless Be Good for Cyprus', *Journal of Ethnopolitics and Minority Issues in Europe'*, 2/2002. Online. Available HTTP: http://www.ecmi.de (accessed July 2003).

Dorussen, H. (2001) 'Mixing Carrots with Sticks: Evaluating the Effectiveness of Positive Incentives', *Journal of Peace Research*, 38:2, pp. 251–62.

Dror, Y. and Pardo, S. (2006) 'Approaches and Principles for an Israeli Grand Strategy Towards the EU', *European Foreign Affairs Review*, 11:1, pp. 17–44.

Ergil, D. (1995) *Doğu Sorunu: Tephisler ve Tesbitler*, Ankara, Türkiye Odalar ve Borsalar Birliği.

Ertuğal, E. (2005) *Strategies for Regional Development: Challenges Facing Turkey on the Road to EU Membership*, European Stability Initiative. Online. Available HTTP: http://www.esiweb.org (accessed December 2005).

Eurasia Insight (2004) 'Saakashvili: Russia to Blame for South Ossetia Crisis', *Eurasia Insight*, 12 July. Online. Available HTTP: http://www.eurasianet.org (accessed July 2004).

European Council (1973) 'Statement of the Nine Foreign Ministers on the Situation in the Middle East', 6 November. Reproduced in C. Hill and K. Smith (2000) *European Foreign Policy: Key Documents*, London, Routledge, p. 300.

– (1977) 'Statement by the European Council on the Middle East', London, 29 June. Reproduced in C. Hill and K. Smith (2000) *European Foreign Policy: Key Documents*, London, Routledge, p. 301.

– (1980) 'Declaration by the European Council on the Situation in the Middle East', Venice, 12–13 June. Reproduced in C. Hill and K. Smith (2000) *European Foreign Policy: Key Documents*, London, Routledge, p. 302.

– (1990) 'Declaration of the European Council on the Middle East', Dublin, 25–26 June. Reproduced in C. Hill and K. Smith (2000) *European Foreign Policy: Key Documents*, London, Routledge, p. 307.

– (1999a) 'Conclusions of the European Council in Berlin', 24–25 March. Reproduced in C. Hill and K. Smith (2000) *European Foreign Policy: Key Documents*, London, Routledge, p. 316.

– (1999b) 'Meeting on 12–13 December 1999 in Helsinki', *Presidency Conclusions*, SN300/99. Online. Available HTTP: http://www.consilium.europa.eu (accessed March 2000).

– (2000) *Zagreb Summit: Final Declaration, November 2000*. Online. Available HTTP: http://www.consilium.europa.eu (accessed December 2005).

– (2001) 'Meeting on 14–15 December 2001 in Laeken', *Presidency Conclusions*, SN300/01. Online. Available HTTP: http://www.consilium.europa.eu (accessed March 2002).

– (2002) 'Meeting on 26–27 June 2002 in Seville', *Presidency Conclusions*, SN 200/02. Online. Available HTTP: http://www.consilium.europa.eu (accessed September 2002).

– (2003a) 'Meeting in Thessaloniki on 21 June 2003', *Presidency Conclusions*, 10229/03. Online. Available HTTP: http://www.consilium.europa.eu (accessed September 2003).

– (2003b) *A Secure Europe in a Better World. European Security Strategy*, 12 December 2003. Online. Available HTTP: http://ue.eu.int/pressdata/EN/reports/78367.pdf (accessed November 2004).

– (2005a) 'Meeting in Brussels on 16–17 June 2005', *Presidency Conclusions*. 10255/1/05. Online. Available HTTP: http://www.consilium.europa.eu (accessed November 2005).

– (2005b) *Negotiating Framework for Turkey*, Online. Available HTTP: http://www.consilium.europa.eu (accessed December 2005).

European Parliament (1990) Resolution on 11 July 1990, *Official Journal*, C231/172, 17 September 1990.

– (2003) *Report on a Proposal for a European Parliament Recommendation to the Council on EU Policy Towards the South Caucasus*, Rapporteur Per Gahrton, 2003/2225(INI). Online. Available HTTP: http://www.europarl.eu.int (accessed January 2003).

Foundation for Middle East Peace (2002) *Report on Israeli Settlements in the Occupied Territories*, Washington, November–December. Online. Available HTTP: http://www.fmep.org (accessed January 2003).

– (2005) *Report on Israeli Settlements in the Occupied Territories*, Washington, November– December. Online. Available HTTP: http://www.fmep.org (accessed December 2005).

Friends of Cyprus (2003) *Still Time*, Report 46, London, Friends of Cyprus.

Fuller, L. (2005) 'Waiting to Exhale in Abkhazia', *Radio Free Europe – Radio Liberty (RFE/RL)*, 21 January. Online. Available HTTP: http://www.rferl.org (accessed January 2005).

– (2006) 'Georgian Parliament Issues Anticipated Ultimatum', *RFE/RL*, 17 February. Online. Available HTTP: http://www.rferl.org (accessed February 2006).

Grabbe, H. (2001) 'How Does Europeanization Affect CEE Governance? Conditionality, Diffusion and Diversity', *Journal of European Public Policy*, 8:6, pp. 1013–31.

Gunter, M. (2000) 'The Continuing Kurdish Problem in Turkey After Öcalan's Capture', *Third World Quarterly*, 21:5, pp. 849–69.

Gürel, A. and Özersay, K. (2006) 'Property and Human Rights in Cyprus: The European Court of Human Rights as a Platform of Political Struggle', paper presented at the European Consortium for Political Research, Joint Sessions, Nicosia, April.

G17 Plus (2003) *State Programme of a European Serbia*, Belgrade, G-17 Plus, May 2003.

Haas, A. (2005) 'After Sharm el-Sheikh', *Bitter Lemons.* Online. Available HTTP: http://www.bitterlemons.org (accessed February 2005).

Haindrava, I. (2005) *Georgia's Incomplete Democracy*, *RFE/RL*, 6 May. Online. Available HTTP: http://www.rferl.org (accessed May 2005).

Halper, J. (2000) 'The 94% Solution: A Matrix of Control', *Middle East Report*, No. 216, Fall 2000. Online. Available HTTP: http://www.merip.org (accessed February 2001).

Hatay, M. (2005) *Beyond Numbers: An Inquiry into the Political Integration of Turkish 'Settlers' in Northern Cyprus*, Peace Research Institute Oslo (PRIO), Nicosia, Cyprus Centre.

Heller, M. (2004) 'Israel–EU Relations: The political dimension', paper presented at the Israeli–European Policy Network Meeting, Berlin, 14 October 2004.

Hill, C. (2001) 'The EU's Capacity for Conflict Prevention', *European Foreign Affairs Review*, 6:3, pp. 315–33.

Hughes, J. and Sasse, G. (2003) 'Monitoring the Monitors: EU Enlargement Conditionality and Minority Protection in the CEECs', Schiffbrucke, European Centre for Minority Issues.

Hughes, J., Sasse, G. and Gordon, C. (2004) 'Conditionality and Compliance in the EU's Eastward Enlargement: Regional Policy and the Reform of Sub-national Government', *Journal of Common Market Studies*, 42:3, pp. 523–51.

Human Rights Watch (2002) *Erased in a Moment: Suicide Bombing Attacks Against Israeli Citizens,* New York, Human Rights Watch.

Huysseune, M. and Noutcheva, G. (2004) 'Serbia and Montenegro', in Bruno Coppieters *et al.* (eds) *Europeanization and Conflict Resolution*, Gent, Academia Press, pp. 107–48.

International Commission on the Balkans (2005) *The Balkans in Europe's Future*, Sofia.

ICG (International Crisis Group) (2001) 'Montenegro: Resolving the Independence Deadlock', *Balkans Report*, 114, Podgorica/Brussels, 1 August.

– (2002) 'Still Buying Time: Montenegro, Serbia and the EU', *Balkans Report*, 129, Podgorica/Belgrade/Brussels, 7 May.

– (2003) 'A Marriage of Inconvenience: Montenegro 2003', *Balkans Report*, 142, Podgorica/Brussels, 16 April.

– (2004) 'Georgia: Avoiding War in South Ossetia', *Europe Report*, 159, Tbilisi/Brussels, 26 November.

– (2005) 'Montenegro's Independence Drive', *Europe Report*, 169, Brussels, 7 December.

– (2006a) 'Conflict Resolution in the South Caucasus: The EU's Role', *Europe Report*, 173, Tbilisi/Brussels, 20 March.

– (2006b) 'Montenegro's Referendum', *Europe Briefing*, 42, Podgorica/Belgrade/Brussels, 30 May.

Katz, Y. (2006) 'Final Borders to Include Kedumim, Karnei Shomron', *The Jerusalem Post*, 23 March. Online. Available HTTP: http://www.jpost.com (accessed March 2006).

Kaymak, E. and Vüral, V. (2006) 'Intra-Communal Dynamics: EU Discourses Among Turkish Cypriot Political Actors Before and After the Failed Referenda', paper presented at the European Consortium for Political Research, Joint Sessions, Nicosia, April.

Kelley, J. (2006) 'Promoting Political Reforms through the ENP', *Journal of Common Market Studies*, 44:1, pp. 29–58.

Khashig, I. and Kupatadze, G. (2005) 'Abkhaz Railway – Light at the End of the Tunnel?', *Institute for War and Peace Reporting*, 12 August. Online. Available HTTP: http://www.iwpr.net (accessed August 2005).

Kirişçi, K. (2005) 'Turkey and the EU: The Domestic Politics of Negotiating Pre-accession', *Macalester International*, 15, pp. 44–80.

Knill, C. and Lehmkuhl, D. (1999) 'How Europe Matters: Mechanisms of Europeanization', *European Integration Online Papers*, 3:7. Online. Available HTTP: http://eiop.or.at/eiop/texte/1999-007a.htm (accessed November 2003).

Koğacıoğlu, D. (2003) 'Dissolution of Political Parties by the Constitutional Court in Turkey', *International Sociology*, 18:1, pp. 258–76.

Krauss, S. (2000) 'The European Parliament in EU External Relations: The Customs Union with Turkey', *European Foreign Affairs Review*, 5:2, pp. 215–37.

Kronenberger, V. and Wouters, J. (eds) (2005) *The EU and Conflict Prevention: Policy and Legal Aspects*, The Hague, Asser Press.

Kurban, D. (2003) 'Confronting Equality: the Need for Constitutional Protection of Minorities in Turkey's Path to the European Union', *Columbia Human Rights Law Review*, 35:1, pp. 151–214.

Kurban, D. (2005) 'Unravelling a Trade-Off: Reconciling Minority Rights and Full Citizenship in Turkey', in *European Yearbook of Minority Issues*, 4 (2004/2005), Bolzano, European Centre for Minority Issues, pp. 341–372.

Kymlicka, W. (2006) 'The Evolving Basis of European Norms of Minority Rights: Rights to Culture, Participation and Autonomy', in J. McGarry and M. Keating (eds) *European Integration and the Nationalities Question*, London, Routledge, pp. 35–63.

Le More, A. (2005) 'Killing with Kindness: Funding the Demise of a Palestinian State', *International Affairs*, 81:5, pp. 983–1001.

Lijphart, A. (1977) *Democracy in Plural Societies*, New Haven, Yale University Press.

Lobjakas, A. (2006) 'Georgia Lobbies for EU Backing in Standoff with Russia', *RFE/RL*, 13 February. Online. Available HTTP: http://www.rferl.org (accessed February 2006).

Lopandic, D. and Bajic, V. (2003) *Serbia and Montenegro on the Road to the EU*, Belgrade, Friedrich Ebert Stiftung.

Lordos, A. (2006) 'Rational Actors or Unthinking Followers?', paper presented at the European Consortium for Political Research, Joint Sessions, Nicosia, April.

Lynch, D. (2004) 'The European Neighbourhood Policy', paper presented at the Workshop 'ENP: Concepts and Instruments', Prague, June.

– (2006) 'Why Georgia Matters', *Chaillot Paper*, 65, Paris, EU Institute for Security Studies.

McGarry, J. and O'Leary, B. (1997) 'Introduction: The Macro-political Regulation of Ethnic Conflict', in J. McGarry and B. O'Leary (eds) *The Politics of Protracted Ethnic Conflict Regulation*, London, Routledge, pp. 1–40.

Manners, I. (2002) 'Normative Power Europe: A Contradiction in Terms?', *Journal of Common Market Studies*, 20:2, pp. 235–58.

Massari, M. (2006) 'All Roads Lead to Brussels? Analysis of the Different Trajectories of Croatia, Serbia–Montenegro and Bosnia-Herzegovina', *Cambridge Review of International Affairs*, 18:2, pp. 259–73.

Mirbagheri, F. (1998) *Cyprus and International Peacemaking*, London, Hurst & Co.

Mossawa Center (2001) *Social, Economic and Political Status of Arab Citizens in Israel*, Haifa, Mossawa.

Nabulsi, K. (2005) 'The State-Building Project: What Went Wrong?', in M. Keating, A. Le More and R. Lowe (eds) *Aid, Diplomacy and Facts on the Ground: the Case of Palestine*, London, Chatham House, pp. 117–28.

Nodia, G. (2005) 'The Dynamics and Sustainability of the Rose Revolution' in M. Emerson (ed.) *Democratization in the European Neighbourhood*, Brussels, Centre for European Policy Studies, pp. 38–52.

Noutcheva, G. (2004) 'The EU and the Western Balkans: A Tale of Mutual Mistrust', *Europa South East Monitor*, 58, Brussels, Centre for European Policy Studies.

Olsen, J.P. (2002) 'The Many Faces of Europeanization', *Journal of Common Market Studies*, 40:5, pp. 921–52.

O'Rourke, B. (2005) 'Ferrero-Waldner: Brussels Says No Point in Near Neighbours Seeking to Join the Union Now' *RFE/RL*, 4 May. Online. Available HTTP: http://www.rferl.org (accessed May 2005).

OSCE (2003) *EU Statements on Georgia*, Permanent Council No. 456, 17 June.

Öcalan, A. (1999) 'Declaration on the Domestic Solution to the Kurdish Question', translated by the Kurdistan Information Centre, London, Mesopotamia Press.

Öktem, K. (2006) 'Return of the Turkish State of Exception', *Middle East Report*, 3 June. Online. Available HTTP: http://www.merip.org (accessed June 2006).

Parsons, R. (2006) 'Council of Europe Warns Georgia', *RFE/RL*, 13 February. Online. Available HTTP: http://www.rferl.org (accessed February 2006).

Patten, C. (2003a) quoted in *Pobjeda*, 1 February. Online. Available HTTP: http://wwwpobjeda.co.yu (accessed February 2003).

– (2003b) 'Commissioner Patten's Reply to Charles Tannock, MEP', 6 November. Online. Available HTTP: http://www.europa.eu.int (accessed January 2004).

– (2004) 'Letter to the Dutch Foreign Minister Bernard Bot and the EU High Representative Javier Solana', reproduced by the Institute for War and Peace Reporting, *Balkan Crisis Report*, 516, 17 September. Online. Available HTTP: http://www.iwpr.net (accessed September 2004).

Pippan, C. (2004) 'The Rocky Road to Europe: The EU's Stabilization and Association Process for the Western Balkans and the Principle of Conditionality', *European Foreign Affairs Review*, 9:2, pp. 219–45.

PLO (2002) *Israel's Pre-emption of a Viable Two State Solution*, Ramallah, PLO Negotiations Affairs Department, Negotiations Support Unit.

– (2003) *Bad Fences Make Bad Neighbours*, Ramallah, PLO Negotiations Affairs Department, Negotiations Support Unit.

– (2005) *Settlement Expansion East of Jerusalem Suggests that Israel is Disengaging from the Two-State Solution*, Ramallah, PLO Negotiations Affairs Department, Negotiations Support Unit.

Pope, H. and Pope, N. (2000) *Turkey Unveiled*, Woodstock, Overlook Press.

Portela, C. (2005) 'Where and Why Does the EU Impose Sanctions?', *Politique Européene*, 17, pp. 83–111.

Prodi, R. (2004) 'Speech by Commission President Romano Prodi to Students and Representatives of Civil Society in Georgia', 18 September. Online. Available HTTP: http://www.europa.eu.int (accessed November 2004).

Quartet's Special Envoy for Disengagement (2006) *Periodic Report*, April, Jerusalem, Office of the Quartet's Special Envoy for Disegagement.

Rehn, O. (2006) 'Brussels Must Offer the Balkans a Credible Future', *Financial Times*, 3 April. p. 2.

Republic of Cyprus (2000) *House of Representatives Resolution*, Nicosia, 11 October. Online. Available HTTP: http://www.pio.gov.cy/news/special_issues/special_issue034. htm (accessed November 2002).

Republic of Turkey (1995) 'Parliamentary Debate', Turkish Grand National Assembly, 21 February 1995.

Republic of Turkey (2004) *Report on Minority Rights and Cultural Rights*, Prime Ministry Advisory Committee on Human Rights, Sub-Committee on Minority Rights and Cultural Rights, Ankara, 1 October.

Reuters (2005) 'Top Palestinian Judge Resigns in Protest of New Appointment Law', 13 October. Online. Available HTTP: http://www.today.reuters.com (accessed February 2005).

Richmond, O. (1998) *Mediating in Cyprus*, London, Frank Cass.

– (2006) 'Shared Sovereignty and the Politics of Peace: Evaluating the EU's 'Catalytic' Framework in the eastern Mediterranean', *International Affairs*, 82:1, pp. 149–67.

Riedel, E. and Will, M. (1999) 'Human Rights Clauses in External Agreements of the EC', in P. Alston (ed.) *The EU and Human Rights*, Oxford, Oxford University Press, pp. 773–54.

Risse, T., Cowles, M. and Caporaso, J. (2001) 'Europeanization and Domestic Change', in T. Risse, M. Cowles and J. Caporaso (eds) *Transforming Europe: Europeanization and Domestic Change*, Ithaca, Cornell University Press, pp. 1–20.

Roberts, N. (2005) 'Hard Lessons from Oslo' in M. Keating, A. Le More and R. Lowe (eds) *Aid, Diplomacy and Facts on the Ground: The Case of Palestine*, London, Chatham House, pp. 17–26.

Rockwell, S. and Shamas, C. (2005) *A Human Rights Review of the EU and Israel – 2003–2004*, Brussels, Euro-Mediterranean Human Rights Network.

Sak, G. (2005) 'Turkey's Transformation Process and the Risk of an Anti-EU Backlash', paper presented at 'The Second Bosphorous Conference' organized by the Centre for European Reform, Istanbul, 14–15 October 2005.

Sasse, G. (2006) 'National Minorities and EU Enlargement: External or Domestic Incentives for Accommodation', in J. McGarry and M. Keating (eds) *European Integration and the Nationalities Question*, London, Routledge, pp. 64–84.

Sayigh, Y. and Shikaki, K. (1999) *Strengthening Palestinian Public Institutions*, Task Force Report, New York, Council of Foreign Relations.

Sayigh, Y. (2005) 'Infighting Threatens Palestinian Democracy', *Financial Times*, 8 August. p. 12.

Schimmelfennig, F., Engert, S. and Knobel, H. (2002) 'Costs, Commitment and Compliance', *EUI Working Paper Series*, Florence, European University Institute, May.

Schimmelfennig, F. and Sedelmeier, U. (2004) 'Governance by Conditionality: EU Rule Transfer to the Candidate Countries of Central and Eastern Europe', *Journal of European Public Policy*, 11:4, pp. 661–79.

Shedada, R. (2005) 'The Basic Law', paper presented at the Conference '10 Years of the Palestinian Authority', 14–17 March 2005, Ramallah.

Sheuftan, D. (1999) *Korah Hahafrada – Disengagement, Israel and the Palestinian Entity*, Tel-Aviv, Zmora-Bitan.

Shikaki, K. (2002) 'Palestinians Divided', *Foreign Affairs*, 81:1, January/February. Online. Available HTTP: http://www.foreignaffairs.org accessed (February 2005).

Smith, K. (1998) 'The Use of Political Conditionality in the EU's Relations with Third Countries: How Effective?', *European Foreign Affairs Review*, 3:1, pp. 253–74.

– (2004) *European Union Foreign Policy in a Changing World*, London, Polity Press.

– (2005) 'The Outsiders: the ENP', *International Affairs*, 81:4, pp. 757–73.

Smith, K. and Sjursen, H. (2004) 'Justifying EU Foreign Policy: The Logics Underpinning EU Enlargement', in B. Tonra and T. Christinsen (eds) *Rethinking EU Foreign Policy*, Manchester, Manchester University Press, pp. 126–41.

Soffer, A. (2001) *Israel, Demography 2000–2020: Dangers and Opportunities*, Haifa, University of Haifa.

Solana, J. (2001) quoted in *Reuters*, 27 November. Online. Available HTTP: http://www.today.reuters.com (accessed November 2001).

Stewart, S. (2003) 'The Role of the UN in the Georgia–Abkhaz Conflict', *Journal of Ethnopolitics and Minority Issues in Europe*, 2/2003. Online. Available HTTP: http://www.ecmi.de (accessed December 2004).

Susser, A. (2000) 'Picking Up the Pieces', *Tel Aviv Notes*, 3, October. Online. Available HTTP: http://www.dayan.org/TAUnotes3.pdf (accessed December 2004).

Sussman, G. (2004) 'The Challenge to the Two-State Solution', *Middle East Report,* July. Online. Available HTTP: http://www.merip.org (accessed August 2004).

Tamari, S. (2002) 'Who Rules Palestine?', *Journal of Palestine Studies*, 31:4, pp. 102–13.

TESEV (Türkiye Ekonomik ve Sosyal Etüdler Vakfı) (2005) 'The Problem of Internal Displacement in Turkey: Assessment and Policy Proposals'. Online. Available HTTP: http://www.tesev.org.tr (accessed December 2005).

The Gallup Organization (2005) 'Georgian National Voter Study', Baltic Surveys, October–November.

The Mattin Group (2005) *Resource Chronology: Israeli Settlement Products and Rules of Origin*, Ramallah.

Tocci, N. (2004a) *Conflict Resolution in the European Neighbourhood: The Role of the EU as a Framework and as an Actor,* EUI Working Paper, 29, Florence, European University Institute.

– (2004b) *EU Accession Dynamics and Conflict Resolution: Catalyzing Peace or Consolidating Partition in Cyprus?*, Aldershot, Ashgate.

Touval, S. and Zartman, W. I. (1989) 'Mediation in International Conflict', in K. Kressel, D. G. Pruitt and Associates (eds) *Mediation Research: The Process and Effectiveness of Third Party Intervention*, San Francisco, Jossey-Bass Publishers, pp. 115–37.

Tovias, A. (2004) *The EU Models of External Relations with EEA Countries and Switzerland in Theory and Practice: How Relevant for Israel?*, paper presented at the Israeli–European Policy Network Meeting, Berlin, 14 October 2004.

Tsakaloyannis, P. (1996) 'Greece: the Limits of Convergence', in C. Hill (ed.) *The Actors in Europe's Foreign Policy*, London, Routledge, pp. 186–207.

(TDN) Turkish Daily News (2002) 'Giscard Remarks cause Uproar in Ankara, and Brussels', *Turkish Daily News,* 11 November.

– (2005) 'Kurdish Politicians Make Their Case Before the European Parliament', *Turkish Daily News,* 20 September.

UNSG (2003a) *Report of the Secretary-General on his Mission of Good Offices in Cyprus,* New York, April.

– (2003b) *Report of the Secretary General*, prepared pursuant to General Assembly Resolution ES-10/13, New York, November.

– (2004) *Report of the Secretary General on his Mission of Good Offices in Cyprus,* New York, May.

– (2006) *Assessment of the Future Humanitarian Risks in the Occupied Palestinian Territory*, New York, April.

Ülgen, S. (2006) 'Dangerous Frustration Is Creeping In', *International Herald Tribune,* 29 March. p. 10.

Wallace, W. (2003) *Looking After the Neighbourhood: Responsibilities for EU-25,* Policy Paper 4, July 2003. Online. Available HTTP: http://www.notre-europe.asso.fr (accessed November 2004).

Weymouth, L. (2006) 'We Are Ready to Charge Israel's Ehud Olmert on His Bold Plan for a New Border', *Newsweek,* 17 April.

Whyte, N. (2005) 'Independently Minded-Montenegro Splits the International Community', *Janes Intelligence Report*, 22 December. Online. Available HTTP: http://www.janes.com (accessed December 2005).

– (2006) 'Serbia–Montenegro'. Email correspondence (15 January 2006).

Wolfers, A. (1962) *Discord and Collaboration: Essays on International Politics*, Baltimore, John Hopkins University Press.

World Bank (2003) *Report on Impact of Intifada*, No. 26313, Jerusalem, 1 June.

Zalewski, P. (2004) *Sticks, Carrots and Great Expectations: Human Rights Conditionality and Turkey's Path towards Membership of the EU*, Report 09/04, Warsaw, Centre for International Relations.

Zartman, W. I and Aurik, J. (1991) 'Power Strategies in De-escalation', in L. Kriesberg and S. J. Thorson (eds) *Timing the De-escalation of International Conflicts*, Syracuse, New York, Syracuse University Press, pp. 152–81.

Index

Page numbers for figures have suffix **f**, those for tables have suffix **t**